IMAGES
of America

TIFFIN

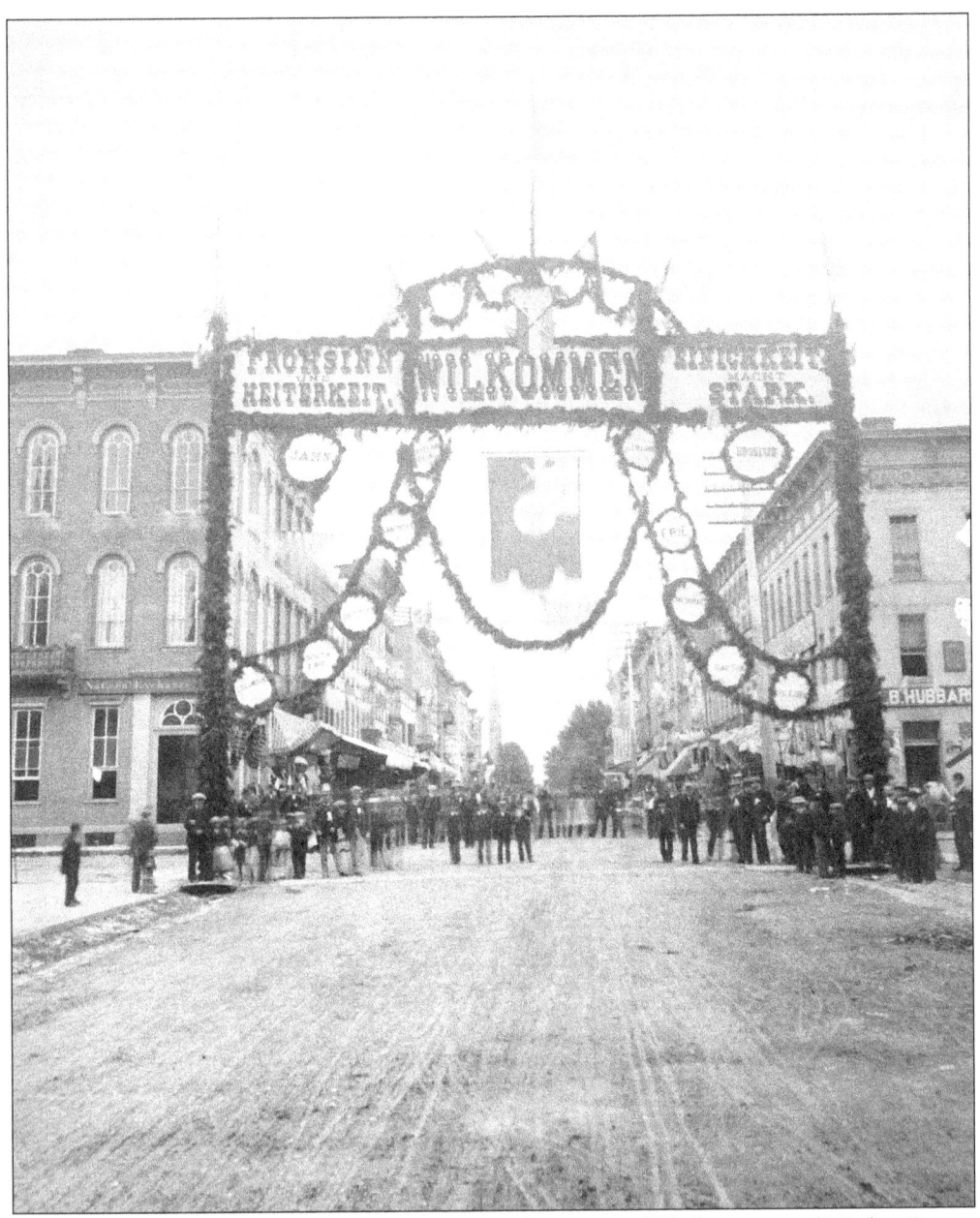

A banner erected by German residents in 1873 at the corner of Washington and Market Streets translates as "Welcome. Be happy and cheerful. Unity is strength." The German influence has been strong in Tiffin's development. Dr. Henry Kuhn was the town's first mayor in 1823, and Tiffin boasted a number of German-language newspapers in the pre–World War I era. (Courtesy of the Seneca County Museum.)

ON THE COVER: The band of the 2nd Regiment of the Ohio National Guard of Tiffin poses for a photograph sometime between 1910 and 1912. The 27-member ensemble was a musically diverse group, featuring a French horn and clarinets among the more traditional trombones, trumpets, and tubas. (Courtesy of the Seneca County Museum.)

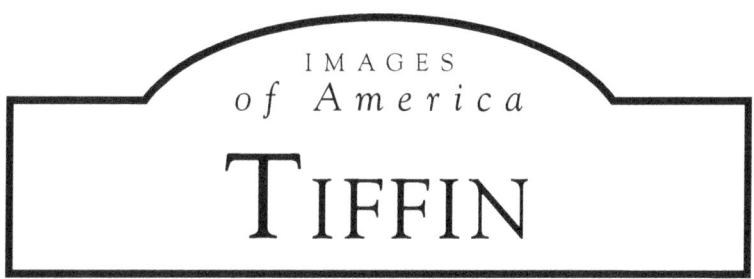

IMAGES
of America

TIFFIN

Keith Elchert and Laura Weston-Elchert
for the Seneca County Historical Society

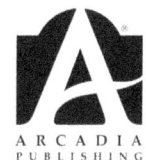

ARCADIA
PUBLISHING

Published by Arcadia Publishing
Charleston, South Carolina

Library of Congress Control Number: 2014947805

For all general information, please contact Arcadia Publishing:
Telephone 843-853-2070
Fax 843-853-0044
E-mail sales@arcadiapublishing.com
For customer service and orders:
Toll-Free 1-888-313-2665

Visit us on the Internet at www.arcadiapublishing.com

To Tiffin and its people, who prove that you can go home again

CONTENTS

ACKNOWLEDGMENTS

How well I remember Tiffin's 1967 sesquicentennial celebration. I remember—as a five-year-old—standing on West Market Street, across from the Gold Crown restaurant, watching the parade go by. I remember having the daylights scared out of me by fireworks as I sat watching the historical pageant unfold at Columbian Stadium. But, most of all, I remember the book—the *Tiffin-Seneca Sesquicentennial Pictorial Issue.*

I could spend hours lost in the past just by picking up that book. It is the inspiration for the book you hold now. With Tiffin nearing its bicentennial in 2022, it is particularly fitting that the Seneca County Museum and members of the Seneca County Historical Society opened archives and allowed us to select the images that appear in these pages. All the images are from their collection, with several exceptions noted.

We owe a particular debt to museum director Tonia Hoffert and trustee Mark Steinmetz, who gave of their time and talents to make sure that this pictorial history of Tiffin is as complete and accurate as it could be. We owe as great a debt to Bill Hoffert, who helped keep our children informed and entertained as we set about our research. The Tiffin-Seneca Public Library staff, particularly Trinity Lescallett, provided skilled research guidance as well. Tina Harrah of the Ohio Historical Society and Linda Lewis of the Dayton public library system were friendly and forthcoming with documents when we needed them quickly. Many thanks go to Emily Justiniano of the US Air Force Band, who helped us research our cover photograph, and Jim Grant, who made an excellent navigator on short notice.

Lastly, we offer thanks to all those Tiffin and Seneca County historians who have come before us and made our path all the easier. We hope this book is a worthy successor to their efforts.

INTRODUCTION

Tiffin's beginnings can be traced to the War of 1812 and to the needs of Gen. William Henry Harrison's army. Seeking to keep the vital supply lines afforded by the Sandusky River and Lake Erie secure against both the British and British-allied Indians, Harrison ordered construction of a strategically placed fort. Fort Ball, named after founder Col. James V. Ball, was established on the northern bank of the Sandusky River. It featured three blockhouses and was fed by a clear-water spring located inside its bayonet-fortified walls. Tiffin's bronze Indian Maiden statue marks the location of the fort and accompanying stockade, which upon completion joined a region-wide defense network. From nearby Fort Seneca, the world first heard the famed declaration Commodore Oliver Hazard Perry made following the Battle of Lake Erie: "We have met the enemy and they are ours."

Erastus Bowe became the area's first white settler in 1817. Bowe had served alongside Commodore Perry and also participated in the 25-day construction of Fort Ball. On his return, Bowe built his cabin in the shadow of the fort and converted half of the cabin into the Pan Yan Tavern, which became a stagecoach stop. Other settlers followed Bowe's path; many spent a night or two in one of Fort Ball's blockhouses as their log cabins went up. The village of Oakley (later known as Fort Ball) began to take shape, primarily under the guidance of mill operator Jesse Spencer, who had invested $3,000 in Oakley in 1823.

Activity soon stirred on the southern bank of the Sandusky River. In 1820, Virginia native Josiah Hedges bought land and began platting the town he named after his friend Edward Tiffin, Ohio's first governor. Tiffin's Perry, Market, Madison, Jefferson, Washington, and Monroe Streets all date from Hedges's original vision. Oakley/Fort Ball was laid out with Adams, Miami, Clay, Sandusky, Franklin, and Water Streets. Growth in the town slowly gained momentum after Tiffin was named seat of the newly established Seneca County. Oddly, it was nearly another two years until the county itself was organized; the legislature recognized Seneca County on January 22, 1824. Tiffin's pace of growth accelerated after 1828, when Hedges successfully lured the Federal Land Office away from Delaware, Ohio.

Friction between the cross-river rivals Spencer and Hedges resulted in Seneca County's first lawsuit. *Ohio Early State and Local History* describes the conflict: "(Spencer) built a brush dam . . . across to the other side of the river, meeting the bank at the triangular space midway between Washington and Monroe Street Bridges on the south side of the river. The brush dam caused much trouble between Mr. Spencer, proprietor of Oakley, and Mr. Hedges, owner of Tiffin, and finally resulted in the arrest of Mr. Hedges, who was imprisoned for a short time in his own courthouse. The first lawsuit and jury trial in the county followed. It seems that the brush dam caused the water to overflow Mr. Hedges' property. One night he and some men whom he hired, dug a trench around the end of the dam. This let the water all out and Spencer's mill could not be operated. He therefore brought suit against Hedges who lost, because at the time the dam was constructed, the property on the Hedges' side belonged to the Government. The costs were $26.75; and thus ended the first jury trial in the county."

Accommodation of other government functions, such as law enforcement, was taking place concurrently. The first log jail was contracted on July 4, 1825, and it cost $450. "It served its purpose," *Early State and Local History* says, "but not very well, for the prisoners very often escaped. They would loosen the logs and crawl out, and there was a usual Sunday morning excursion to the jail to see who had escaped." A more secure brick-and-stone structure replaced that jail in 1843. The building, which also served as the sheriff's residence, was in use until it was replaced in 1877. The current facility, the first located outside the city limits, opened in May 1994. Its construction followed years of lawsuits over jail conditions.

Early State and Local History also recounts a brief history of one of Tiffin's most recognizable landmarks. "As early as 1822," it notes, "Mr. Hedges erected a grist mill one half mile north of the present Washington street bridge, along the east side of the river, and in 1833 a saw mill on the west side opposite. The same dam operated both mills. This first mill . . . is the pioneer mill of the city. It is on the same site of the first mill erected in 1822. Having burned in 1874, it had to be rebuilt in 1875. The mill on the west side of the river has been razed and no vestige of it remains." Pioneer Mill withstood the Flood of 1913 (it was known as Bacon's Mill at that time) and was rebuilt a second time after being struck by fire in 1937. It continued as an active mill, grinding flour and meal, until 1950. A succession of businesses cycled through the building for more than 20 years until the Pioneer Mill—which had attained status in the National Register of Historic Places—opened as a fine-dining restaurant in 1974.

The year 1829 saw the beginnings of St. Mary's Catholic Church, when Hedges sold an acre of land to the archbishop of Cincinnati for $33. It was not until 1831 that a priest shortage subsided, and Father Edmund Quinn was sent to the recently established parish. And quite a parish it was, as it was the first established in northwest Ohio. As local historian Stephen J. Hartzell describes it, "Its area of responsibility extended from Lake Erie and the Michigan border to the north, to Springfield on the south, and from the Indiana line on the west, to Norwalk on the east." The first Mass was said in the home of parishioner John Julian; confessions had been heard beforehand in Julian's corncrib. The present St. Mary's Church, the parish's third, was built in 1905.

In 1845, a group of German families received permission from the Cincinnati diocese to form another parish in Tiffin; this was the beginning of St. Joseph Catholic Church. Under the leadership of the Rev. Joseph Bihn, the parish founded the Citizen's Hospital and Orphans Asylum in 1867. Hundreds of orphaned children lived there between 1869 and 1936. Now known as the St. Francis Home after the sisters in residence, the facility provides a variety of living and ministry options for senior citizens.

On March 7, 1835, Tiffin was incorporated by decree of the Ohio legislature. Fort Ball and Tiffin continued as rivals for the next 15 years before agreeing to merge in March 1850. But even as the young towns competed, Josiah Hedges saw the need to bridge their differences—literally. His first attempt to span the Sandusky in 1833 lasted only about a year. His wooden bridge was smashed when, driven by heavy rains, an unmoored bridge carried northward from Tymochtee struck it broadside. Hedges replaced the structure with a toll bridge. He dropped the toll when a rival free bridge was completed upriver at Market Street.

Railway service first reached Tiffin in 1841 on the Mad River & Lake Erie Railroad. But in 1842, it was by stagecoach that Tiffin's most famous visitor to date arrived. An 1870 article in the *Atlantic* recounts "Four Months With Charles Dickens" by G.W. Putnam: "Our stage - coach ride across Ohio ended at Tiffin, a small town which we reached about noon, from whence was a railroad to Sandusky City on Lake Erie. The good landlord at Tiffin, finding who were his guests, did his best to please, and also to let the entire town know that 'Dickens was at his hotel.' And when we left the house for the depot he had a large kind of open wagon on springs, with seats very high, on which Mr. and Mrs. Dickens were perched. I think the driver was instructed to pass through all the principal streets of the place before he reached the railroad station, for we went at a slow pace and were a long time going; and the people awaited us in groups, as if by appointment, at the street-corners and at the windows and doors of the houses; and if the inhabitants of Tiffin, Ohio, did not on that occasion see 'Boz' and his wife, it certainly was not the fault of that good landlord or of his carriage-driver."

Literacy and education continued to play a large role in the developing community. In 1850, members of the German Reformed Church (now known as the United Church of Christ) established Heidelberg College in Tiffin. The first classes for the five students enrolled took place in a downtown storefront building. The town's other institution of higher learning, Tiffin University, was founded in 1888 as Tiffin Business University. Between 1918 and 1956, the school operated out of the Remmele Building downtown. After obtaining the former Miami Street School, the campus was moved to the site from which it operates today. An aggressive expansion plan has increased Tiffin University's campus to 130 acres, overtaking Heidelberg's 110 acres.

The years encompassing the Civil War and Reconstruction were fruitful ones for Tiffin, as its population doubled from 4,000 to 8,000. And in 1882, the city landed its biggest industrial prize to date when Meshech Frost led the successful effort for the National Machinery Company. The establishment of a pair of glass plants in the late 1880s helped to further define Tiffin and cement its reputation as a manufacturing center.

Historian Myron Barnes summarized the state of 1880s Tiffin as "still a self-sufficient community." "The entire county had learned to meet most of its daily needs through local industry . . . We took care of our own poor and were generous to local charities . . . We built and maintained our own school system, built our own bridges, and maintained our own roads and streets," he said.

Perhaps Tiffin's most acclaimed resident was Gen. William Harvey Gibson, who is commemorated with a statue on the courthouse square. An attorney, Gibson was an early organizer of Ohio's Republican Party and served as state treasurer after his election in 1855. He was forced to resign in 1857 after being accused of covering up a nearly $750,000 fund shortage courtesy of his predecessor. Upon the start of the Civil War, Gibson enlisted and was appointed colonel of the 49th Regiment, Ohio Volunteer Infantry. Whitelaw Reid, author of *Ohio in the War*, describes Gibson's experience: "He entered the service under a cloud. . . . General sympathy was felt for him, and it was felt that his entry into the military service was a manly effort to wipe out the stigma which weakness, rather than intentional guilt had placed on him. His career did this, and gave him an honored name among the soldiers of the state." Gibson's troops saw action at Chickamauga and Atlanta, among other decisive battles. At Shiloh, Gibson had three horses shot out from underneath him and was bayoneted. He returned to Tiffin after his service and was a highly sought-after speaker for Independence Day and similar celebrations. When Gibson died in 1894, he was eulogized by governor and future president William McKinley.

March 23, 1913, Easter Sunday, marked the start of Tiffin's most pivotal period. Unrelenting rainfall sent the Sandusky River surging out of its banks. The floodwaters reached their crest on Wednesday, March 26, and a total of 19 people were killed as the homes along the riverbank in which they were huddled were torn from their foundations. The degree of devastation was mind-boggling. Losses were estimated to total $1 million (nearly $22 million in today's dollars). The city was essentially cut in half, as every bridge save one connecting Tiffin's two sides was destroyed. Reconstruction of the bridges, deepening the channel of the river to the city, and erecting retaining walls was a process of recovery that would take years.

In addition to the reconfigured physical landscape, the early decades of the 20th century saw numerous dramatic changes in the pace and manner of life, both in Tiffin and nationwide. Barnes laments in his city history *Between the Eighties*: "Tiffin lost its individual character rather rapidly after the advent of the automobile, paved roads, radio and eventually television. As early as the 1920's, citizens were patterning their value systems on the national figures who were in the news." Barnes also traces the gradually changing face of Tiffin's retail component. "Washington Street," he writes, "which had only one chain store by World War I, was a community of local proprietors who often owned their own buildings. The wealth generated by these proprietorships remained in Tiffin, and the owners were generous in their support of civic enterprises . . . [B]y 1977 we find that there are only two locally owned establishments which date from the 19th century."

We find also that the retail landscape of downtown is much changed. The exodus began in the late 1950s as the lure of Westgate proved too attractive for businesses such as Kresge's and Islay's to resist. This sparked a development boom on West Market Street, stretching all the way to US 224 and culminating in the opening of the Tiffin Mall in 1980.

Tiffin's emphasis on education continued to be keen, as evidenced by a mid-20th century construction boom. This included the Lincoln, Washington, Krout, and Columbian buildings. "From 1953 to 1960 Tiffin had rebuilt three of its grade schools, and the high school, and added the additional junior high," Barnes summarizes. "This is an impressive seven years, and clearly reflects the progressive attitude which Tiffin citizens can display when they want to."

The early years of the 21st century find Tiffin as a city again in transition. Industrial giants such as Tiffin Glass, General Electric, and American Standard have departed the scene. As city luminaries debate the best path forward, the past celebrated in these pages can offer both a lesson and an inspiration.

One

A Tale of Two Cities

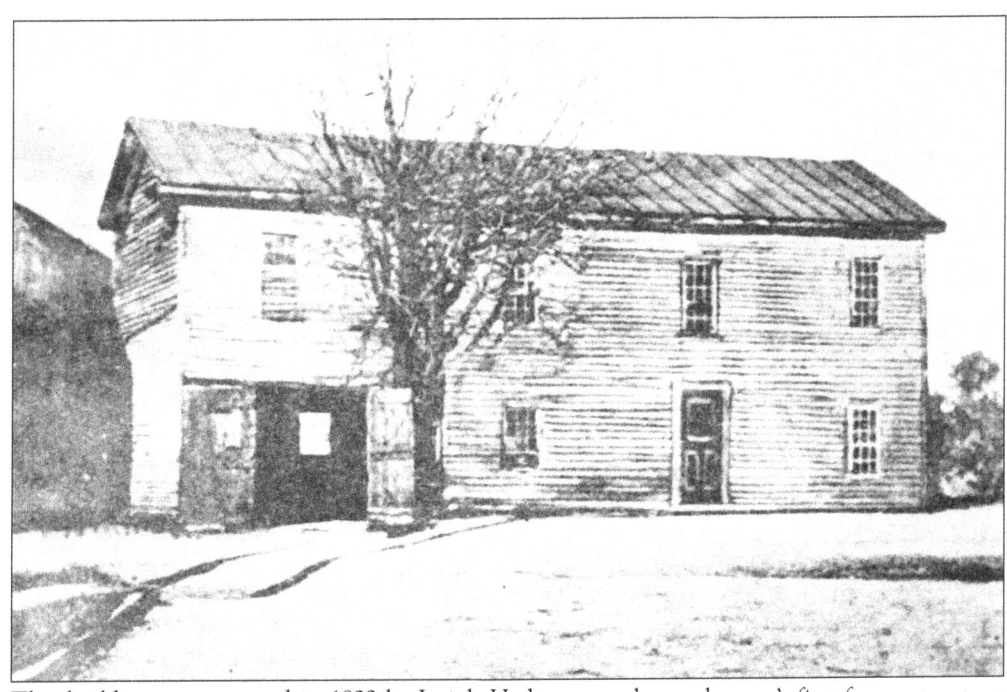

This building, constructed in 1822 by Josiah Hedges, was the settlement's first frame structure and served as Seneca County's first courthouse. It was originally situated on the north side of present-day Court Street, east of Washington Street, but was later moved to the riverbank at the end of Jefferson Street. The building was lost to the floodwaters of 1913.

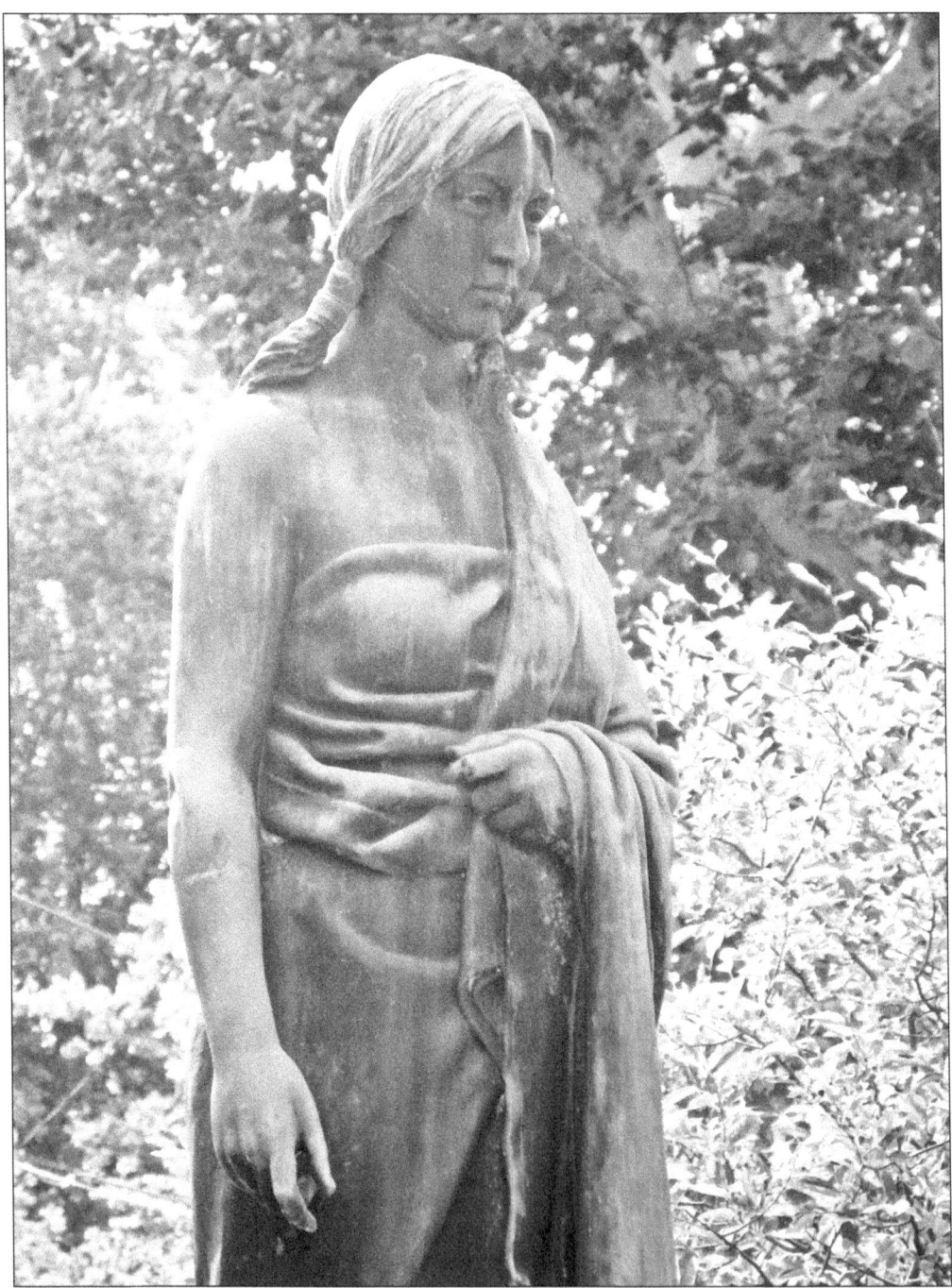

This Indian Maiden statue stands on the grounds of Fort Ball along present-day Frost Parkway. The inscription on the statue reads, "This Indian maid keeps ceaseless watch where red men and sturdy pioneers drank from a spring whose sparkling waters flowed within the stockade of old Fort Ball / Presented to the City of Tiffin by Meshech Frost June 1926." (Authors' collection.)

Dr. Eli Dresbach was the first physician in the territory that became Seneca County. He originally settled in Fort Ball but moved across the river after a few years. In 1824, Dresbach constructed this building at the northwest corner of present-day North Sandusky and Miami Streets. It was Seneca County's first brick structure, but the building was razed in 1911.

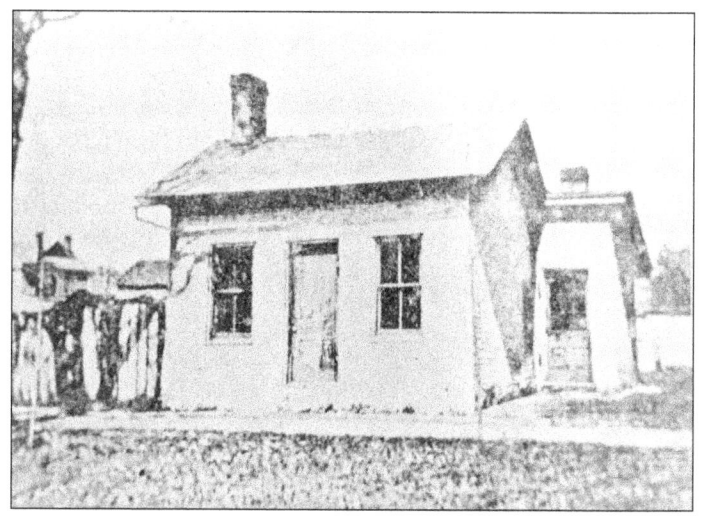

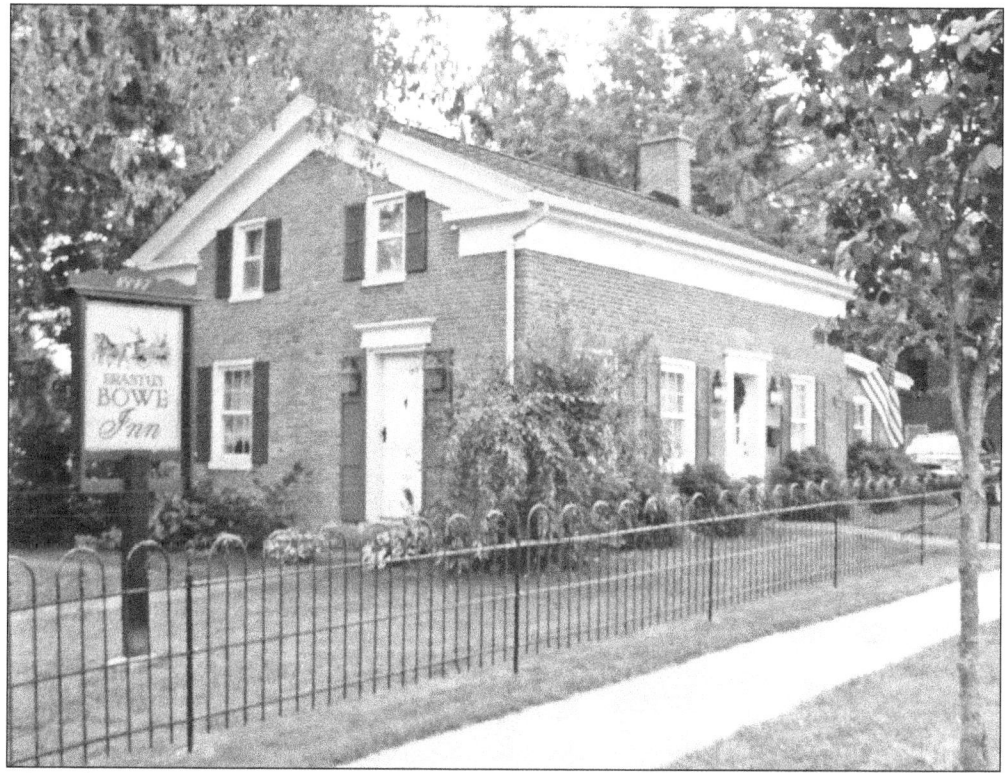

The redbrick, tin-roof Erastus Bowe residence at 108 Franklin Street was built by Seneca County's first white settler in 1837 (other sources say 1847), several decades after Bowe first arrived in Fort Ball. The home was restored in the early 2000s by Tiffin preservationists Phil and Rayella Engle. As part of their research, the Engles visited the birthplace of Thomas Edison in Milan, Ohio—the Edison house has the identical blueprint to the Bowe house. (Authors' collection.)

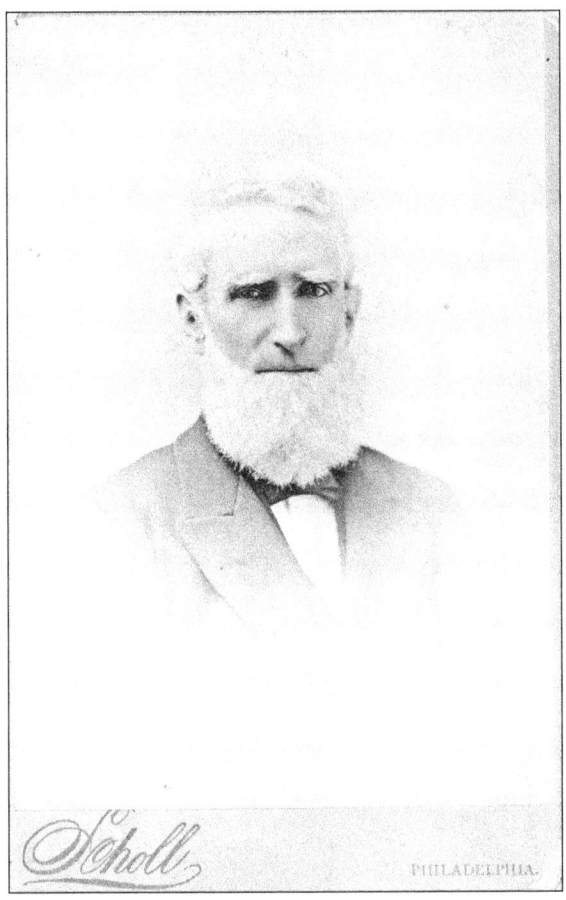

Rezin Shawhan is regarded as Tiffin's first millionaire. He and his family arrived from Virginia in 1832. Shawhan's success in the mercantile business allowed him to invest in the growing town and eventually to turn to real estate, banking, and hotel construction full-time. When Shawhan died in 1887, his will stipulated a $2,000 gift for a Tiffin library and $1,000 to every church in the city, as well as a bequest to Heidelberg College.

The Rezin Shawhan house, built in 1853, is now the Seneca County Museum. "It was a good example of late Greek Revival architecture," wrote former museum director Myron Barnes, "and it had seventeen rooms plus a large two story carriage house. It easily housed the museum collection, and had room for further expansion." Among its myriad displays is a collection of Tiffin glass and the contents of the demolished courthouse's cornerstone.

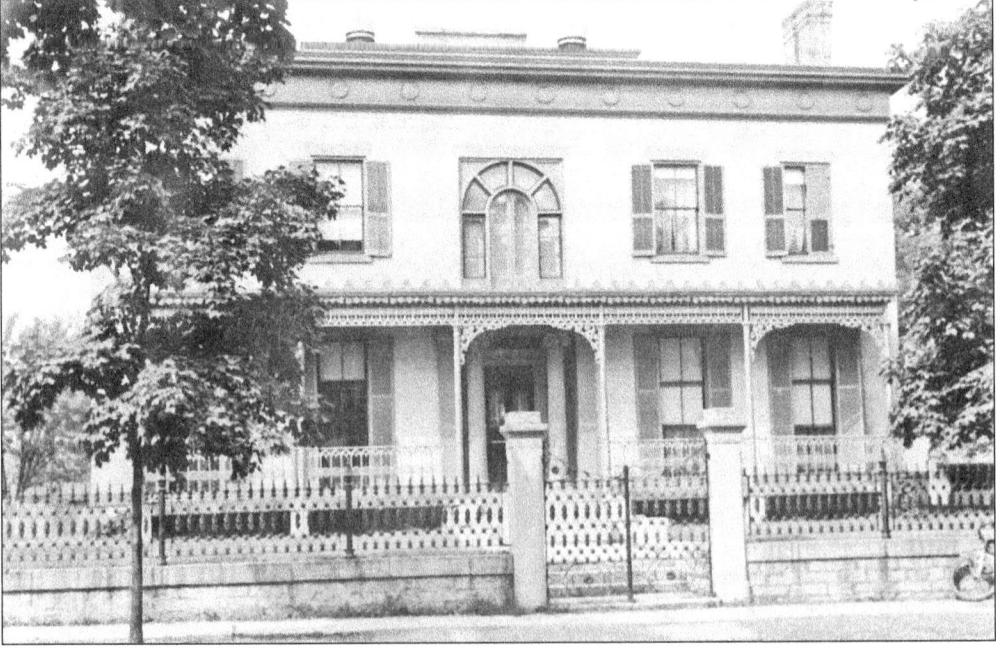

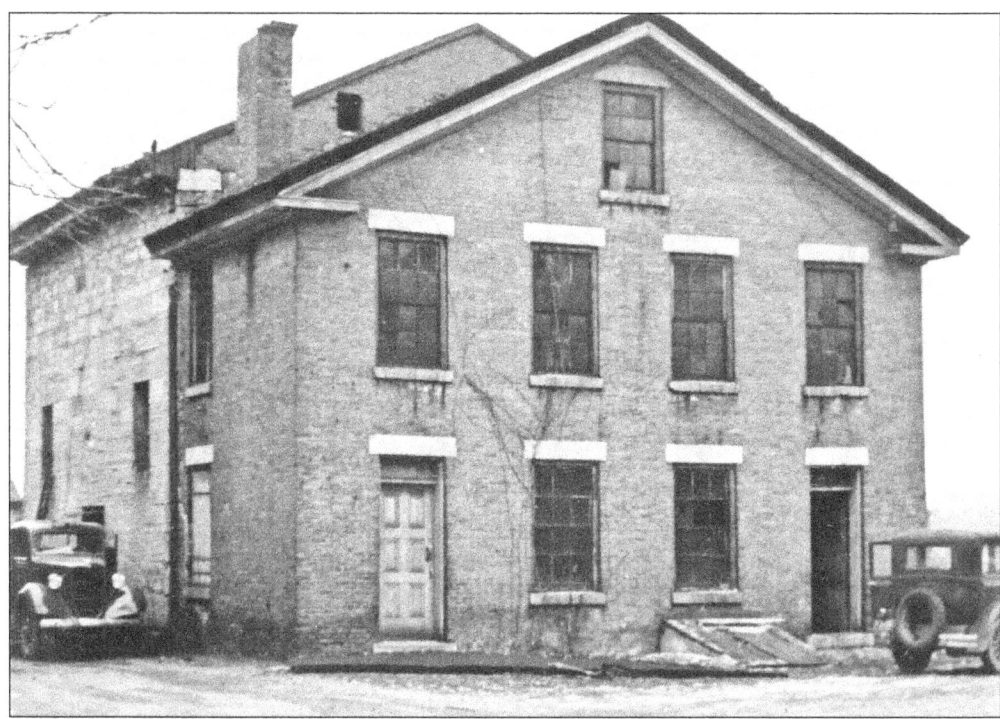

Seneca County's first freestanding jail, situated along Madison Street, was built in 1843, replacing a log structure that lent itself easily to jailbreaks by enterprising inmates. The original structure, which features particularly narrow windows, is to the rear of the photograph. A new jail, complete with a sheriff's residence, took the place of this one in 1878.

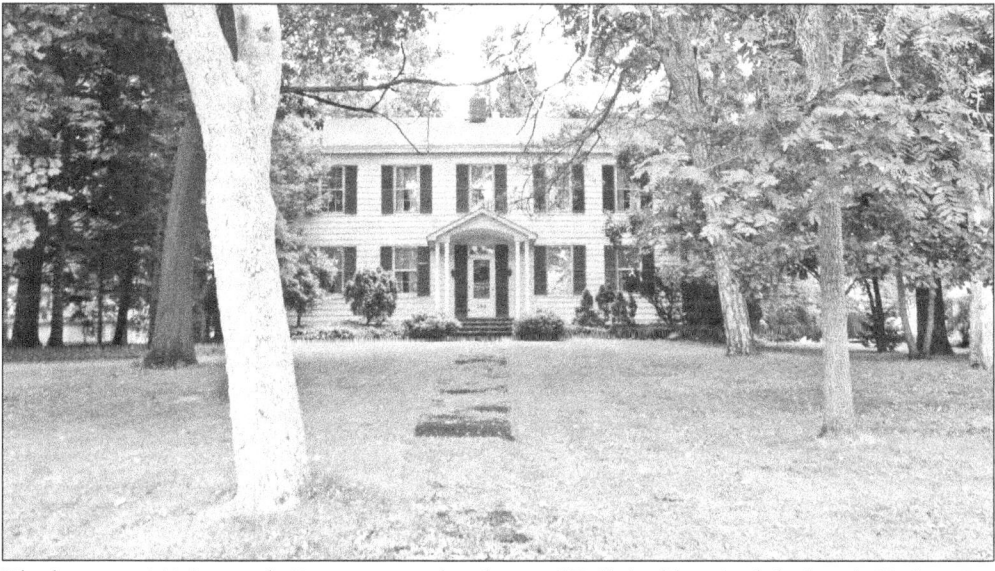

The house at 260 Riverside Drive is considered one of Tiffin's oldest, built by Josiah Hedges. For more than a century, the home was the property of the Bacon family. Frank Bacon could walk down the stone front walkway and across the road to his business at Bacon's (now the Pioneer) Mill. Frank's son Roger assisted in the conversion of the Pioneer Mill into the restaurant it is today. (Authors' collection.)

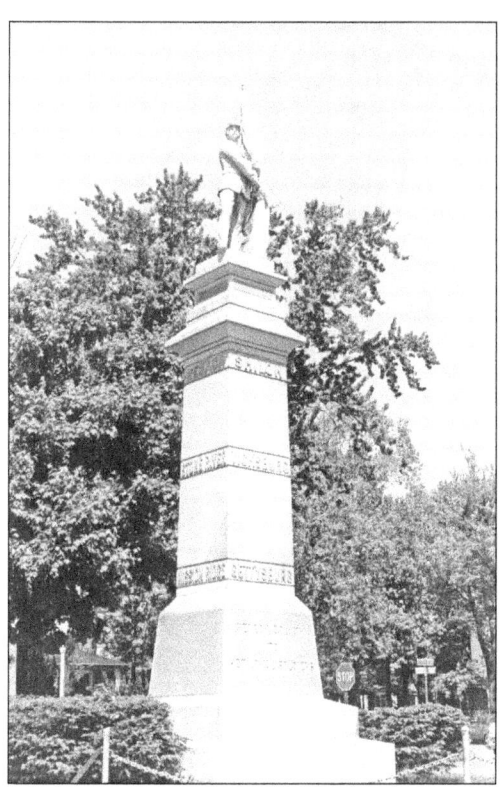

The Soldiers and Sailors Monument is the centerpiece of Tiffin's Civil War memorial on Frost Parkway. Dedicated on July 3, 1885, the granite standard bearer monument, built at a cost of $8,000, is inscribed: "Seneca County / To her loyal soldiers / Resaca / Stone River / Mission Ridge / Shiloh / Vicksburg / Atlanta / Antietam / Appomattox / Nashville / Cedar Creek / Wilderness." H.W. Yeager is credited as the monument's sculptor.

Now wedged between a pair of modern businesses, the Jacob Oster residence, 259 South Washington Street, is a Greek Revival throwback. Inside, the house's walls are a foot thick, with hand-forged nails still visible. Oster was a tinsmith who built his home in 1841, making it one of Tiffin's oldest residences. (Authors' collection.)

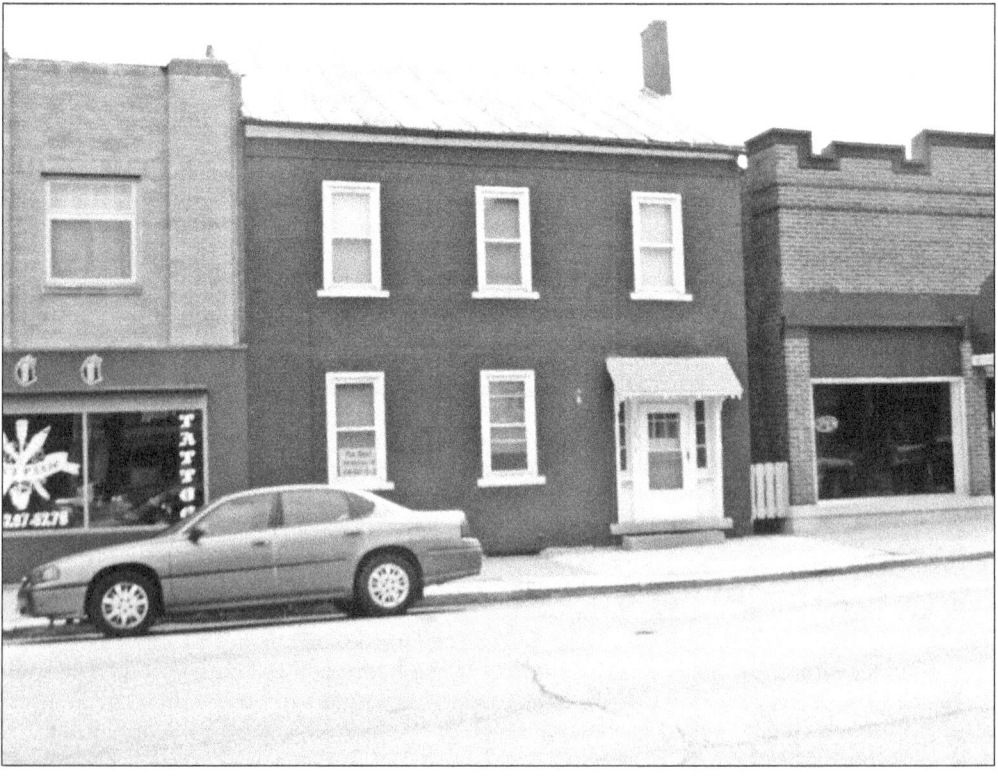

Two

A City of
Law and Order

Tiffin's police
department in 1900
consisted of eight
officers and their
marshal, protecting
the town's nearly
11,000 residents. The
slaying of Officer
Sweeney (second row,
second from left)
by business robber
Butch Hoffman led
to the department's
reorganization into
the structure familiar
today. Hoffman
hopped a train to
Toledo and was never
arrested. In 1915, the
department added
the services of a
motorcycle patrolman.

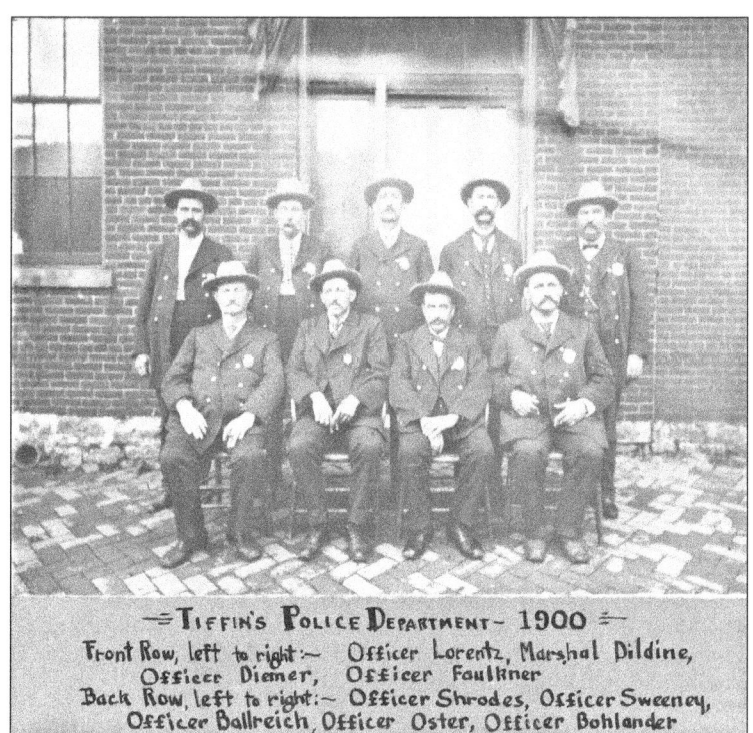

≈TIFFIN'S POLICE DEPARTMENT- 1900 ≈
Front Row, left to right:— Officer Lorentz, Marshal Dildine,
Officer Diemer, Officer Faulkner
Back Row, left to right:— Officer Shrodes, Officer Sweeney,
Officer Ballreich, Officer Oster, Officer Bohlander

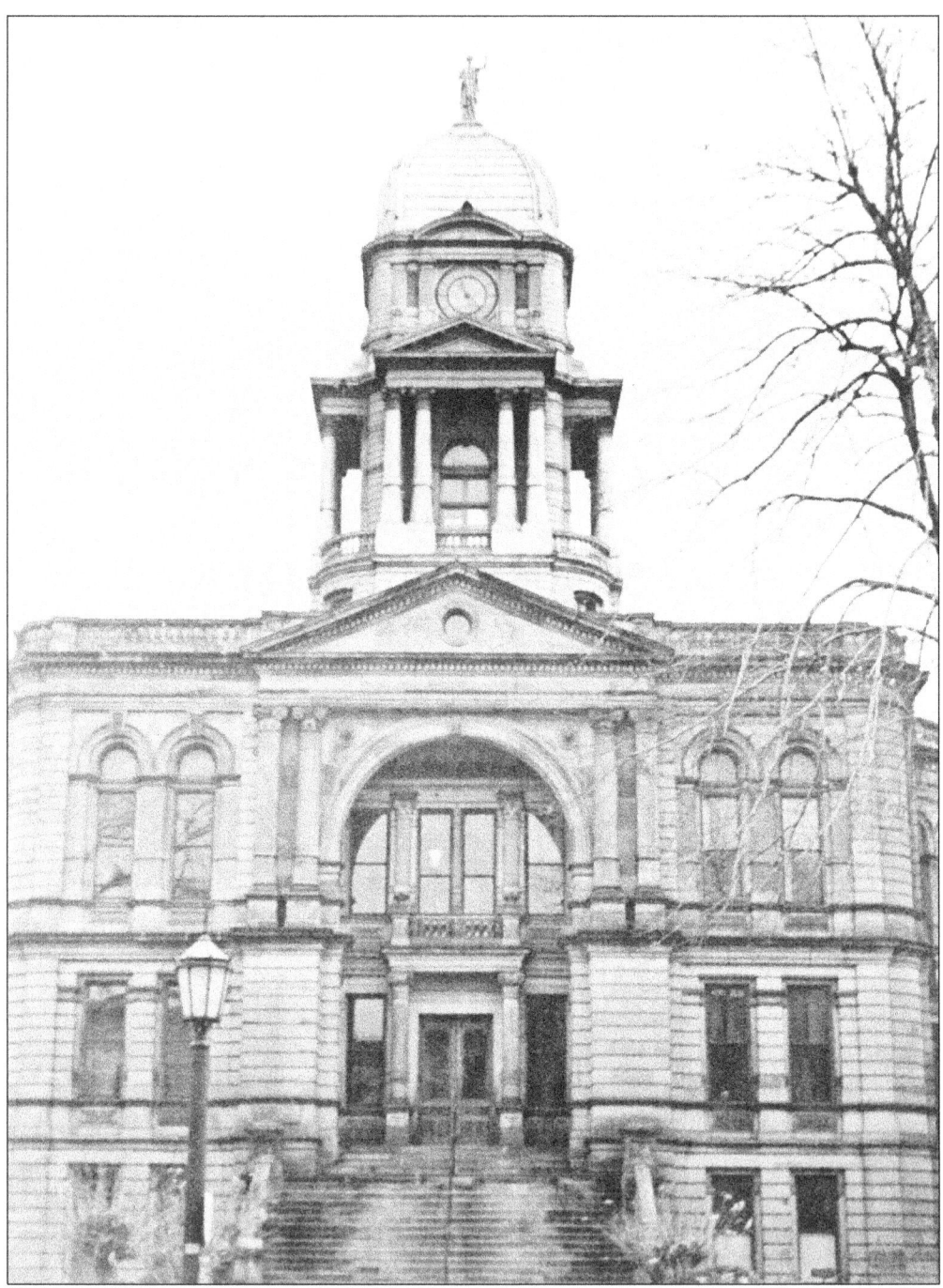

The third Seneca County Courthouse, designed by Elijah E. Myers, was built in 1884. The building, which was listed in the National Register of Historic Places, served the county's judicial and administrative needs until it was abandoned by the courts in 2004 due to its deteriorating condition. County commissioners opted to raze the building in January 2012 rather than invest in a multimillion-dollar upgrade.

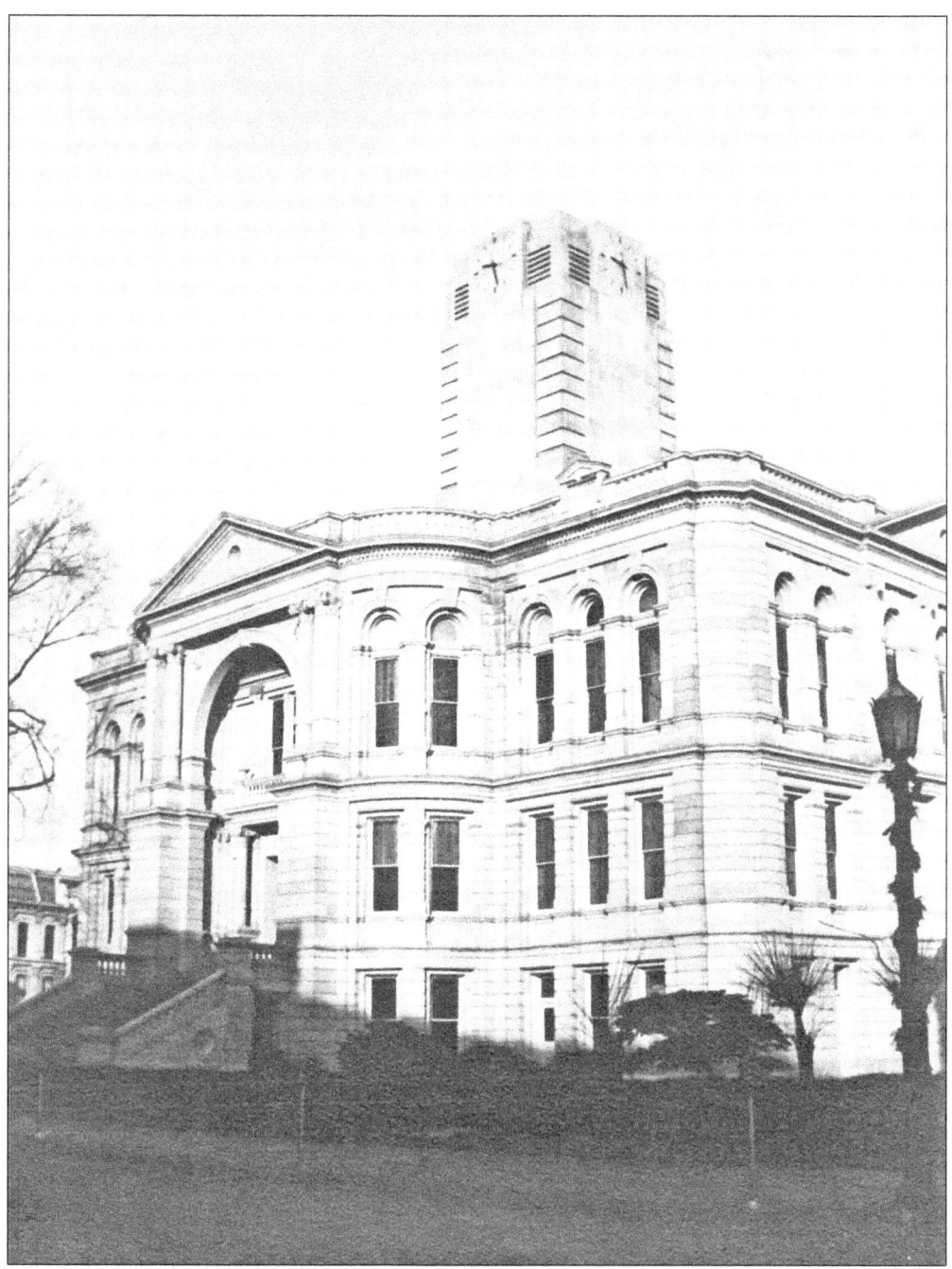

From 1944 forward, the Beaux-Arts facade of the Seneca County Courthouse was offset by an Art Deco clock tower. The courthouse's original clock tower served from the building's 1884 dedication until 1943, when deterioration forced its demolition. A plan to similarly reclad the rest of the courthouse fell through for lack of funding. The architectural incongruity lasted until the courthouse's demolition.

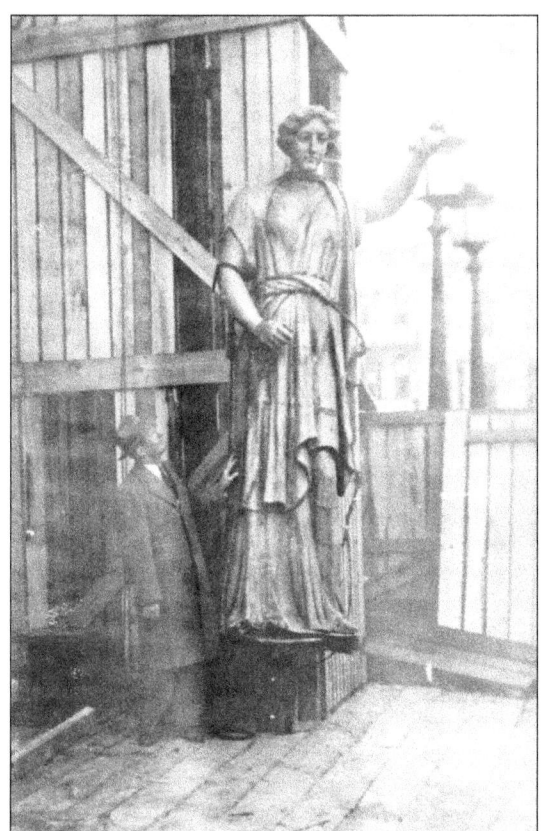

The Lady Liberty statue that had topped the Seneca County courthouse until 1943 sits at ground level in this 1945 photograph. According to legend, the statue was to be melted down to aid in the World War II effort, but employees at Rosenblatt's scrapyard could not bear to comply and buried Lady Liberty instead. A foreman who had heard of his employees' actions ordered them reversed.

A Power Company trolley, with a lone female passenger in an elegant hat, passes in front of the Seneca County Courthouse on South Washington Street in this pre-1906 photograph. The General Gibson statue has yet to be erected, but the 1878 jail and sheriff's residence stands prominently at the rear right. On the left, Court Street is a thriving commercial row.

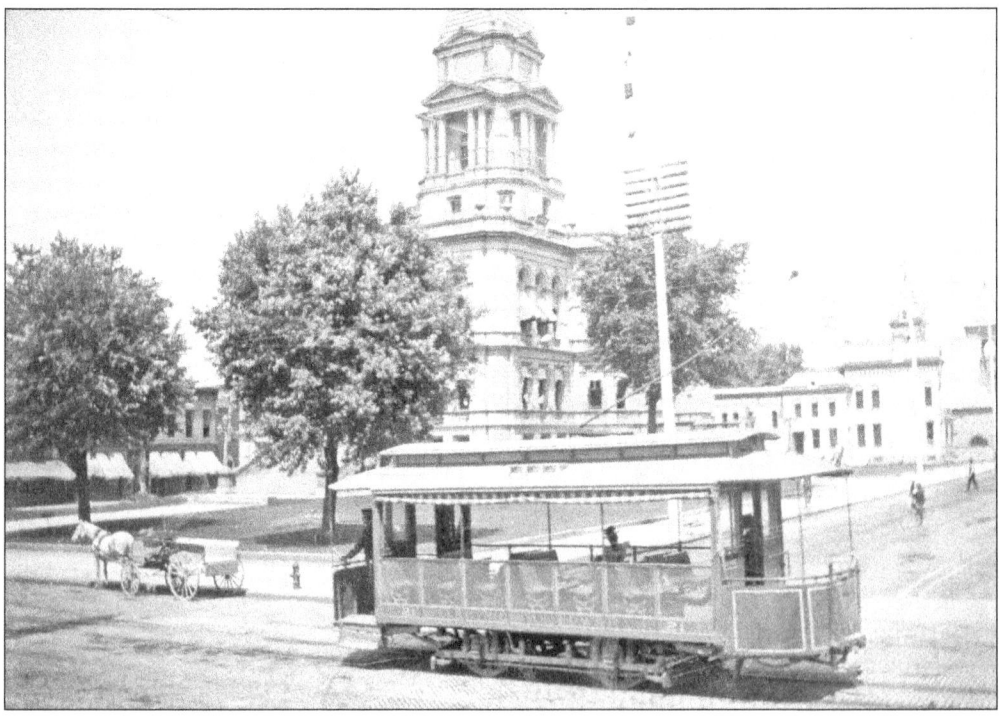

Before 1938, Tiffin's city hall sat at the intersection of East Market and Monroe Streets, as it does today. The fire station, however, faced Market and not Monroe. The reconstruction took place under the auspices of the Works Progress Administration, Pres. Franklin Delano Roosevelt's program to lift the nation out of the Great Depression. The new building was occupied in 1940.

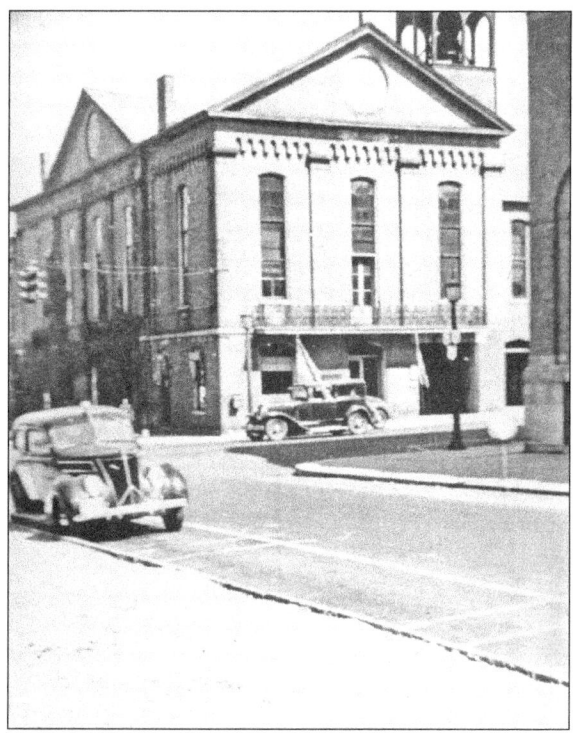

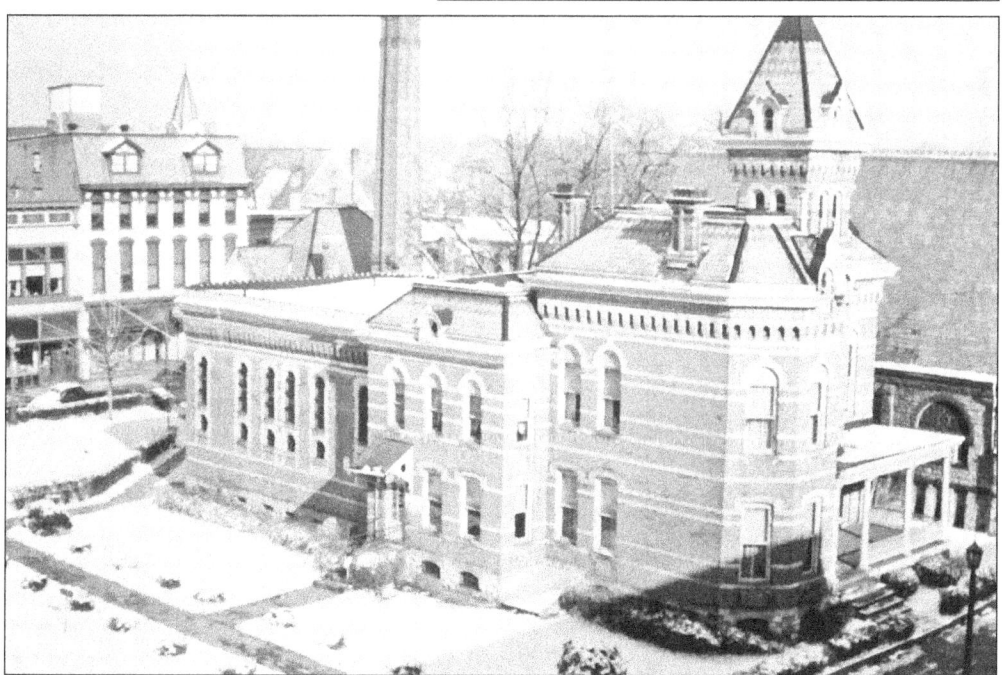

The 1878 Seneca County Jail served for about a century before declining conditions and an inmate lawsuit forced its court-ordered closure. Built on the site of the home of Tiffin's first mayor, Dr. Henry Kuhn, the jail cost $20,600 (plus $10,000 in land acquisition). The building was eventually razed and replaced with a county office building, the facade of which mimics the old jail's banding.

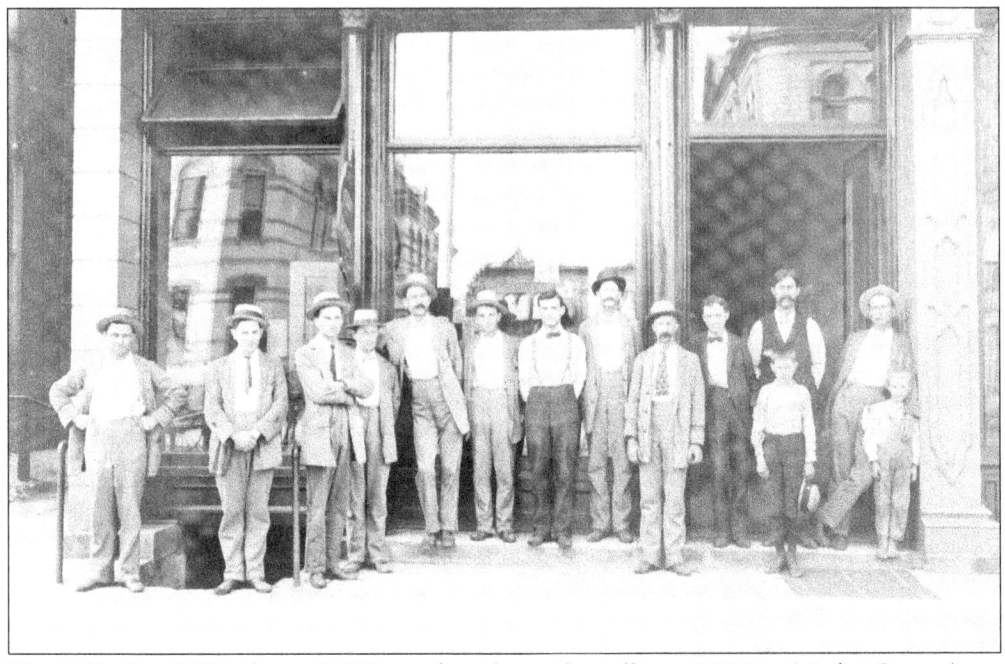

The Tiffin Post Office force of 1898 stands in front of its office at 100 East Market Street (note the reflection of the courthouse in the window at the left). This storefront would serve until completion of the South Washington Street building in 1916. By 1967, the carriers had moved to the present-day facility on South Monroe Street.

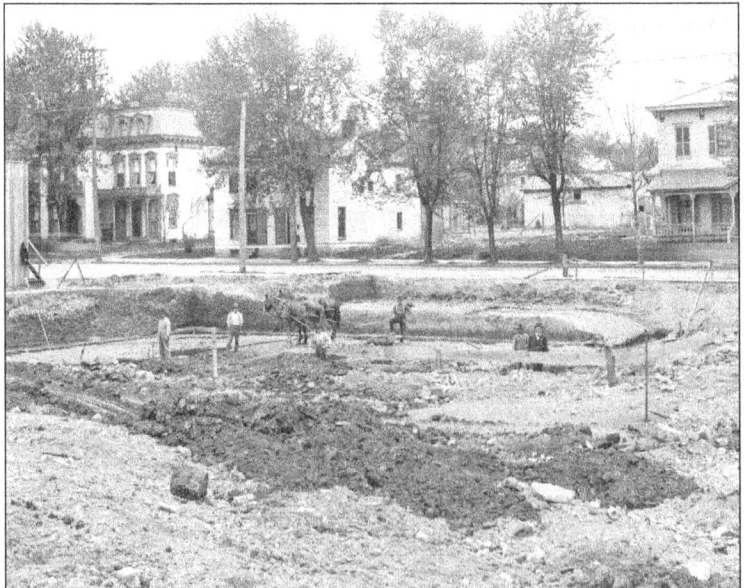

Post office construction gets under way as the foundation for the building is dug at its 217 South Washington Street location on May 1, 1915 (the back of the photograph is signed by a Mr. Cramer, the superintendent of construction). The location, where Main Street dead-ends into South Washington, had previously been the site of the Western Exchange Hotel.

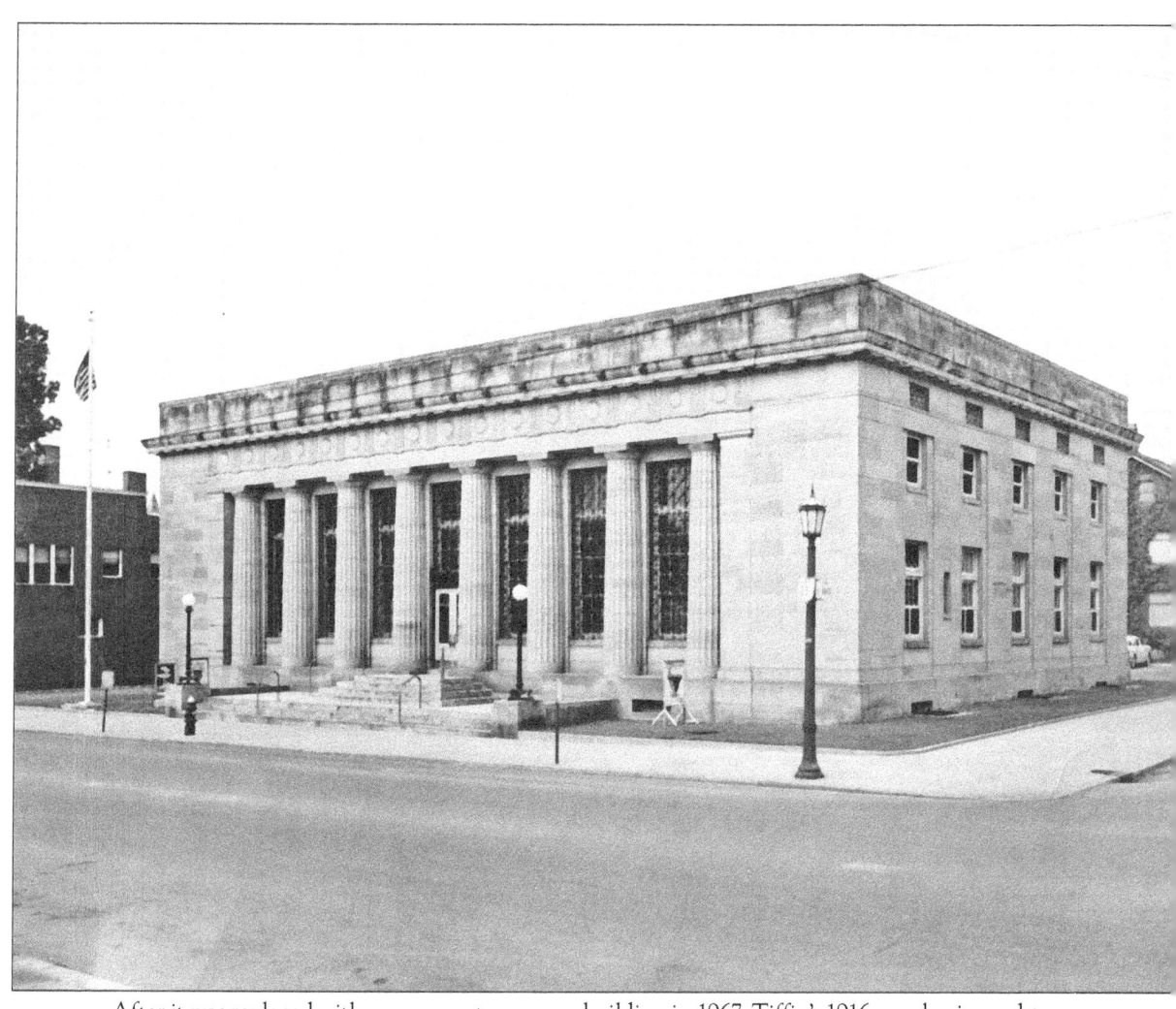

After it was replaced with a more contemporary building in 1967, Tiffin's 1916 neoclassic sandstone post office served as an annex to Columbian High School. Since January 2011, the building has been home to the American Civil War Museum of Ohio. The museum's numerous exhibits trace the 17th state's role in aiding the effort to preserve the union.

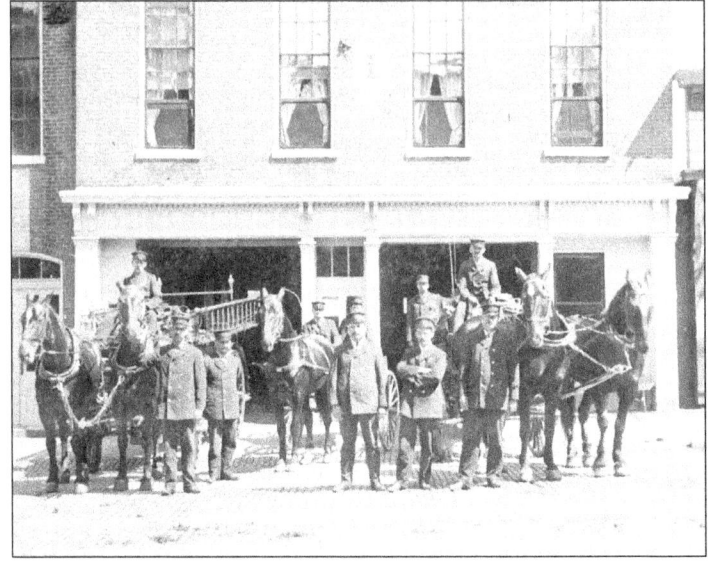

Horse carts, carriages, and hook-and-ladder wagons were the state-of-the-art firefighting tools in the days before the advent of motorized transportation. Though this photograph is from around 1910, similar equipment was in use at the time of Tiffin's Great Fire in 1872. In the wake of that fire, Tiffin received aid from Chicago (among other cities), reciprocating the aid Tiffin had sent Chicago after that city's devastating 1871 fire.

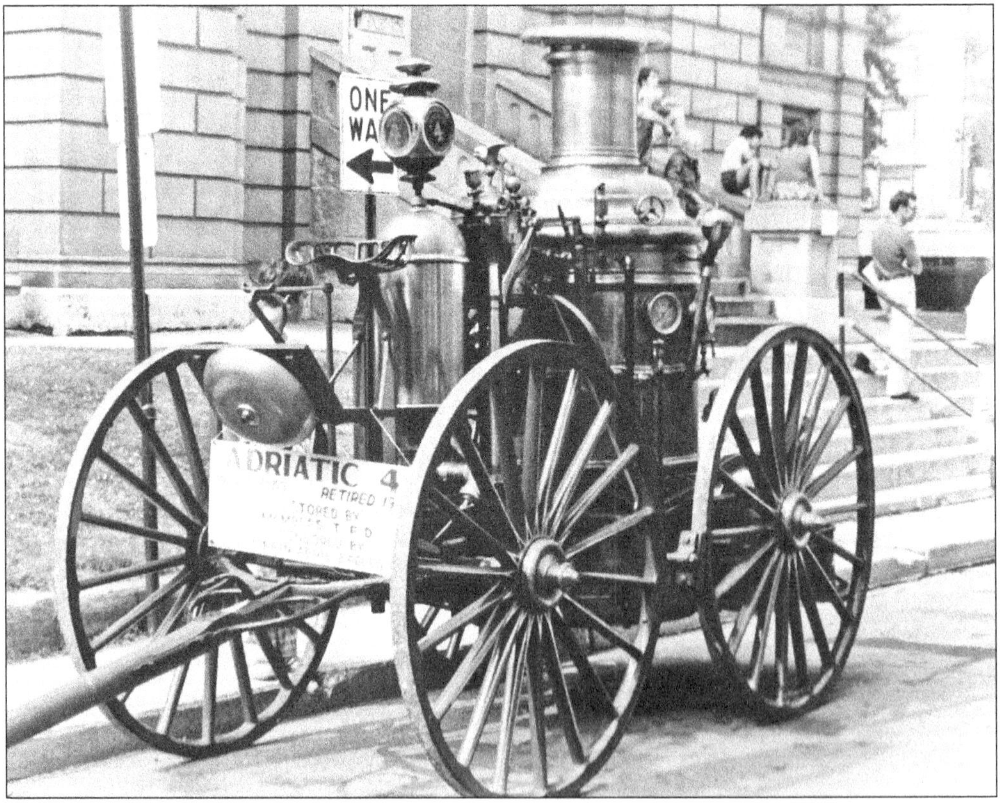

The fire department's vintage pumper, the *Adriatic*, was on public display next to the courthouse in 1978. The *Adriatic* ran for 22 hours straight during Tiffin's Great Fire of April 13, 1872. That blaze consumed 35 homes, as well as numerous barns, sheds, and several businesses. In today's dollars, the fire is estimated to have done more than $1.5 million in damage on both sides of the Sandusky River.

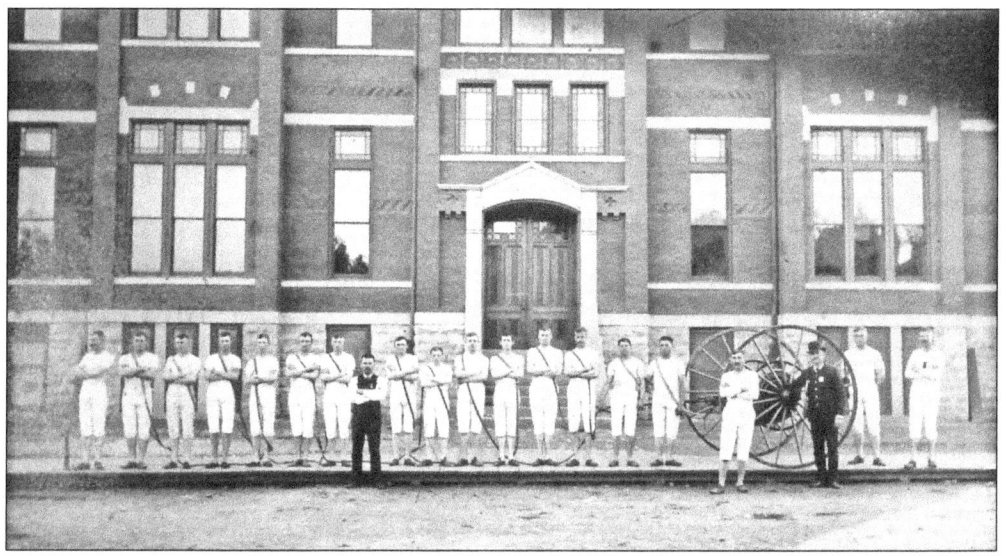

Volunteer firefighters of the Alert Hose Company pose in their tournament uniforms in front of the Miami Street School (now part of Tiffin University). The hose cart they are standing with is now part of the collection of the Seneca County Museum.

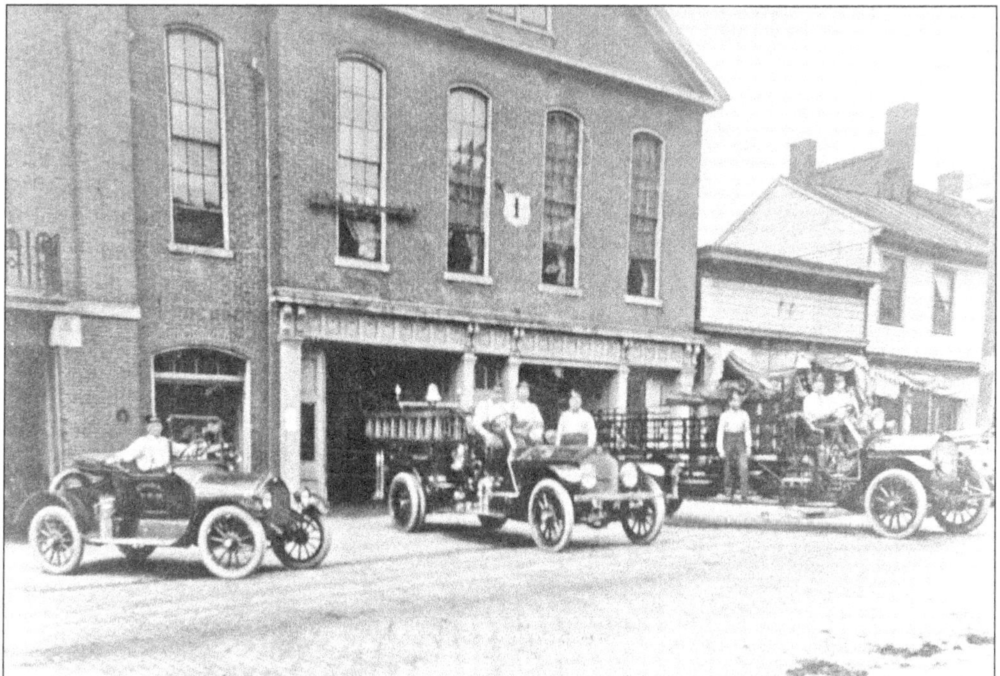

The city's firefighters pose with their equipment outside Firehouse No. 1. The firehouse was located on Market Street, just east of Monroe Street. No. 1 was the sole firehouse to remain in operation after Tiffin's city council decided in 1893 to move from a volunteer force to a full-time, paid firefighting staff. This building was replaced by the South Monroe Street station in 1940.

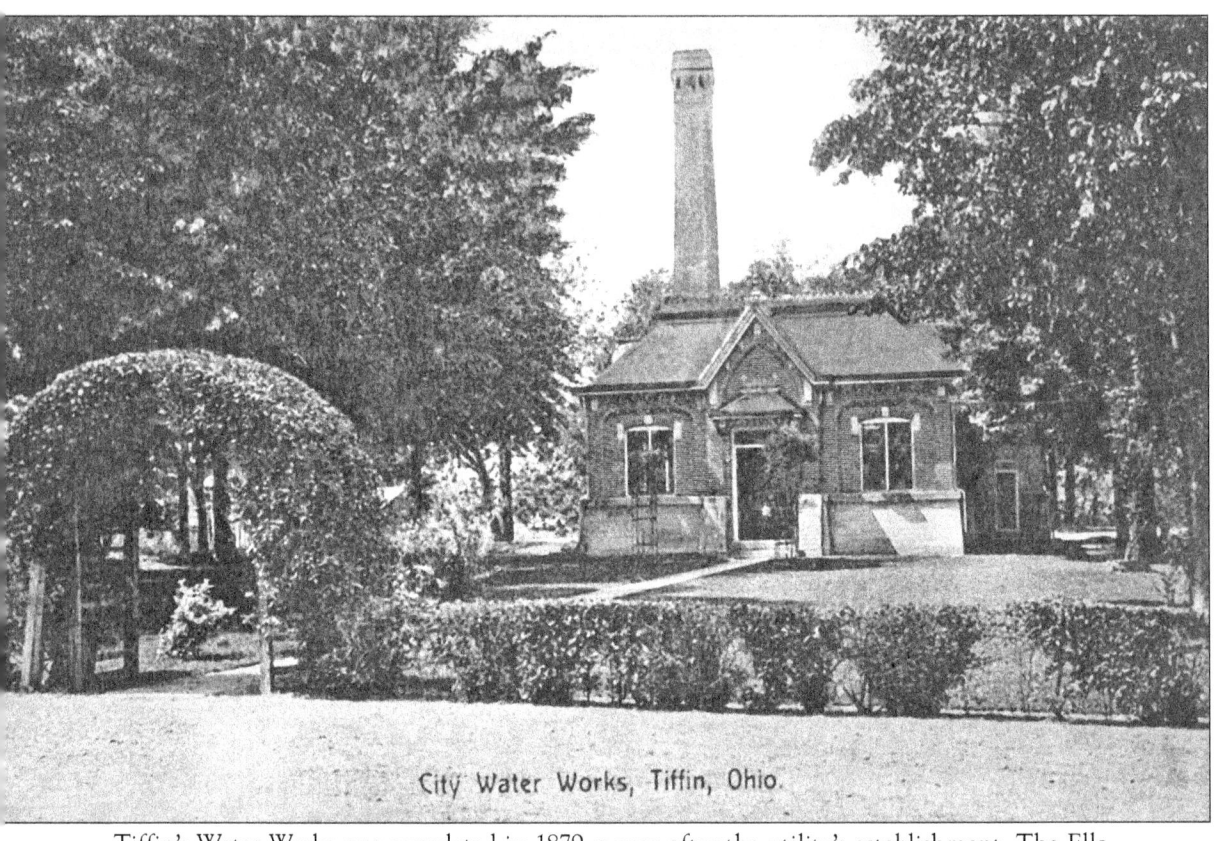

City Water Works, Tiffin, Ohio.

Tiffin's Water Works was completed in 1879, a year after the utility's establishment. The Ella Street facility originally drew its water from on-site artesian wells; the Sandusky River—along the bank of which the plant is situated—was not tapped as a water source until 1918. The building was added to the National Register of Historic Places in 1980.

Three

A City of Business

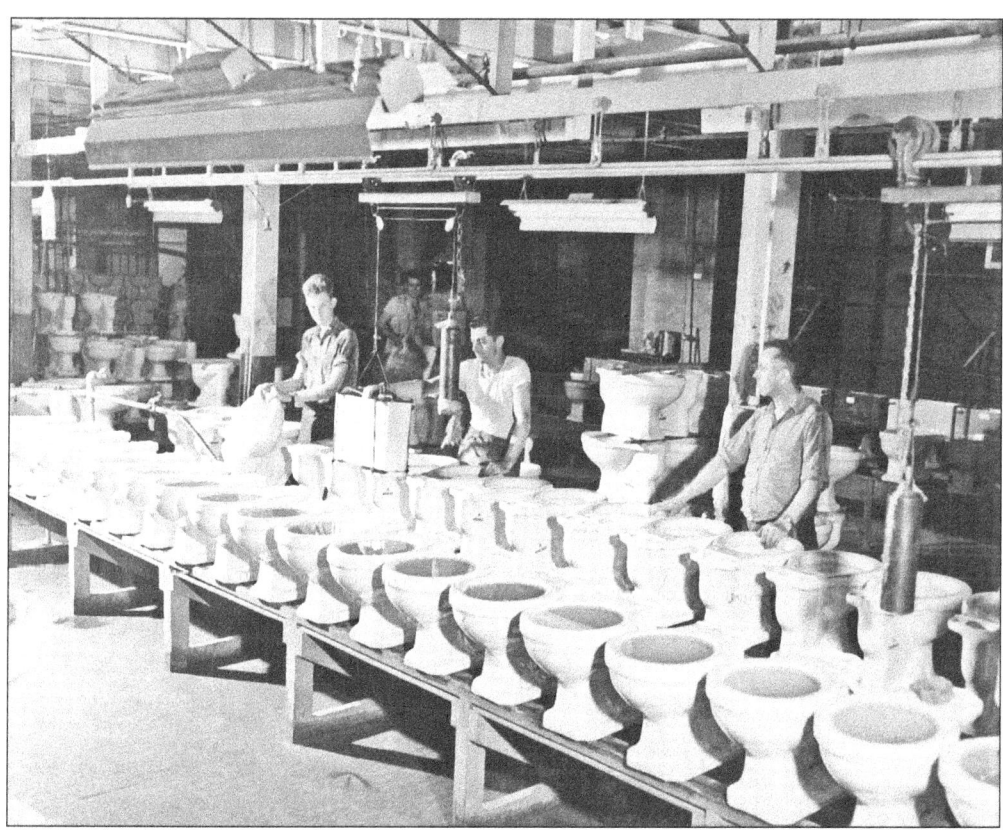

American Standard in Tiffin was known for its production of toilets, a logical extension of predecessor Great Western's specialization in sanitary ware for bedrooms. By the late 1960s, the Tiffin plant was producing 1.2 million toilet bowl and tank units a year. Myron Barnes credits the plant as "the largest vitreous china manufacturing facility in the United States, and one of the largest in the world."

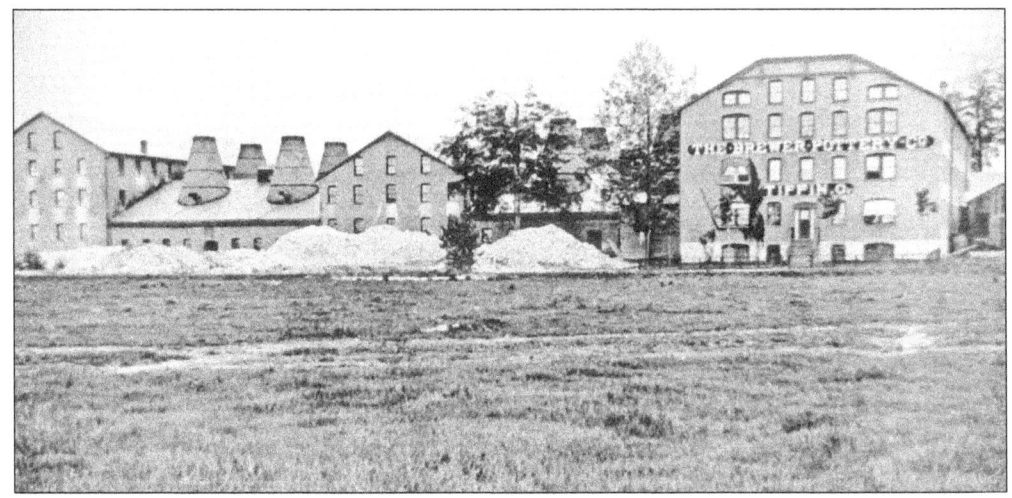

The Brewer Pottery Co. was a forerunner of Tiffin's American Standard plant. Its Tiffin roots trace to 1889; industrialist Meshech Frost helped to lure Brewer officials. A decade later, the foundering plant was acquired by Great Western Pottery of Kokomo, Indiana. In 1913, Great Western sold the Tiffin plant to Standard Manufacturing, which merged with the American Radiator Company in 1929.

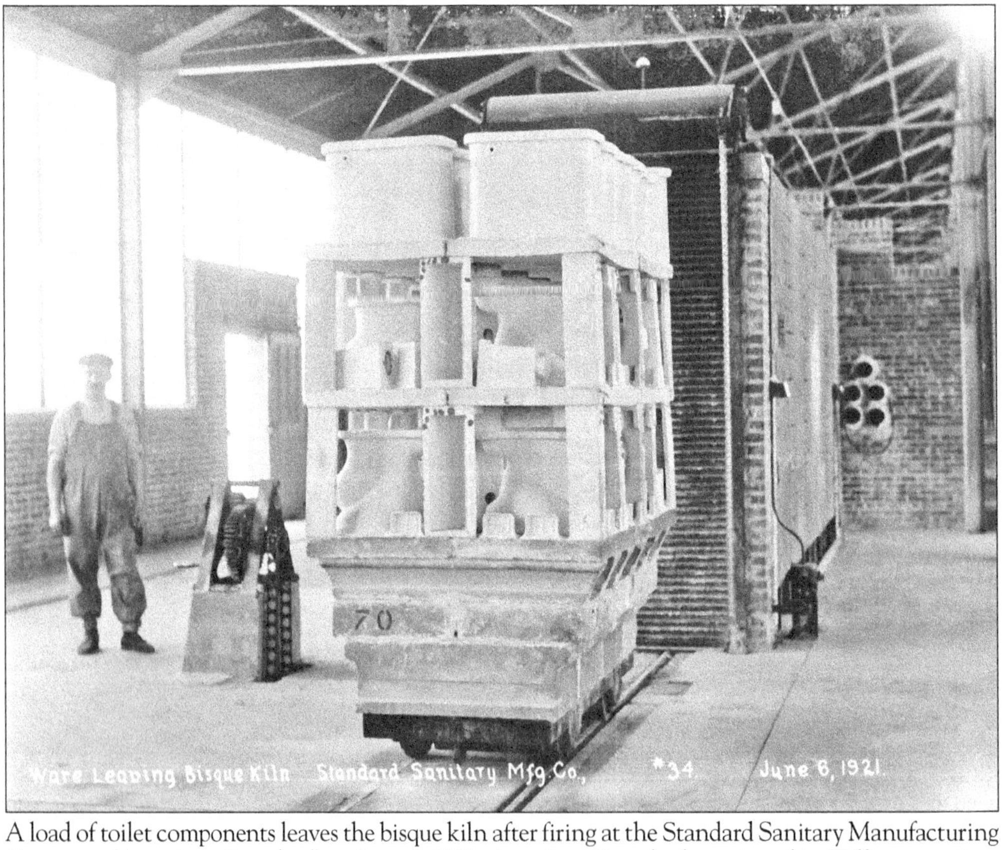

Ware Leaving Bisque Kiln Standard Sanitary Mfg.Co.,   #34.   June 6, 1921.

A load of toilet components leaves the bisque kiln after firing at the Standard Sanitary Manufacturing Company (American Standard) on June 6, 1921. American Standard continued its Tiffin operations until 2008, citing a downturn in the housing market in its decision to close the plant.

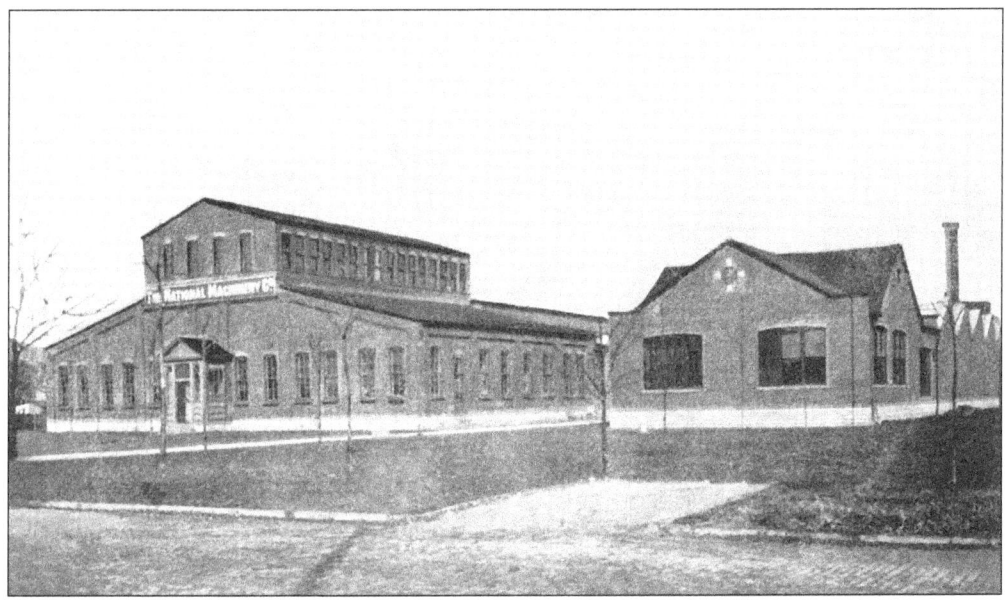

In 1882, Meshech Frost was instrumental in luring the National Bolt and Pipe Machinery Company from Cleveland to Tiffin. From the Greenfield Street plant would come machines that made wire nails, fencing, and even stone crushers. The National went international in 1958 with the acquisition of a plant in Nuremberg, Germany. The plant closed briefly in 2002 but is again under local family ownership.

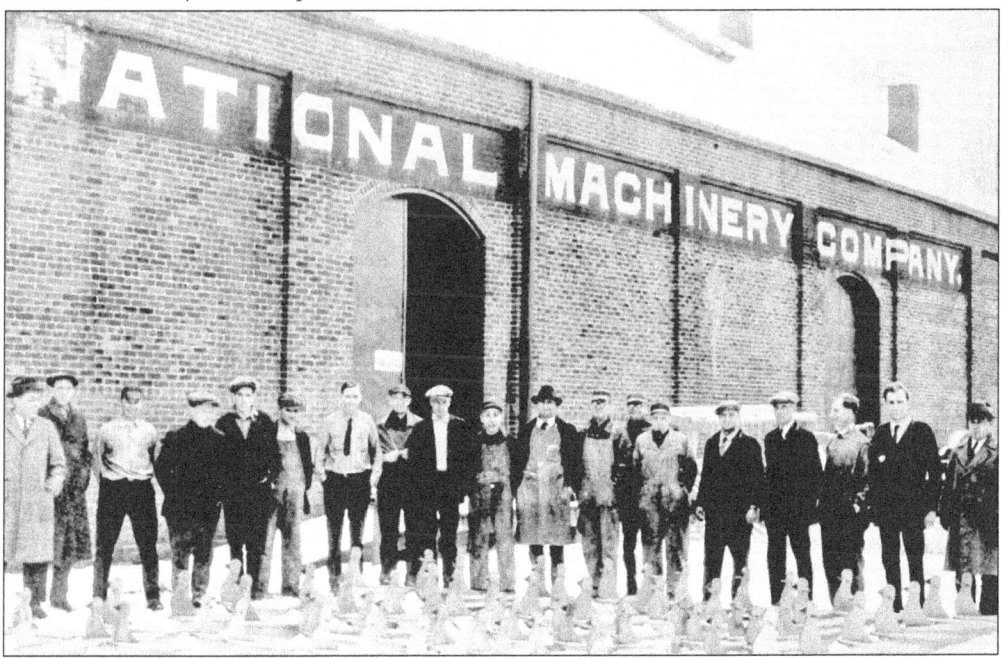

Early 20th-century employees of the National pose with toy ducks they had made as Christmas gifts for Junior Home children. The Frost family, National's owners, have shown an abiding interest in giving back to the community the National calls home, largely through the National Machinery Foundation. Since 1948, it has contributed to worthy causes from the community YMCA to education at all levels.

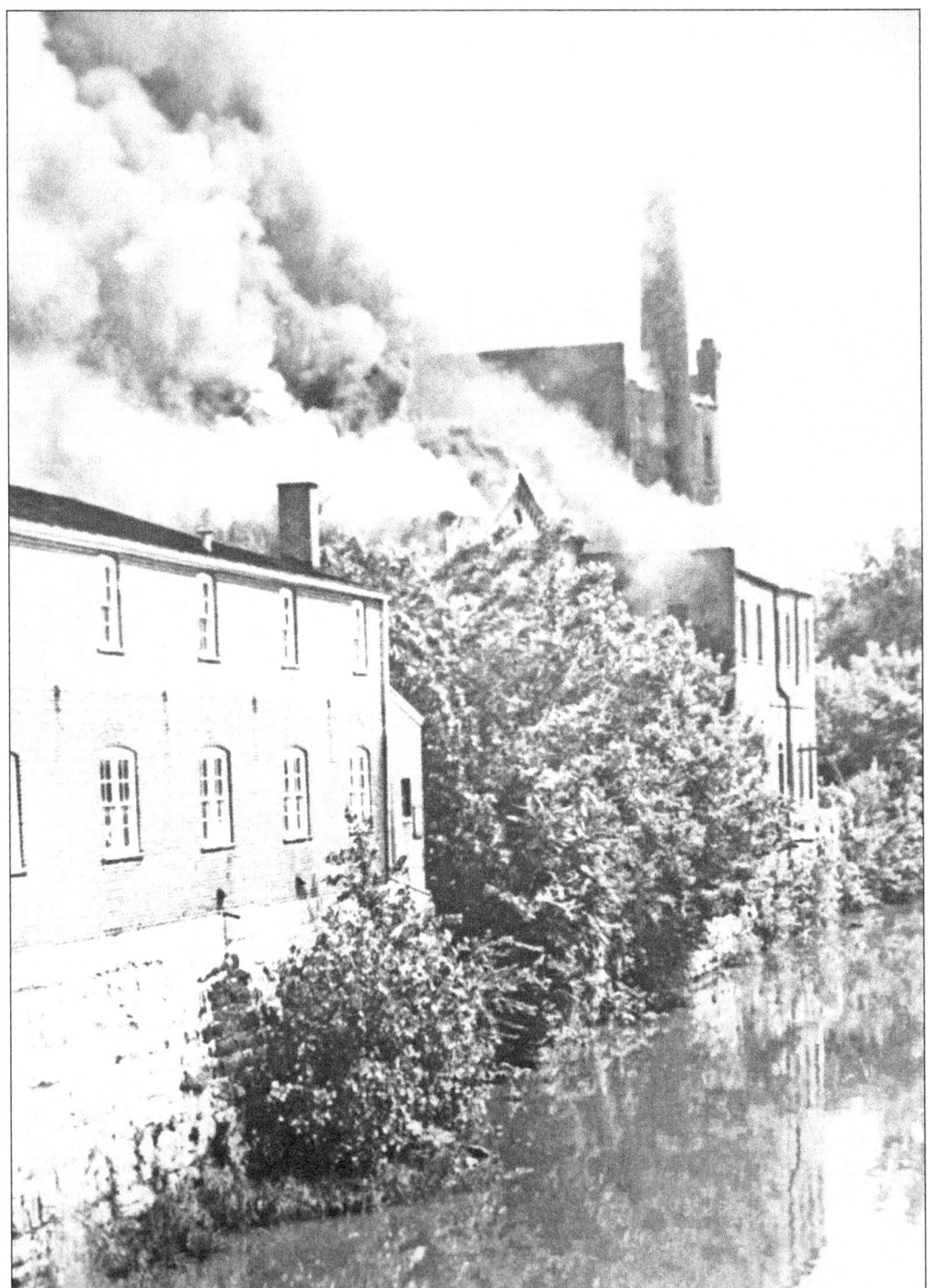

The former Hubach Brewery was struck by fire in August 1966. The Madison Street business began as the City Brewery in 1859. After passing through the hands of several owners, it was bought by Henry Hubach in the late 1870s. The brewery was family-owned until Prohibition, when it was converted into a milk and ice cream plant. Beatrice Foods was the owner at the time of the fire.

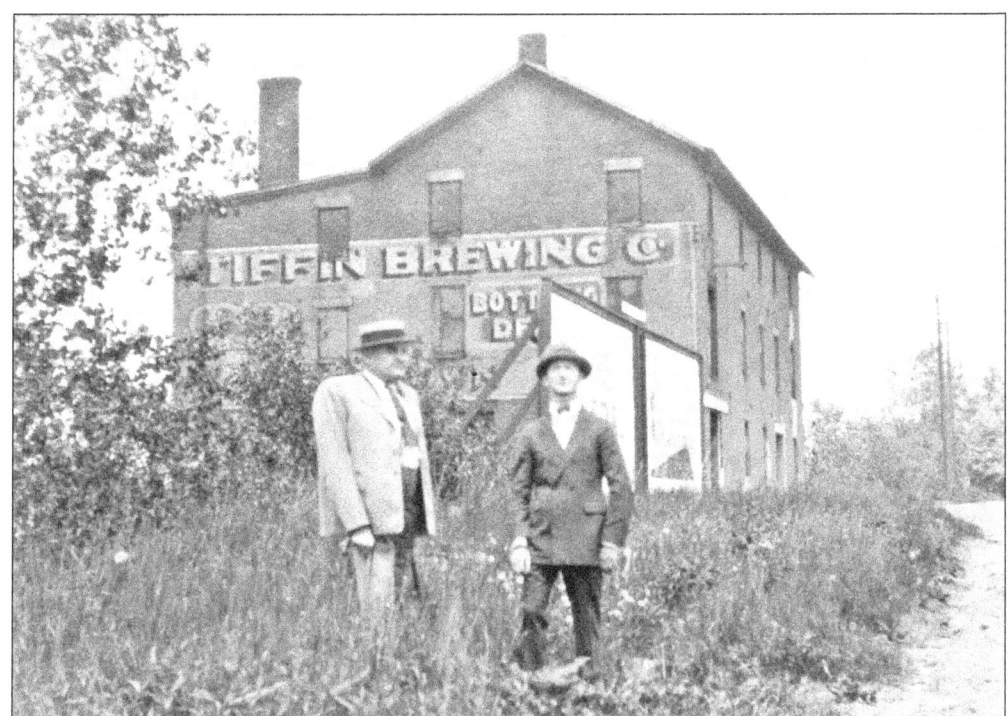

The Tiffin Brewing Co. operated from 1848 to 1920 along present-day Riverside Drive. The plant survived both the Great Fire of 1872 and the Flood of 1913; water collapsed a portion of the brewery in 1920. A portion of the former plant remains in use by Tiffin Scenic Studio, which makes rigging, curtains, and scenic drops for theaters and auditoriums.

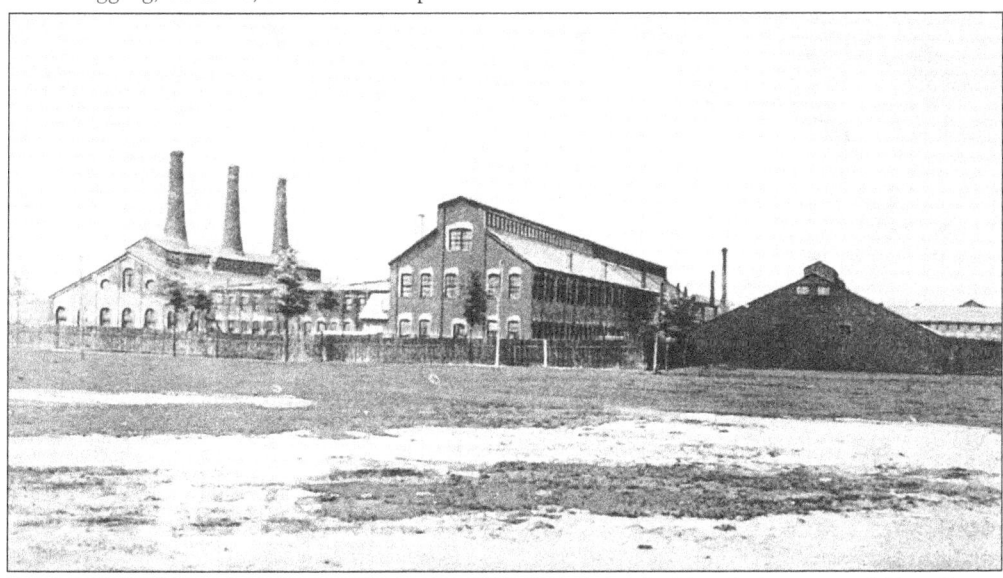

August 19, 1889, marked the initial pouring of Tiffin Glass; the Fourth Avenue and Vine Street plant came to be known for its stemware and other collectible glass. The plant attracted craftsmen from across Europe, and Tiffin Glass gained such a reputation that it was at one time sold through Tiffany's. Production ceased on May 1, 1980, and the city demolished a portion of the plant five years later.

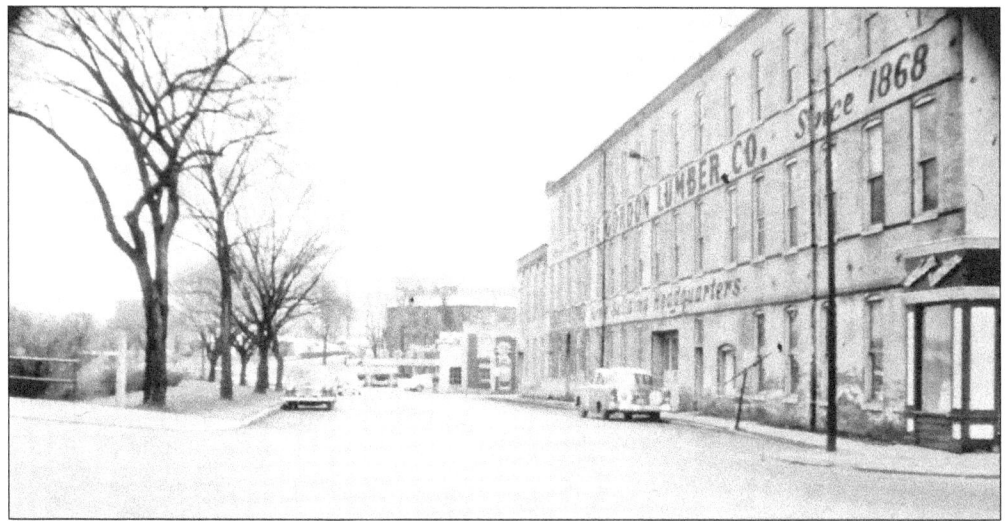

The Gordon Lumber Company later occupied the three-story brick building at Washington Street and River Road (now Riverside Drive) first known as home to the Tiffin Woolen Mills. Rezin Shawhan and others founded the mills with capitalization of $100,000 in 1867; they were in operation until shortly after the turn of the century. The site is now the location of the Seneca County Commission on Aging.

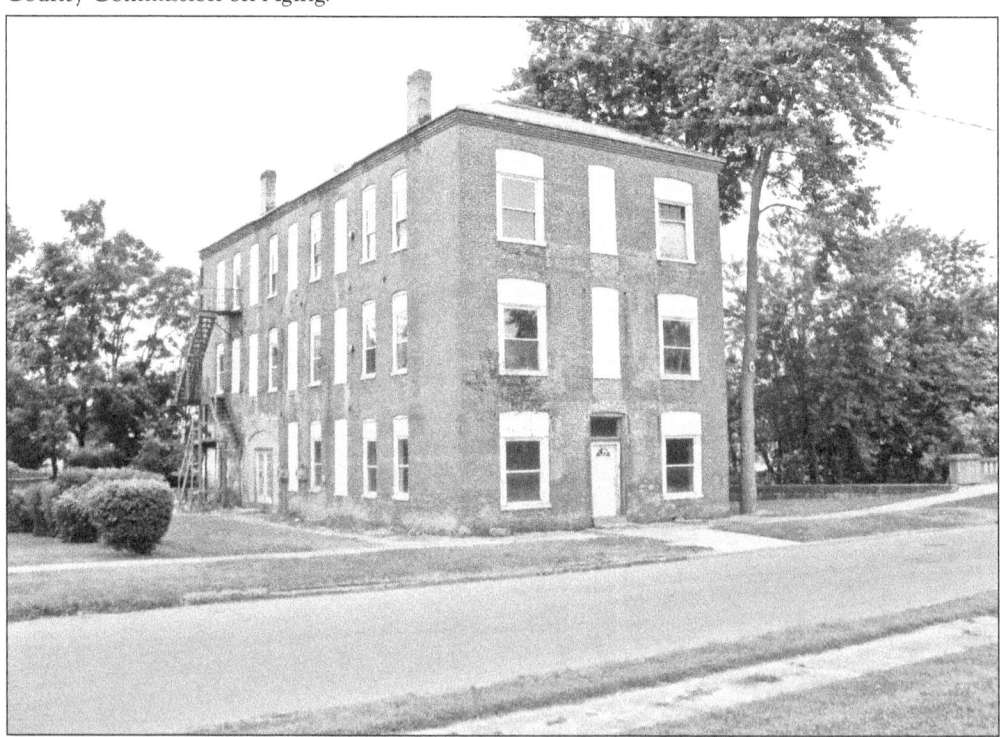

The first location of the Tiffin Shoe Factory was a building along Rock Creek on a triangle of land formed by Jefferson and Liberty Streets and Riverside Drive. After the shoe factory moved into a downtown storefront, the three-story brick building was converted for apartment living. In photographs of the Flood of 1913, the VanNette apartments can be seen standing defiantly against the rising water. (Authors' collection.)

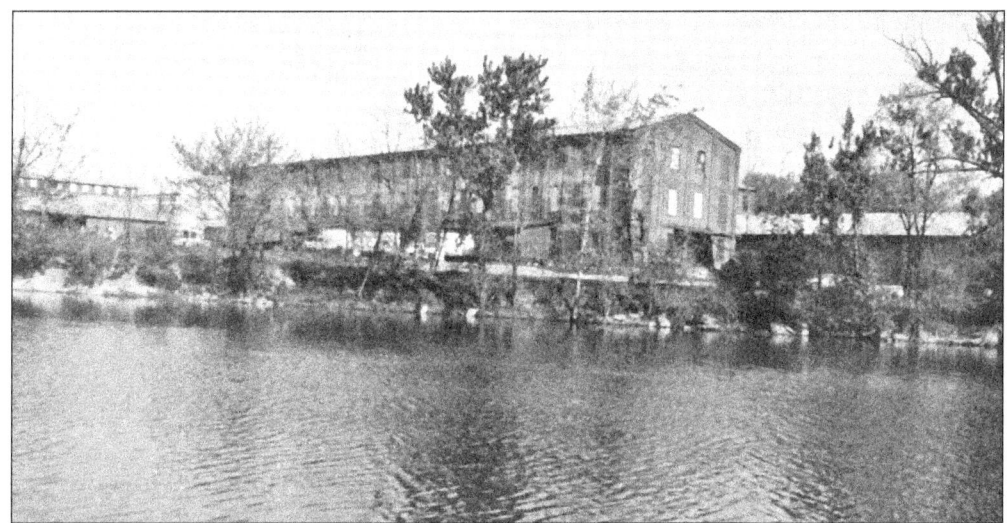

Established in 1858, Tiffin Agricultural (later Wagon) Works manufactured farm implements at its plant at Harrison and Minerva Streets. After emerging from receivership in 1899, the business came to focus on the production of farm wagons. Historian Myron Barnes tells of his brother seeing a Tiffin wagon on a deserted French farm during World War I. The emergence of the automobile led to the company's dissolution sometime shortly after 1914.

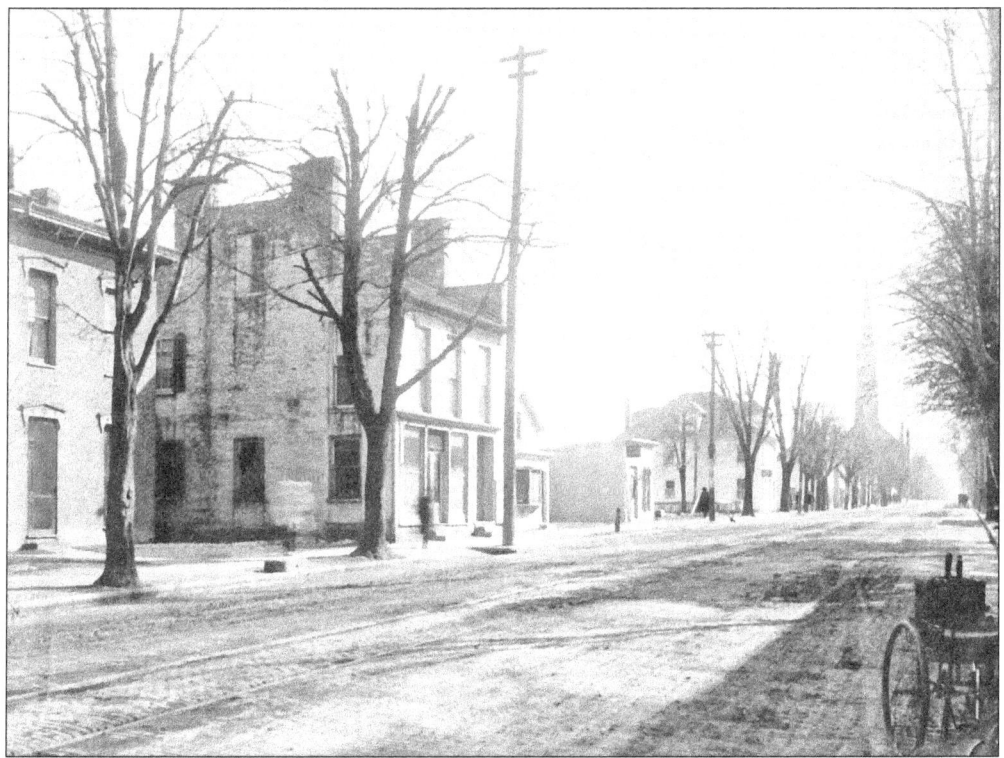

This South Washington Street scene features the Western Exchange Hotel in the foreground. Built in 1836 by Calvin Bradley, the four-chimney brick building is showing considerable wear at the time of this undated late 19th-century photograph. The Western Exchange was where Tiffin founder Josiah Hedges died; he lived at the hotel in his final years.

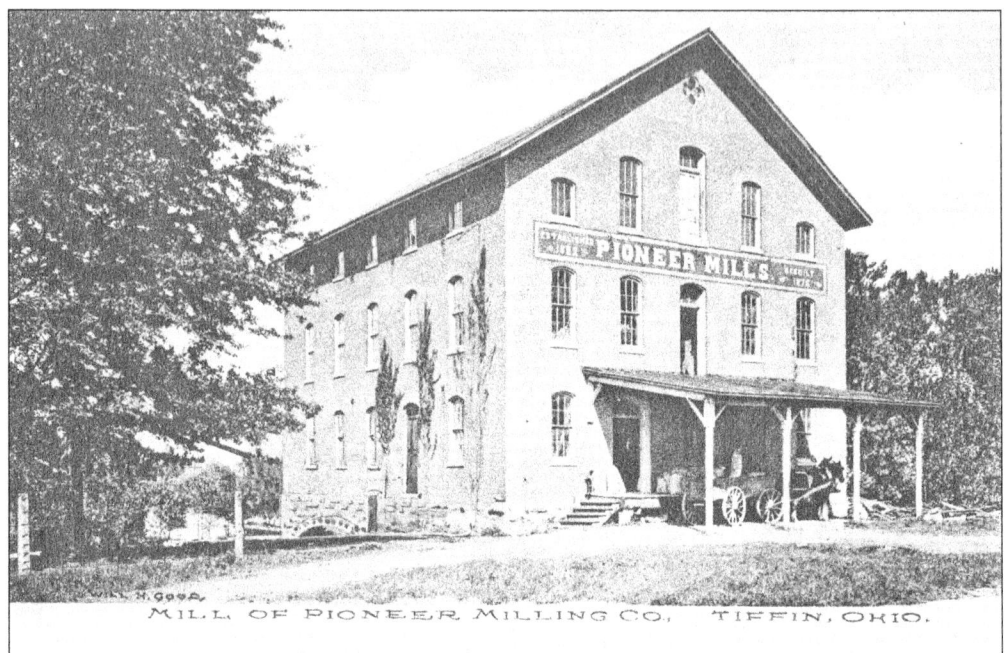

A postcard depicts the Pioneer Mill on Riverside Drive in its post-1875 reconstruction. The mill withstood both the 1913 flood and a second fire in 1937. The milling business was abandoned in 1950, with the mill eventually repurposed into a restaurant. Roger Bacon, who owned the milling business at the turn of the 20th century, estimates that, at its height, Seneca County was home to 25 waterwheels.

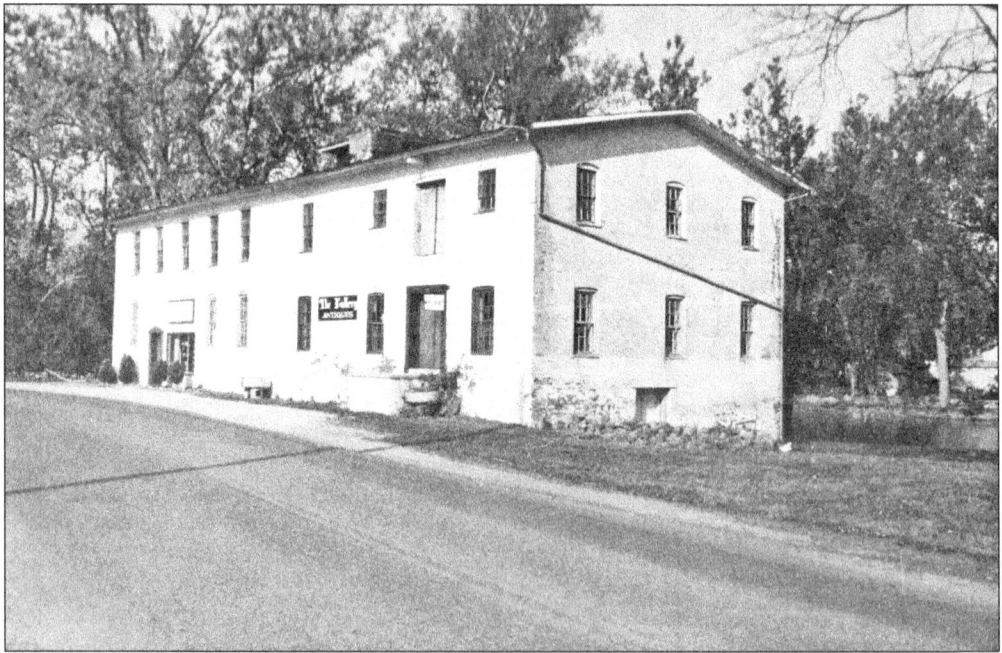

This Riverside Drive building, next to the Pioneer Mill, was constructed in the early 1860s as the Eagle Rye Distillery. In the 1890s, it became a soap factory before being used as the Tiffin Robe and Tanning Company. Today, it houses an antiques store.

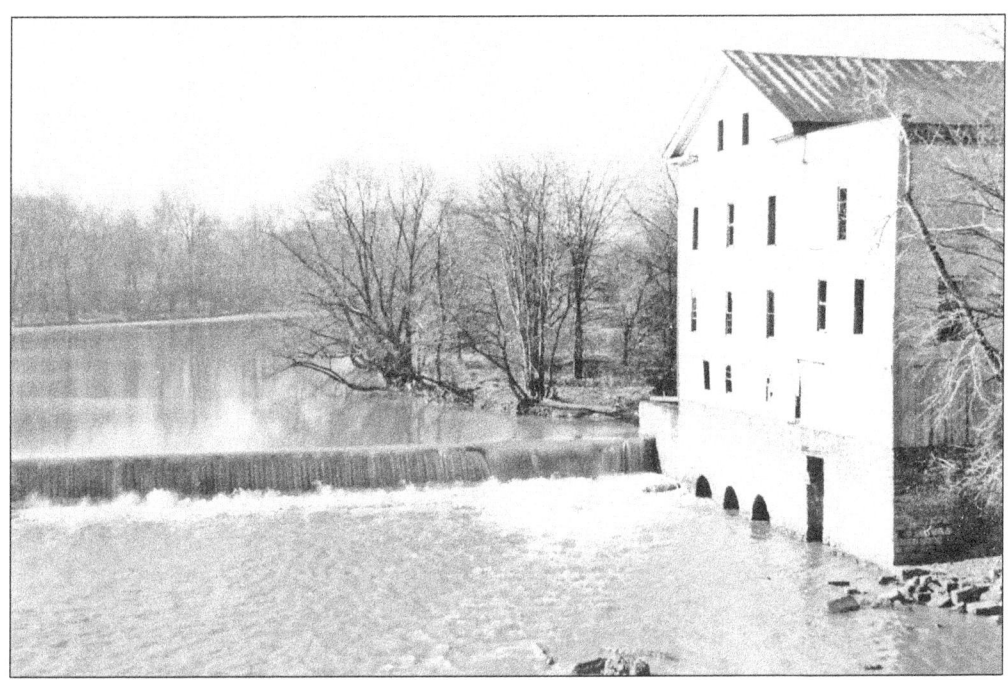

Speck's Mill sat south of the present-day Huss Street Bridge, on the western bank of the Sandusky River (this view is looking southward downriver). Harry Speck's massive gristmill, which ground both corn and wheat, was built in 1846 and operated well into the 20th century after withstanding the floodwaters of 1913. The mill was demolished in 1947.

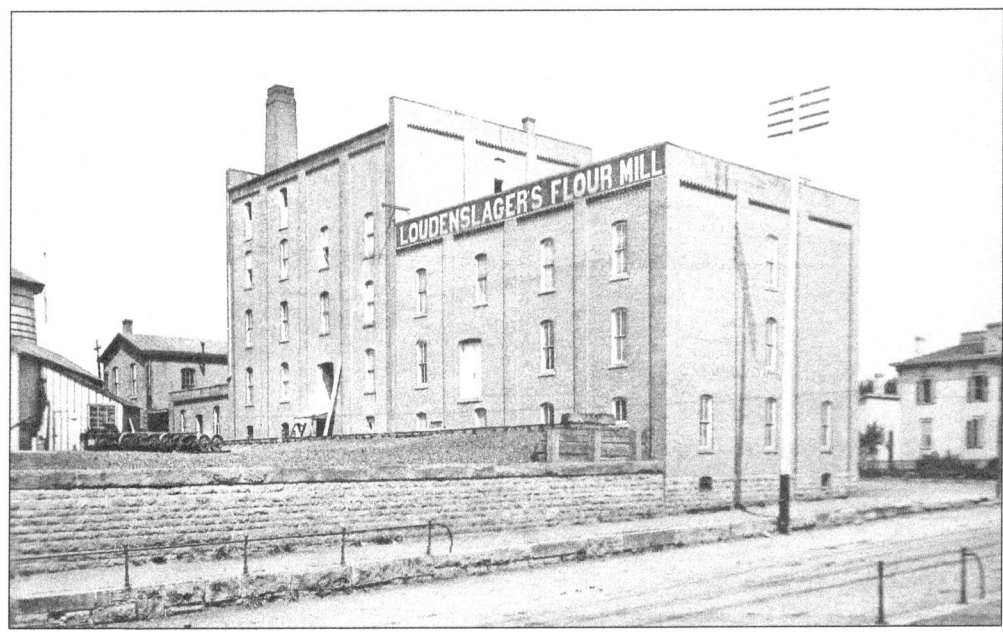

In 1895, Joseph Loudenslager purchased the flour mill that he ran until his death 30 years later. The facility had been built in 1884 as the McAdoo, Einsel & Shears Steam Flouring Mill. At the time of its 1885 opening, it was claimed the mill could produce 200 barrels of flour in 24 hours, milling 1,000 bushels of wheat.

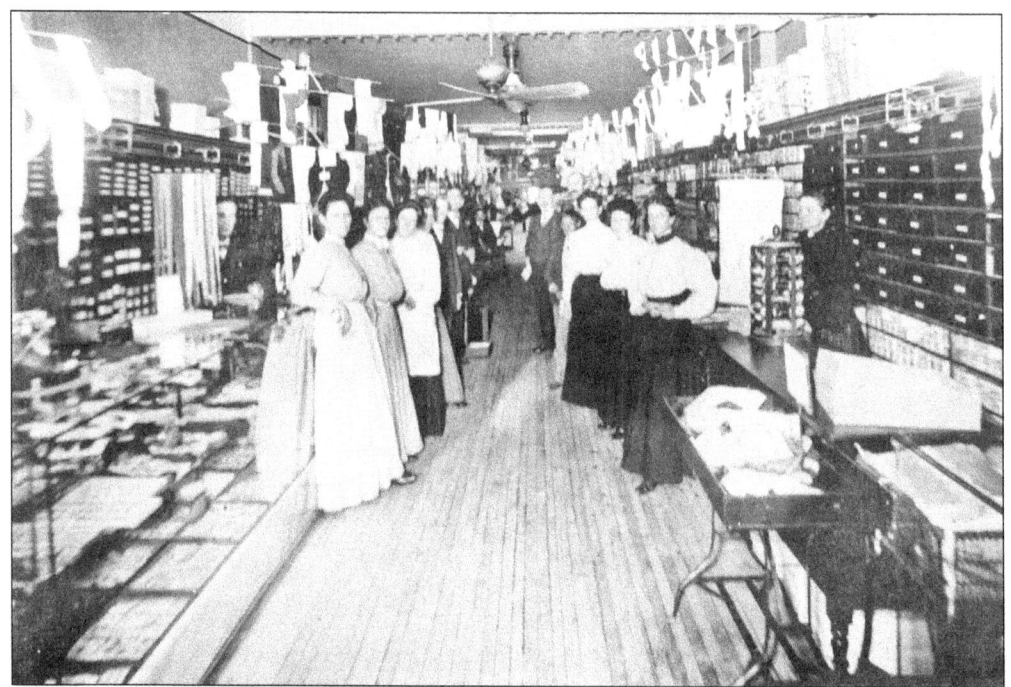

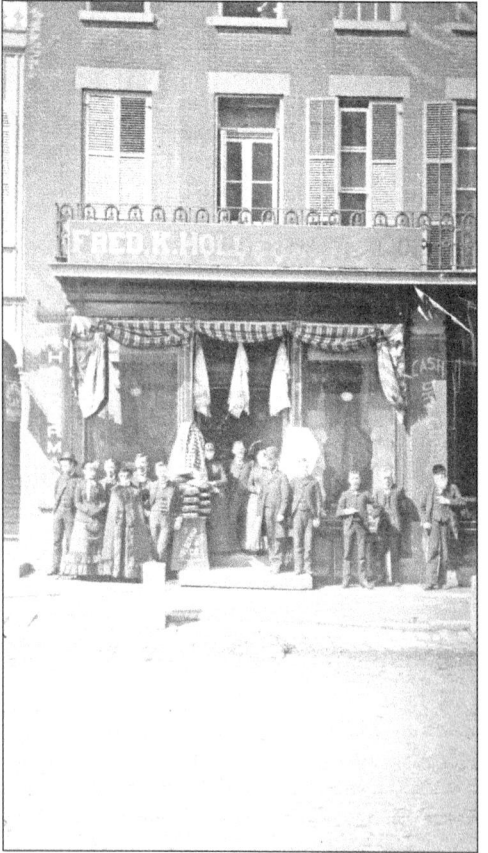

The staff of Holderman's dry goods store poses for an 1895 photograph. Holderman's, at 106 South Washington Street, remained in business into the 1930s. A notice in the 1903 book *Historical Sketches of the Churches and Schools of Tiffin, Ohio* advertises "fine dress goods," including "new grenadines," and "French and Persian lawns." "We are also prepared to show an unsurpassed line of Lace and Trimmings," it announces.

Fred K. Holderman's staff poses in their finest outside the Washington Street dry goods store. The female members of the staff are particularly well dressed, with one decked out in fur and another carrying a beaded purse.

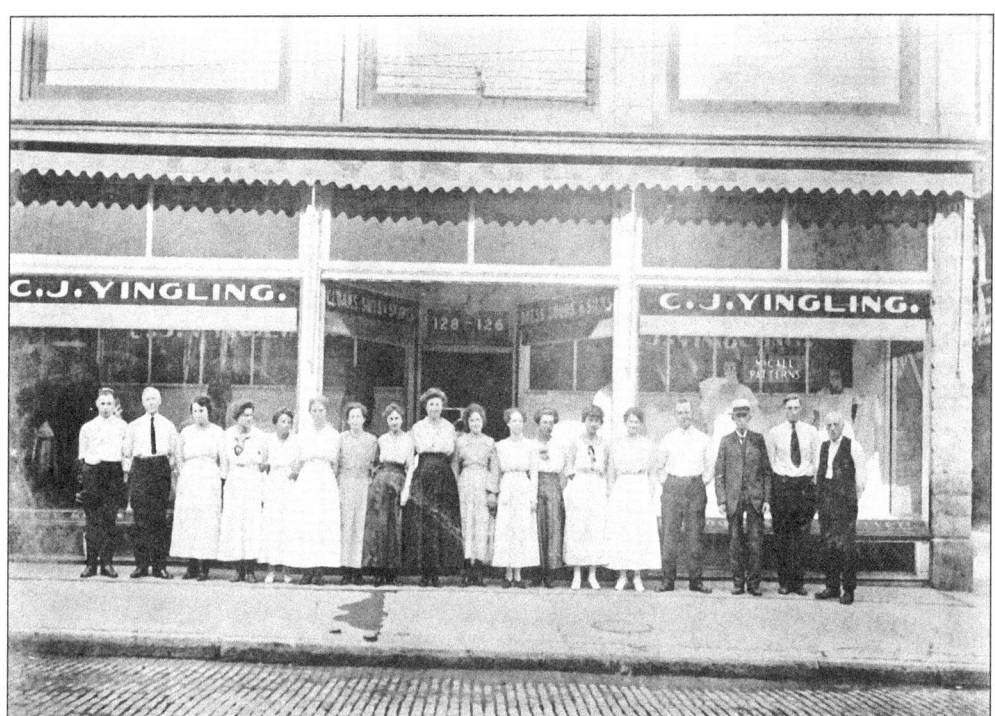

C.J. Yingling's was one of six dry-goods stores along Washington Street in 1880s Tiffin, and one of three that survived into the 1930s. "Ladies bought dress materials by the yard at one of the dry goods stores where they also looked through fashion plates to select a stylish pattern," writes historian Myron Barnes. The wraparound above the store's entrance advertises "cloaks, suits & skirts/dress goods & silks."

Berson's Boston Store was a Washington Street fixture through the mid-1950s. The department store, run by proprietors Max and Leah Berson, carried both women's and men's clothes (ladies' hats and men's dress shirts and ties are both visible in the window displays). The three-story brick building was destroyed by fire in July 1955. The loss was estimated at $150,000.

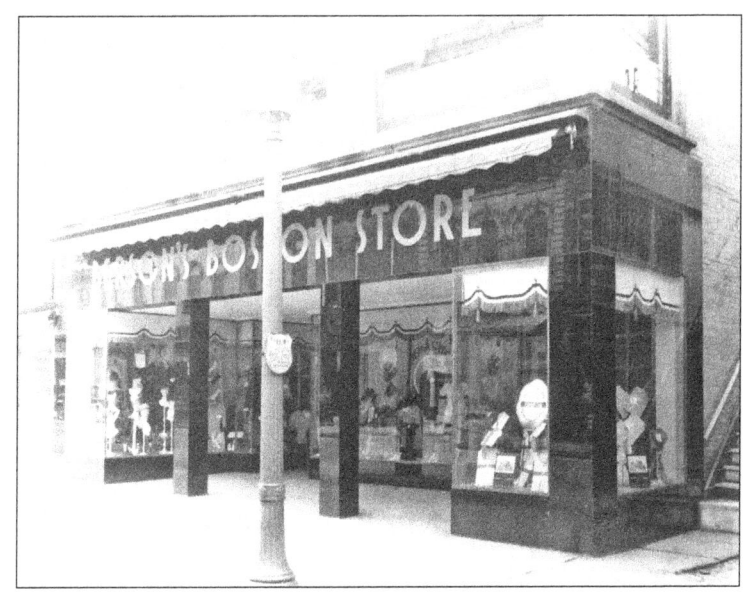

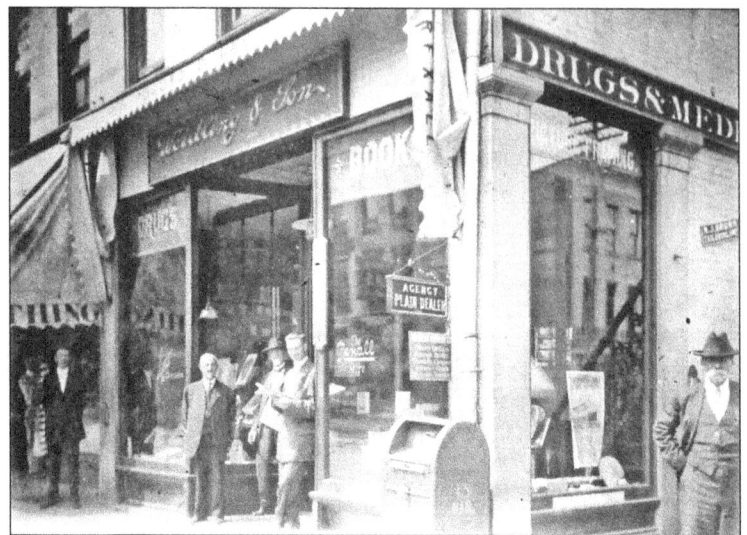

Welding & Son was Tiffin's Rexall Store at 108 South Washington Street. The drugstore offered numerous other services as well—from money orders and travelers checks to photograph framing. Fine chocolates are on display in the far left window.

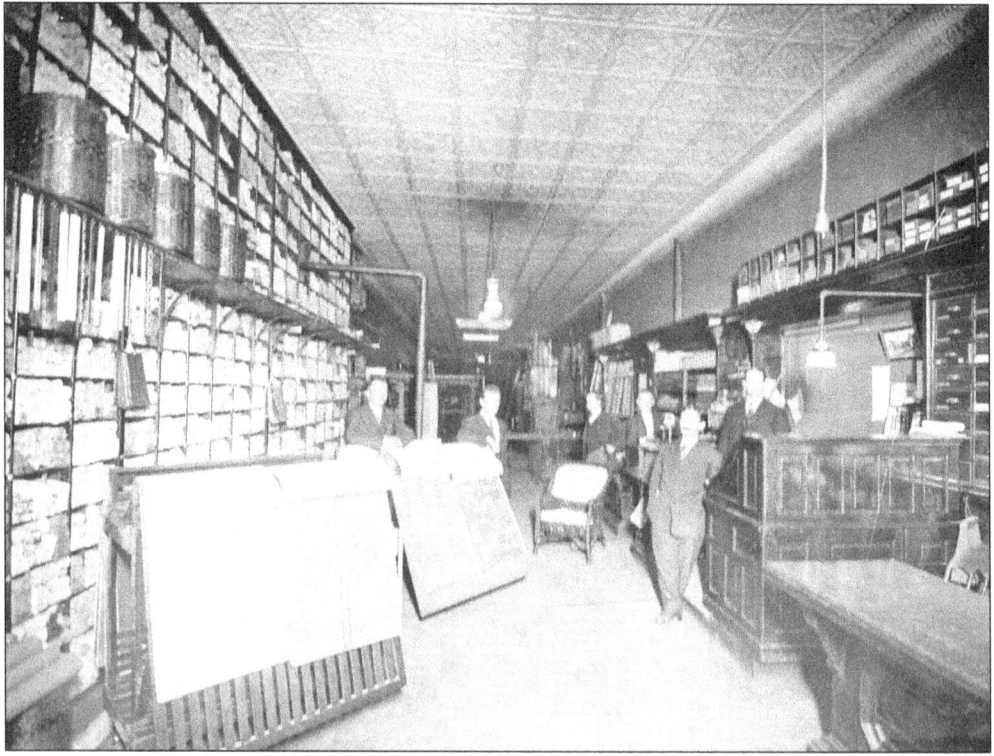

The Tiffin Carpet Store was at 117 (later renumbered as 135) South Washington Street. The store also sold curtains, wallpaper, and window shades. Tiffin Carpet was the successor to Sneath & Baker, which bills itself as "The Carpet, Curtain and Wall Paper House" in a 1903 advertisement, which also touts "a full stock at right prices."

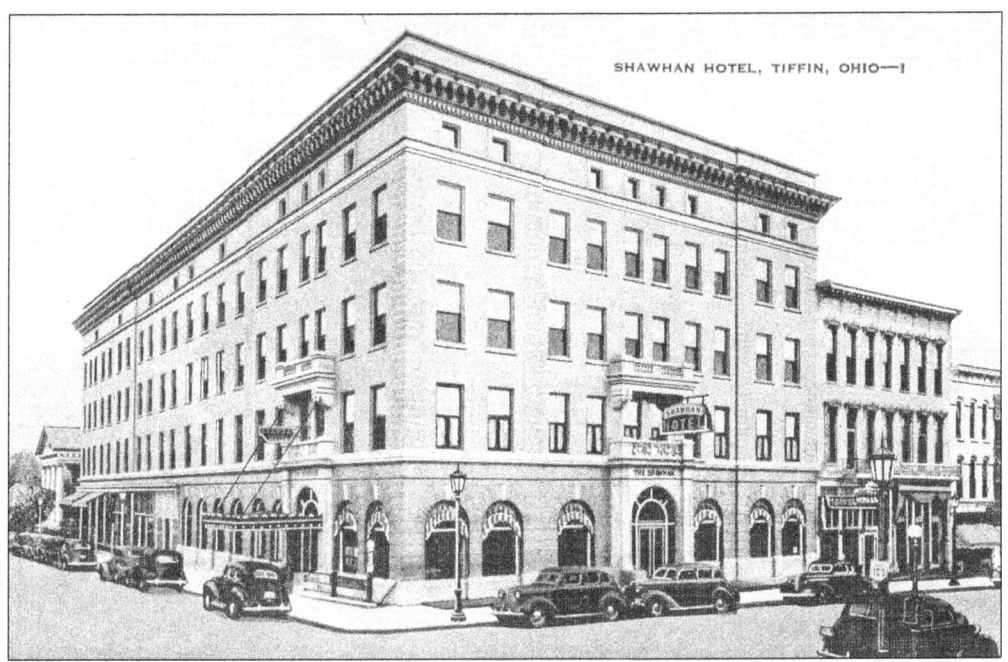

The first Shawhan Hotel dates to 1850, when Rezin Shawhan took over the Eagle House. The building that stands today at the intersection of East Perry and South Washington Streets was erected in 1903 as a tribute by Shawhan's widow. A decade later, the Shawhan's patrons had to be evacuated by lifeboat as the flood-swollen Sandusky River a block north reached the hotel lobby.

Fire gutted the vacant Shawhan Hotel on December 7, 1976—the last in a series of five fires that struck downtown Tiffin in 18 months. As the fire raged on a frigid night, the letters "H-O-T" on the sign at East Perry and South Washington Streets continued to glow eerily (the sign was connected to a separate, off-site power source). The Shawhan's shell sat vacant for 22 years before being redeveloped as assisted-living apartments.

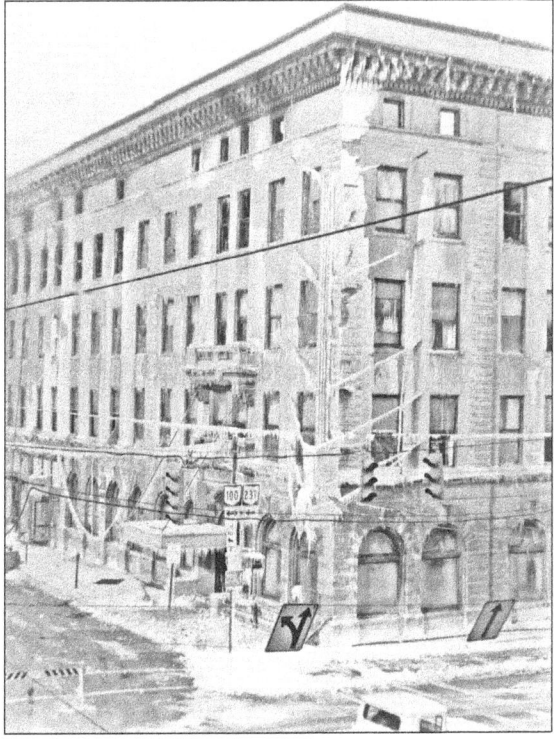

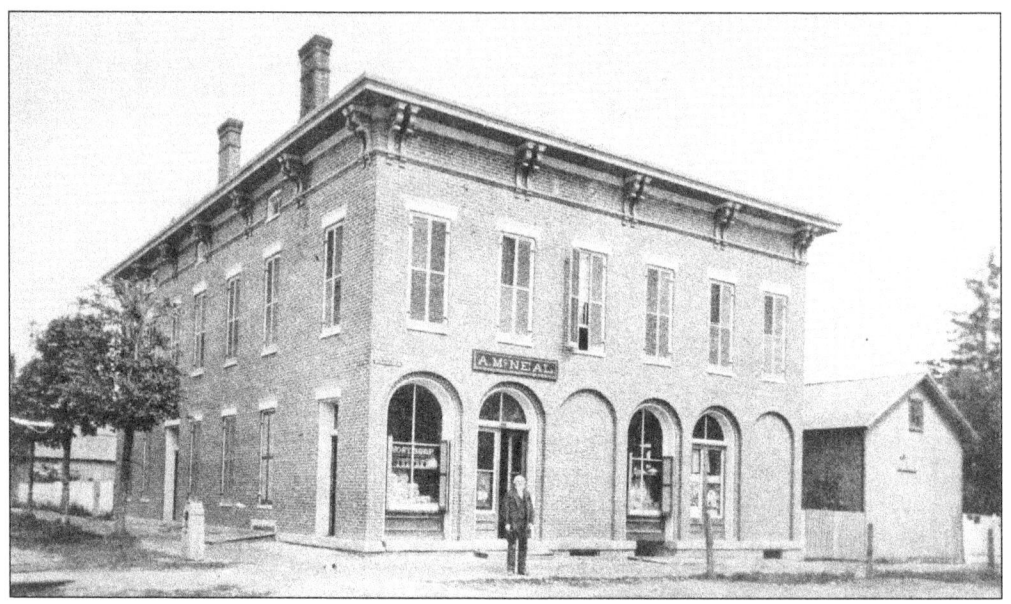

The Austin McNeal grocery stands at North Sandusky and Miami Streets, the point of origin of Tiffin's 1872 fire. Austin's father, Milton, sited the store across from what was intended as Fort Ball's town square. A newspaper article remarked at the time of the closing that McNeal's would "no longer be a lure to the children wanting candy, (and) buying slate pencils."

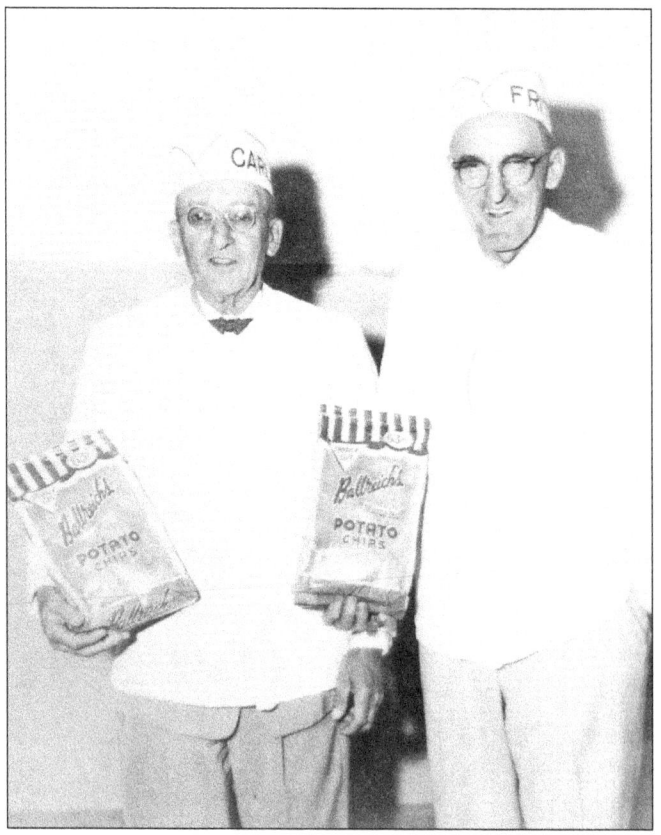

Brothers Carl (left) and Fred Ballreich show off bags of their signature potato chip. Fred and his wife, Ethel, processed the first potatoes on the site of the Ballreichs' plant at 186 Ohio Avenue in 1920. The chips are famously marketed as "marcelled," indicative of the wave created when the potatoes are cut and fried. (Courtesy of Ballreich's Potato Chips.)

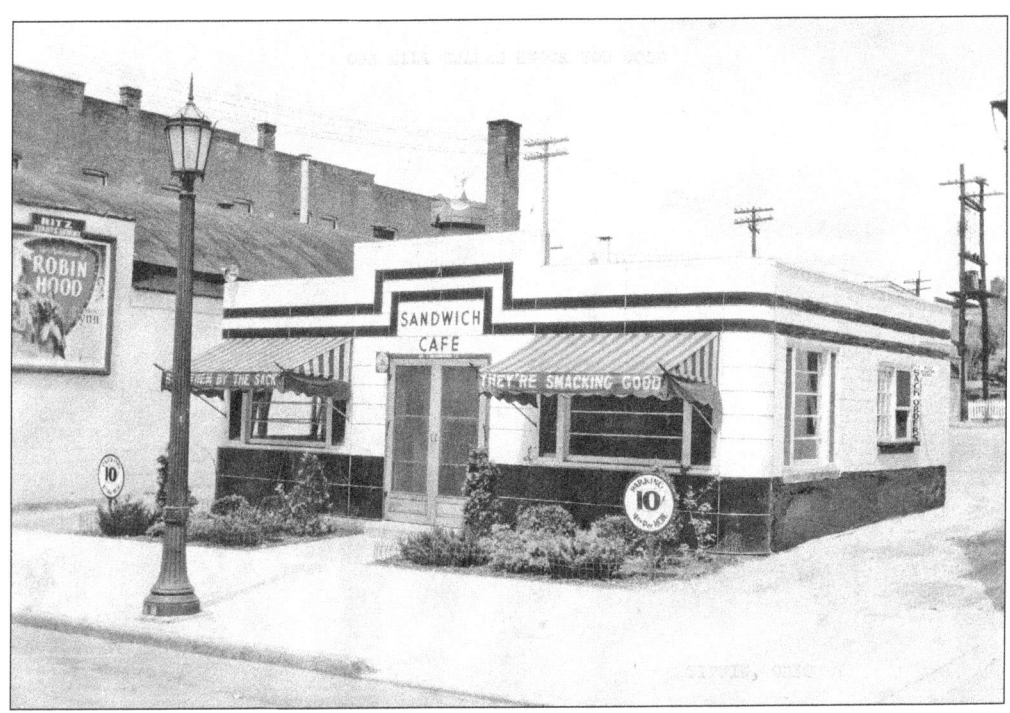

The Sandwich Café at 45 South Washington Street featured one of Tiffin's first drive-through windows (note the sign for sack orders at the right rear of the building). Note also the Ritz Theatre advertisement for Errol Flynn's *Robin Hood*, which was released in 1938. A succession of restaurants, including Reino's and Phat Cakes & Café, has occupied the site through the years.

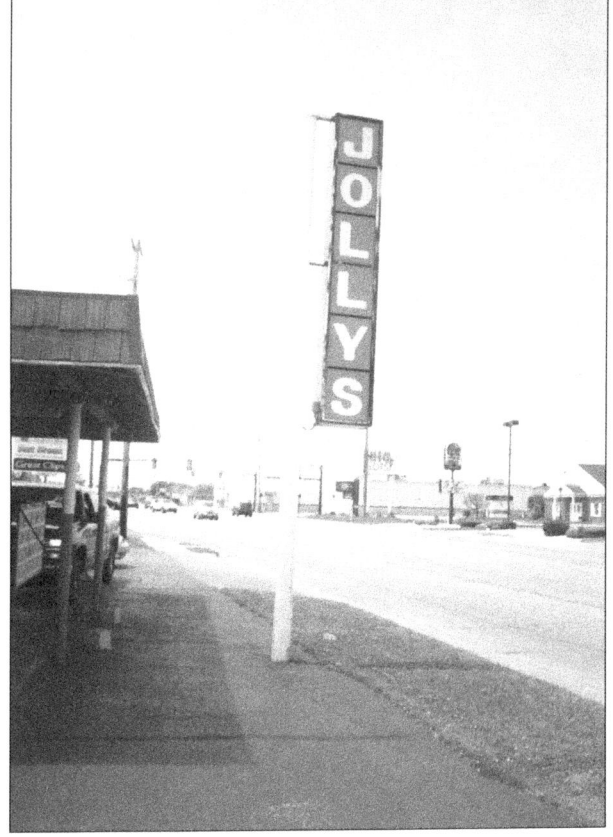

Jolly's Drive-in has been a Tiffin institution since 1947. The summertime favorite, located at 1630 West Market Street, was named after founder Roy "Jolly" Jolivette. The original building stood until 1975, when a new generation of owners built the familiar root beer stand of today. That original structure was towed behind the family home and converted into a potting shed. (Authors' collection.)

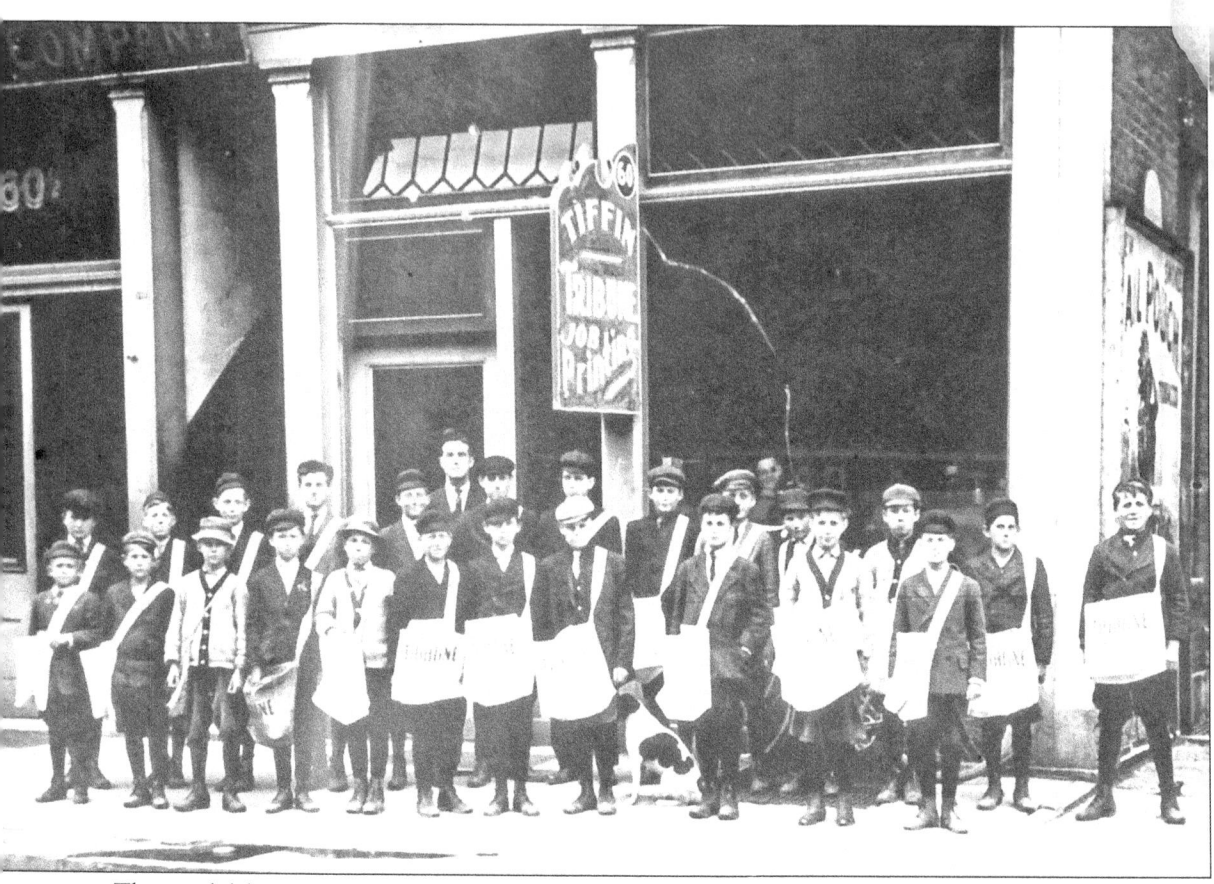

The youthful carrier staff of the *Tiffin Tribune* poses outside the newspaper's offices. The paper was established by W. Gray in 1855 and competed with the *Seneca Advertiser*. The Republican-leaning *Tribune* and the Democrat-affiliated *Advertiser* merged during the Great Depression, with the first edition of the *Advertiser-Tribune* published on January 10, 1933.

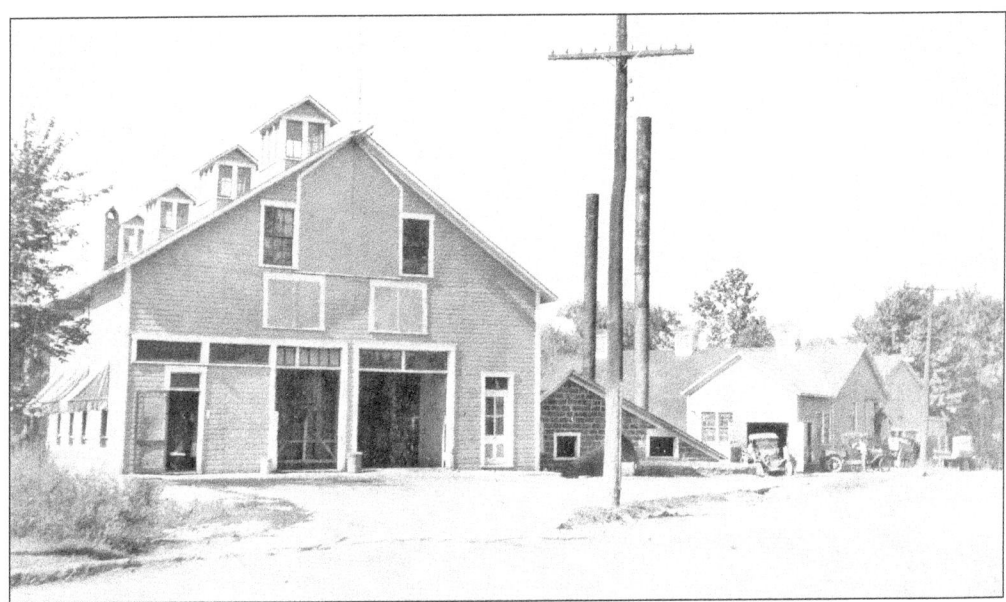

In 1900, Tiffin's Pure Milk and Dairy Co. was opened at the corner of Sycamore and Ella Streets by Clarence Hatcher. Milk was culled from Hatcher's own dairy herd and bottled in jars for sale. The switch to bottles was made after the herd was sold in 1910. Pure Milk was sold in August 1949 and became part of Beatrice Foods.

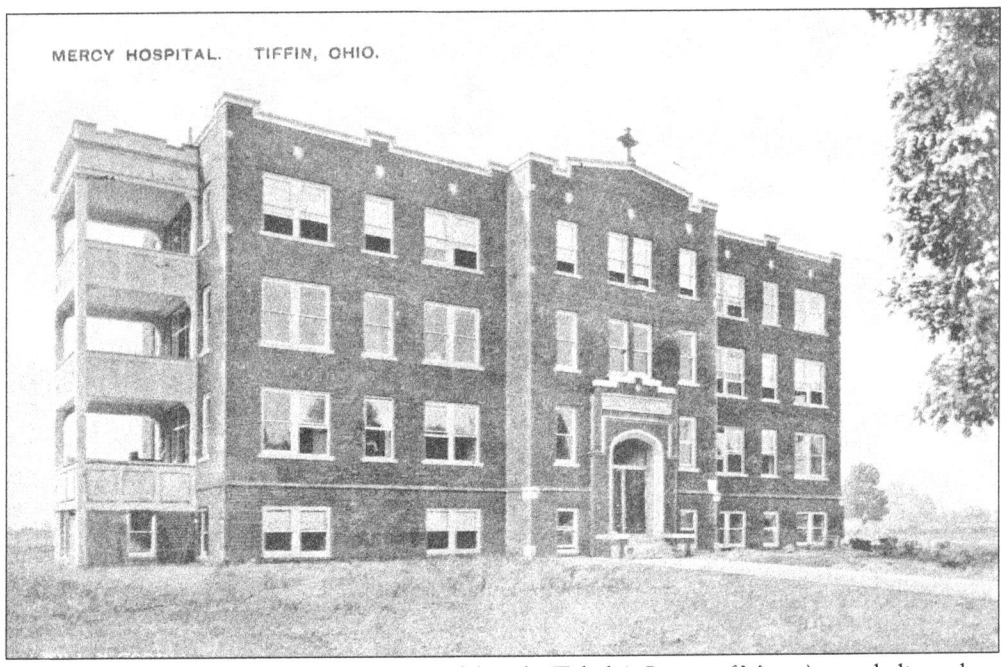

Following a 1912 fund drive, Mercy Hospital (run by Toledo's Sisters of Mercy), was dedicated on October 26, 1913. Its original capacity was 35 patients, with bassinets for 10 newborns as well. Wings were added in 1947 and 1959, with a facility-wide upgrade in the early 1980s. A new Mercy Hospital opened in 2008, and the Market Street hospital shown here has been razed.

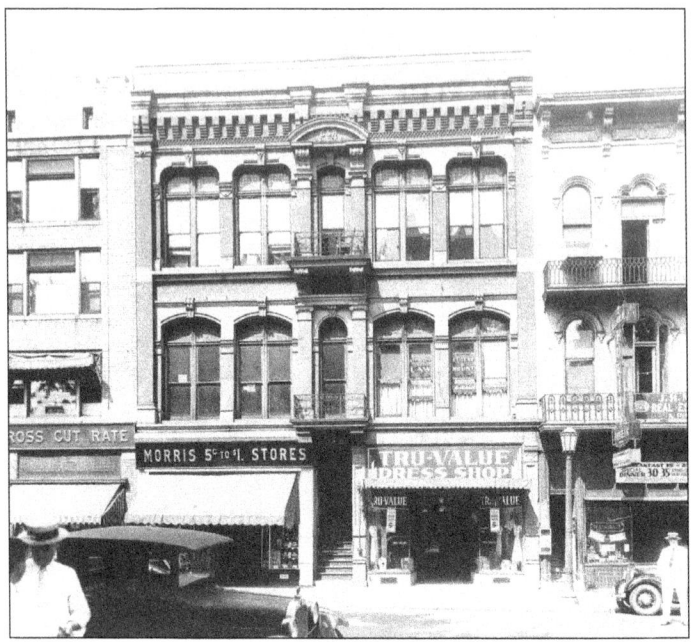

The block directly across South Washington Street from the courthouse was known as the Grummel Block; its namesake was Philip Grummel. Grummel ran a brewery and also was proprietor of a hardware store on Washington Street. The pediment at the top of the building dates the G&R Block (the *R* may stand for John A. Remmele, who developed the block two south of this one) to 1881.

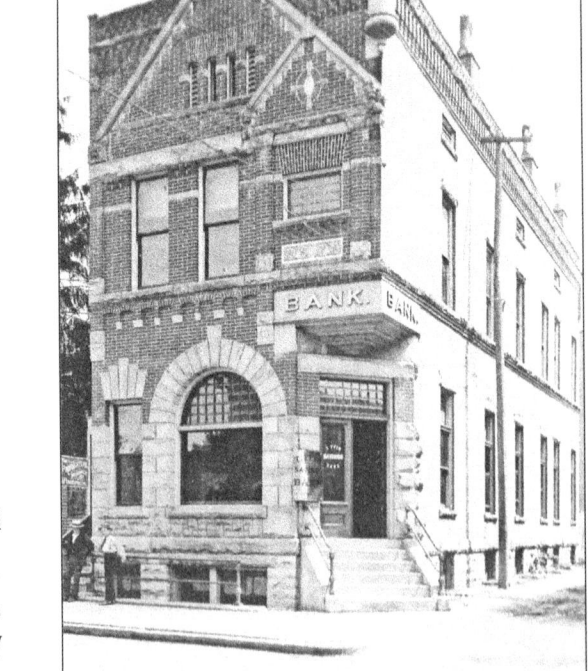

The Tiffin Savings Bank was organized in 1873 and called this distinctive East Perry Street building home. The sturdy Romanesque Revival structure, with its arched window, leaded glass, and heavy masonry, helped to convey an image of wealth and substance.

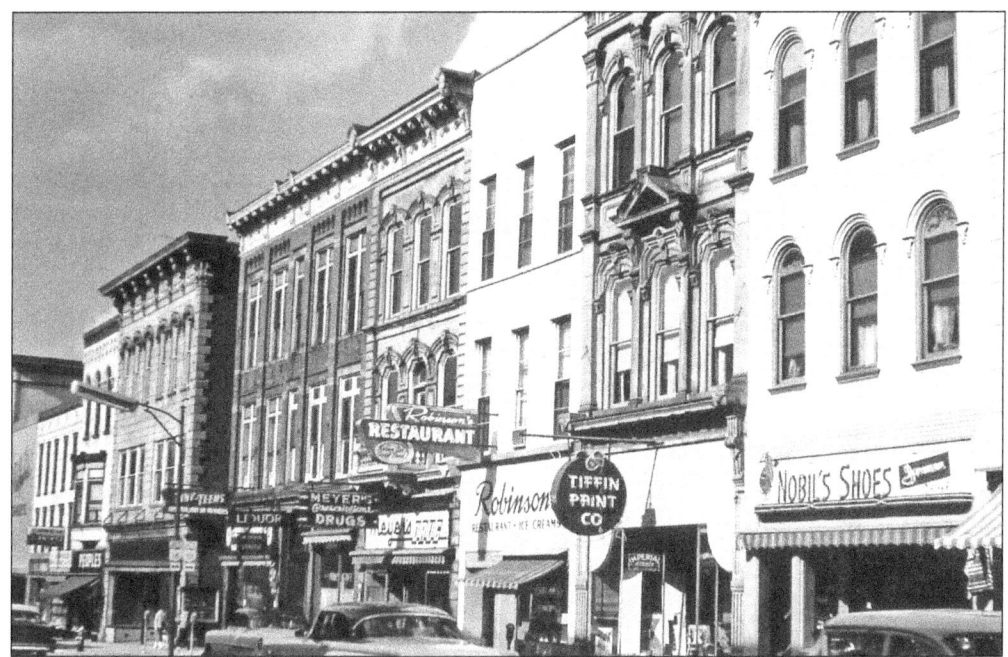

A 1940s-era view looking northward on Washington Street, just south of Market Street, reveals a Tiffin in transition. Gaudy neon signs stand in stark contrast to the three-story Victorian storefronts in which the shoe stores, drugstores, and restaurants are housed. The facade of Ralph's Shoes, at the far end of the block, remained unchanged for more than 30 years.

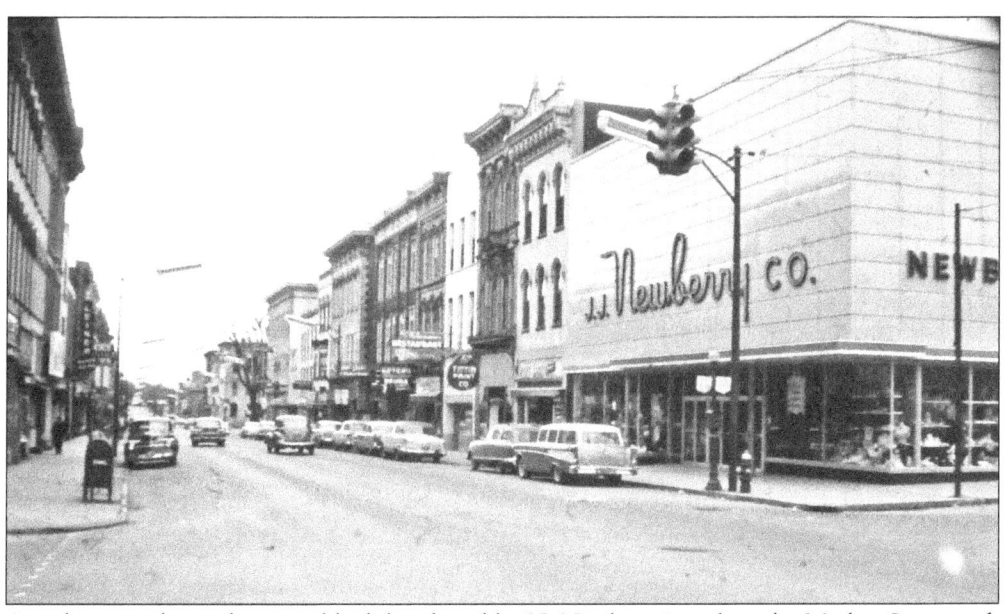

A wider view shows the same block bracketed by J.J. Newberry's and, at the Market Street end, the Tiffin National Bank with its distinctive T-shaped sign. Tiffin National was chartered as the National Exchange Bank about a month before the assassination of President Lincoln in 1865. And Newberry, along with J.C. Penney and LaSalle's, was an anchor of the pre-Westgate shopping district.

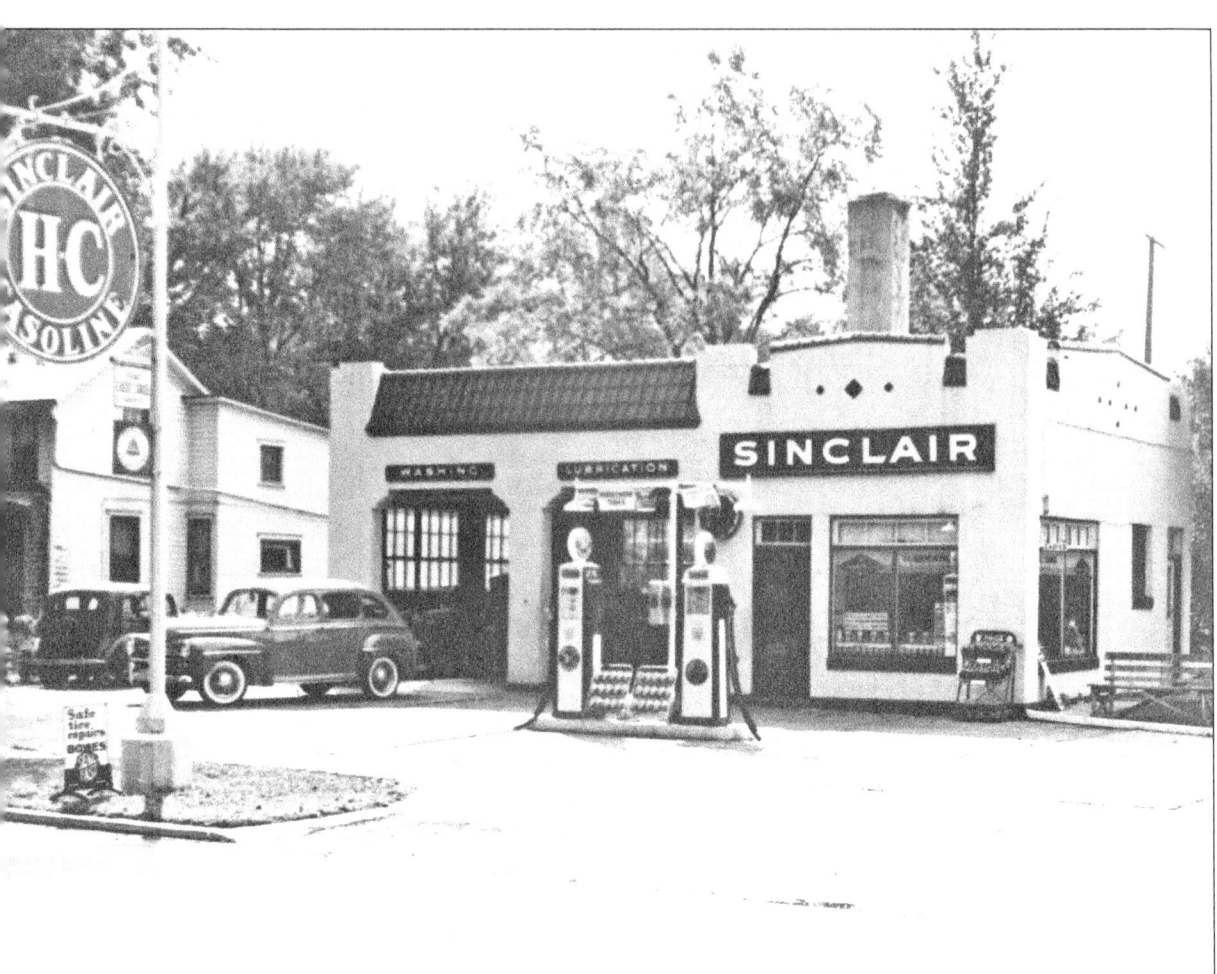

This Sinclair Oil service station along Melmore Street was typical of many of its era, both in architecture and in service. Each Sinclair station was architecturally unique; this one featured a terra-cotta roofline. Customers could receive either a car wash or lubrication services in the station's two bays, and a sign at the roadside advertises "safe tire repairs" using Bowes Seal Fast. Colas were available in a rack outside the front door.

The Associated Tire and Auto Service featured Gulf brand products and was located at the point where Jefferson Street dead ends into Melmore. A pair of uniformed attendants offered personal service, making sure all the driver's needs were fulfilled. The distinctive, dark-brick building still stands in the triangle today.

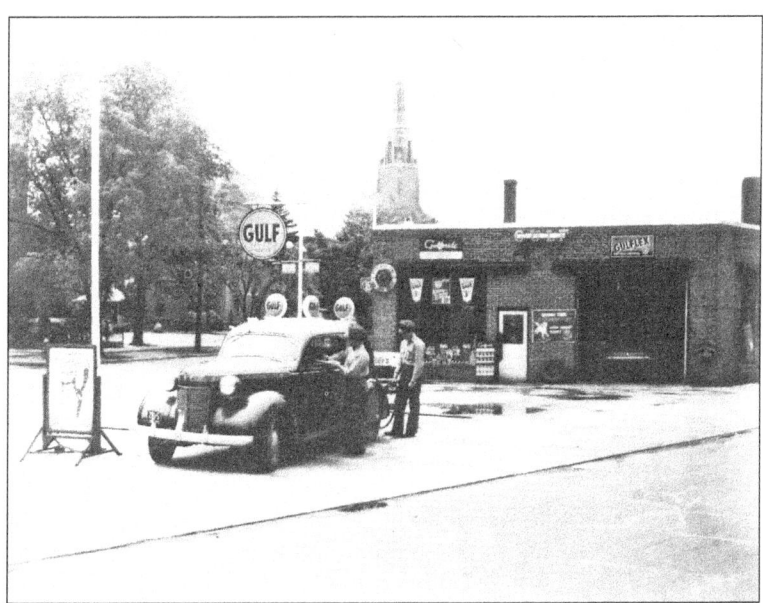

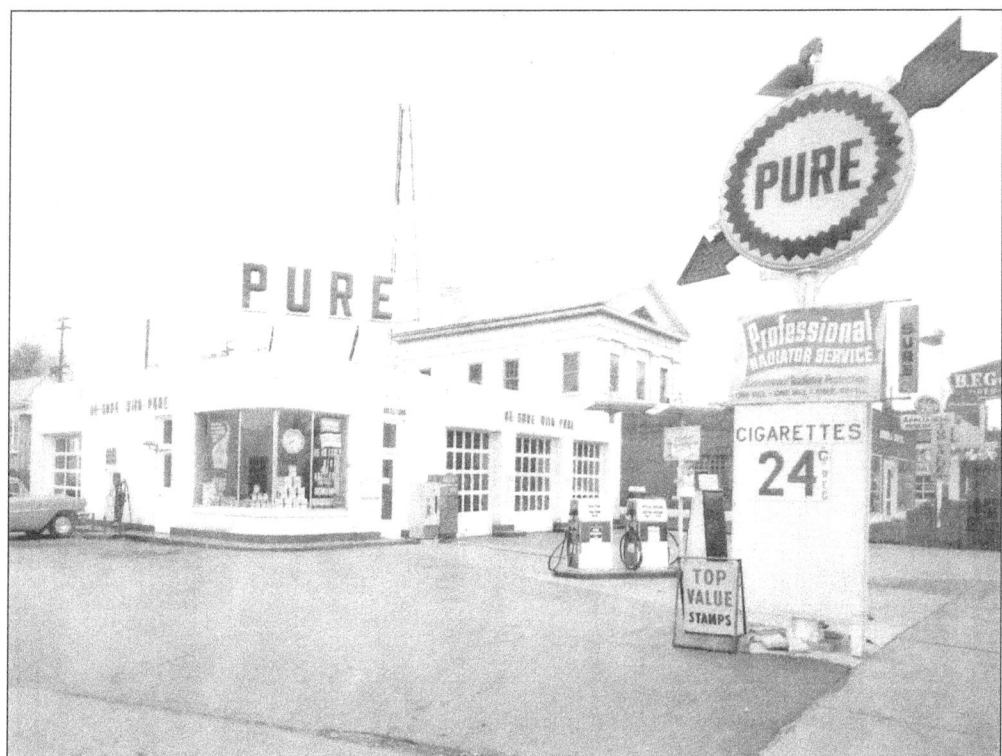

Customers could "Be Sure With Pure" Oil, which was for sale at Tunes Pure Oil location at 17 North Washington Street during the 1950s. The streamlining of the building and its white color were chosen for specific reasons—to convey a sense of cleanliness and to make women as well as men feel welcome.

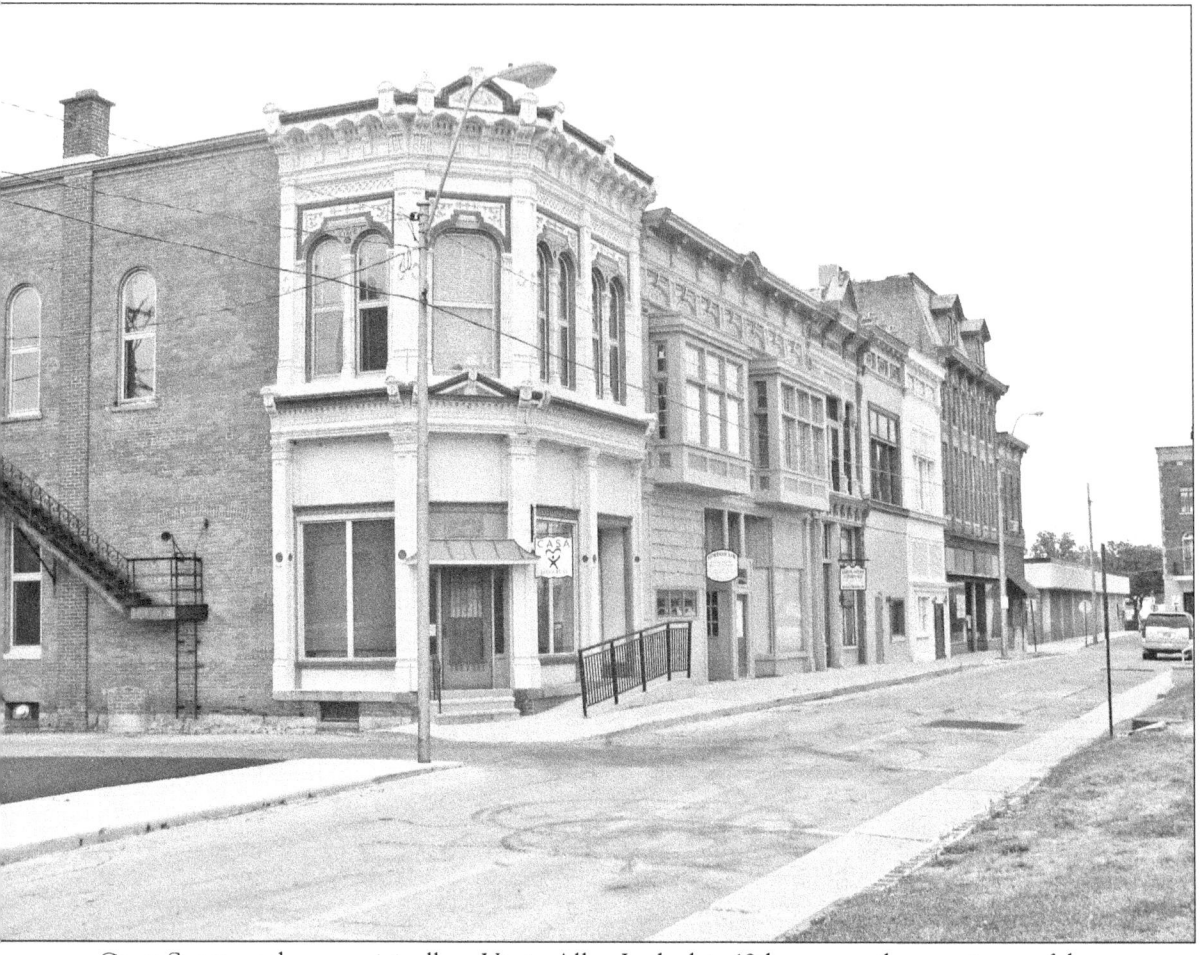

Court Street was known originally as Virgin Alley. In the late 19th century, the proprietors of the *Daily Advertiser* moved their newspaper offices to Court Street, where they added a commercial print business and bindery. The storefronts also have proven popular offices for attorneys, and the Seneca County Board of Elections once had its offices in the building in the foreground. (Authors' collection.)

Four

A CITY OF WORSHIP

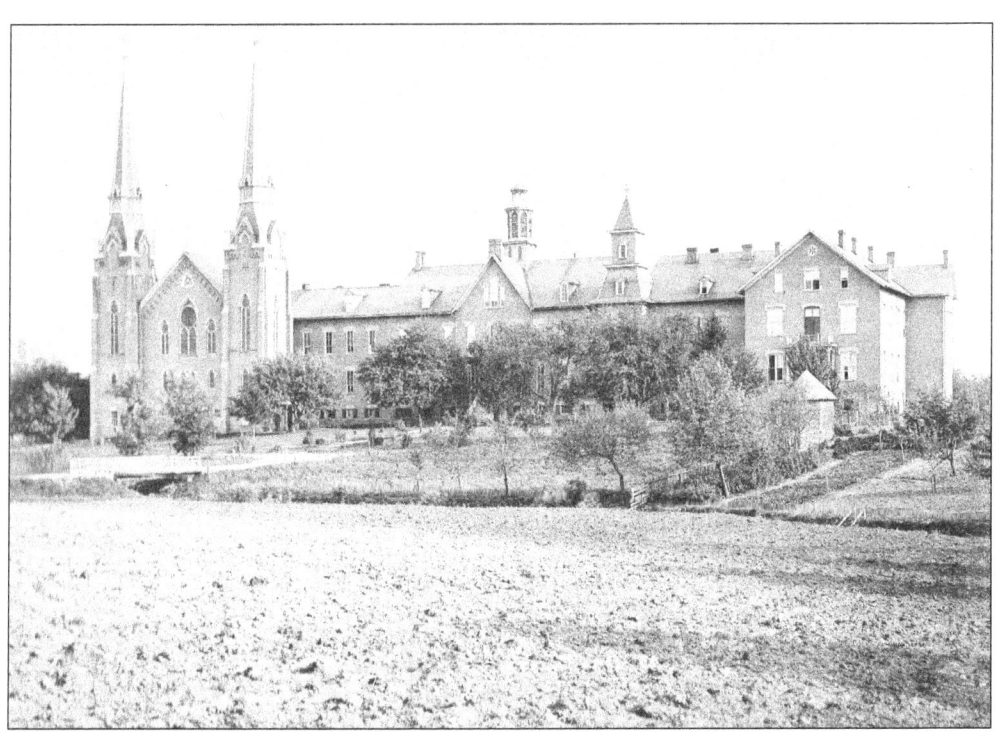

The three phases of the St. Francis Home are all visible in this photograph, taken sometime after 1884. The center core was built around 1871, with the chapel added in 1878. A final wing was added to the west in 1884. The field in the foreground was at one time home to a vineyard. St. Francis was a home for both orphans and the aged; the orphanage was discontinued in 1936 after 67 years of service.

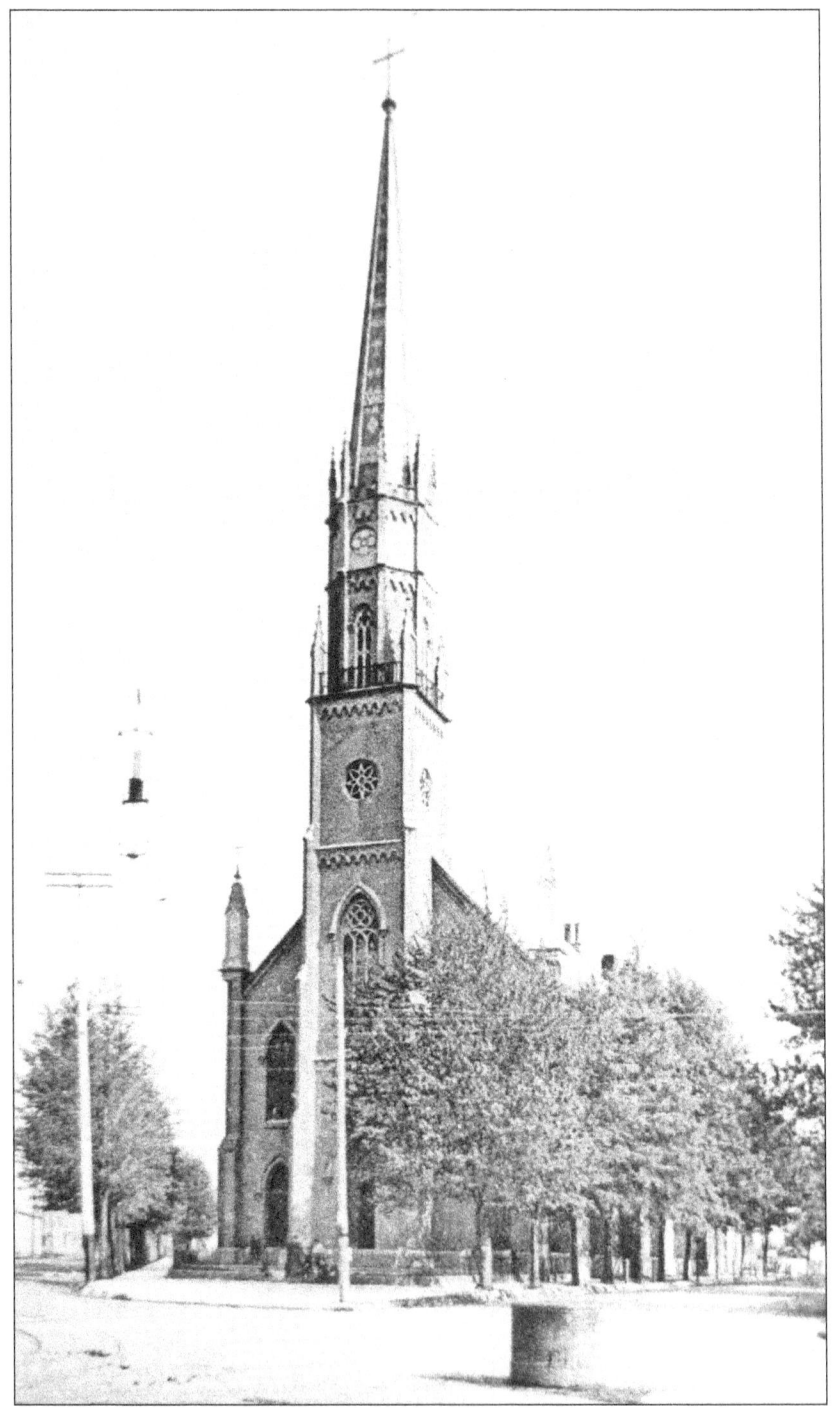

"St. Joseph's has from the first been one of the vital forces within the community," notes historian Myron Barnes. Among the Catholic church's achievements are the establishment of both Tiffin's Ursuline convent and St. Francis Orphanage. The parish traces its roots to 1845 as a German-centric offshoot of St. Mary's Catholic Church. St. Joseph's has been in continuous operation at the intersection of South Washington and Melmore Streets since 1862.

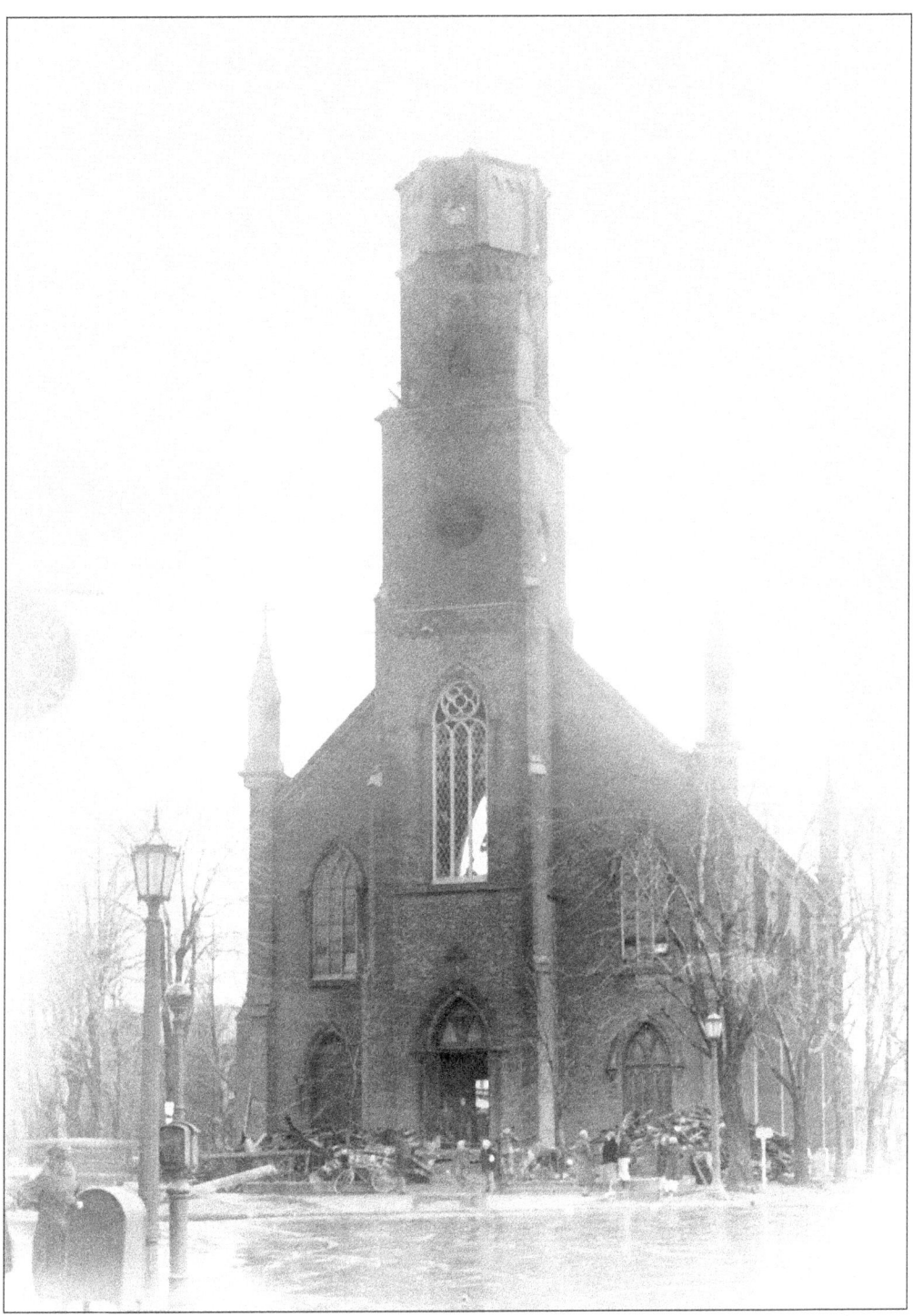

Passersby gawk at the ruins of St. Joseph's Catholic Church after a devastating 1934 fire. Lightning struck the church's steeple, causing the blaze that destroyed much of the structure's interior. Parish priests were able to save a number of sacred vessels and vestments, according to a Tiffin Fire Department history. Several firefighters narrowly avoided the church's collapsing bell tower.

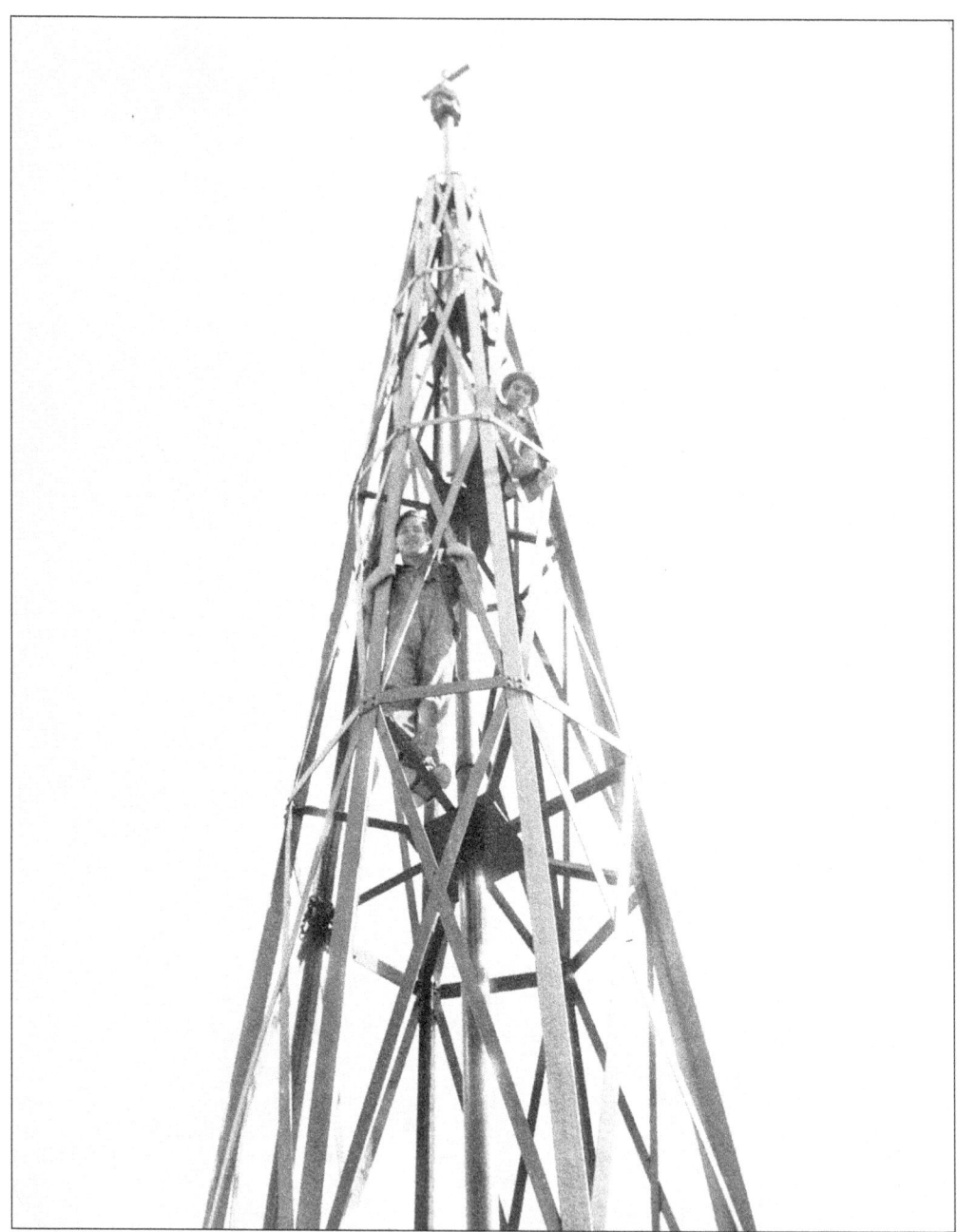

Workers pose at the apex of the steeple as St. Joseph's Catholic Church undergoes reconstruction after the fire in 1934. While it is noticeably shorter than in its original 180-foot incarnation, St. Joseph's steeple long has been the focal point of the Tiffin skyline. Note the many photographs throughout this book in which the steeple figures prominently in the background.

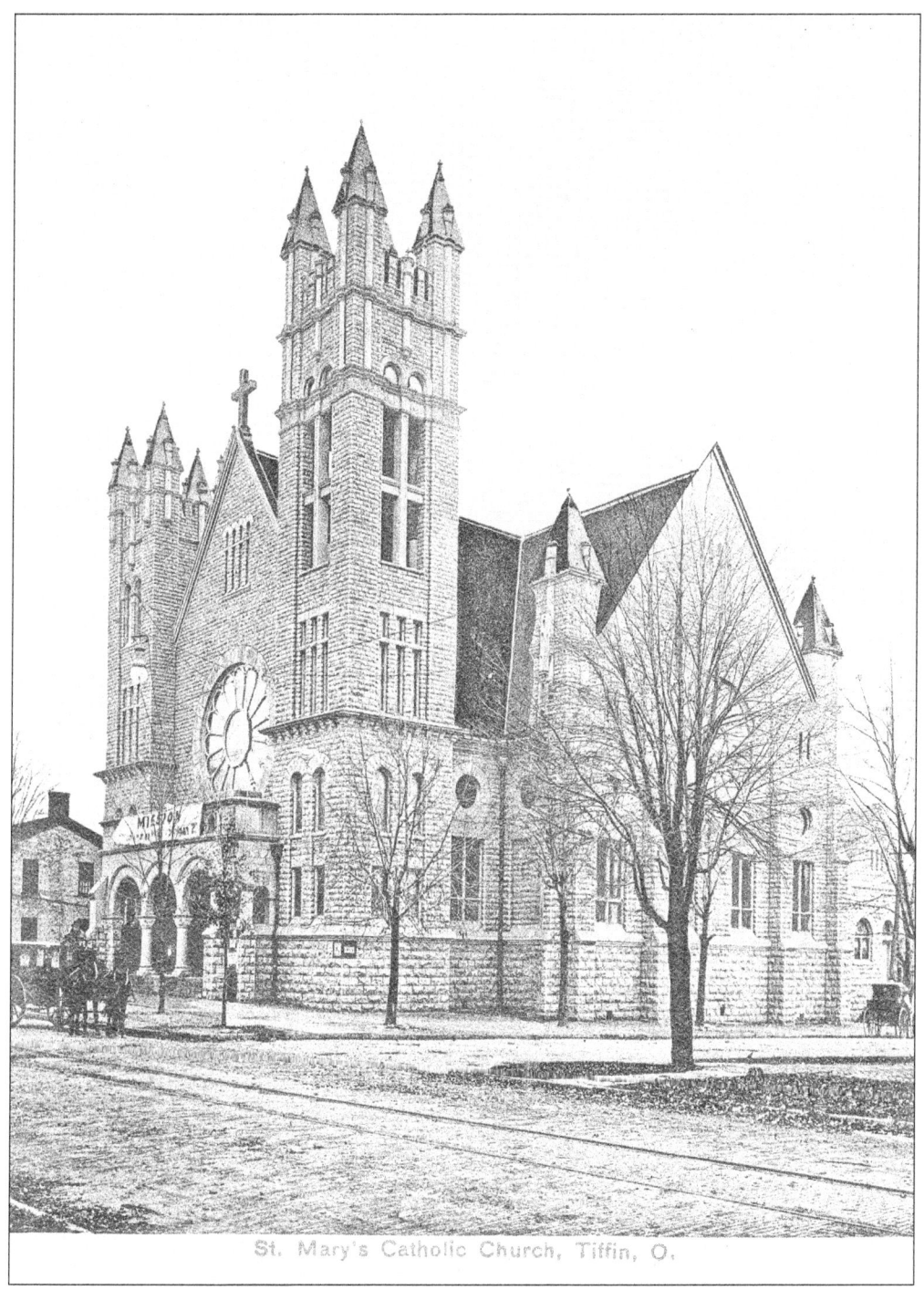

St. Mary's Catholic Church, Tiffin, O.

The third church to bear the name St. Mary's Catholic Church was erected at South Sandusky and Clay Streets in 1905. The parish house and St. Mary's School sit immediately to the north. The stone church's interior features 14 marble carvings of the Stations of the Cross; the wall hangings depict Christ's crucifixion. Through the years since its 1831 founding, St. Mary's Parish has assimilated Tiffin's Irish, German, and Italian immigrant populations.

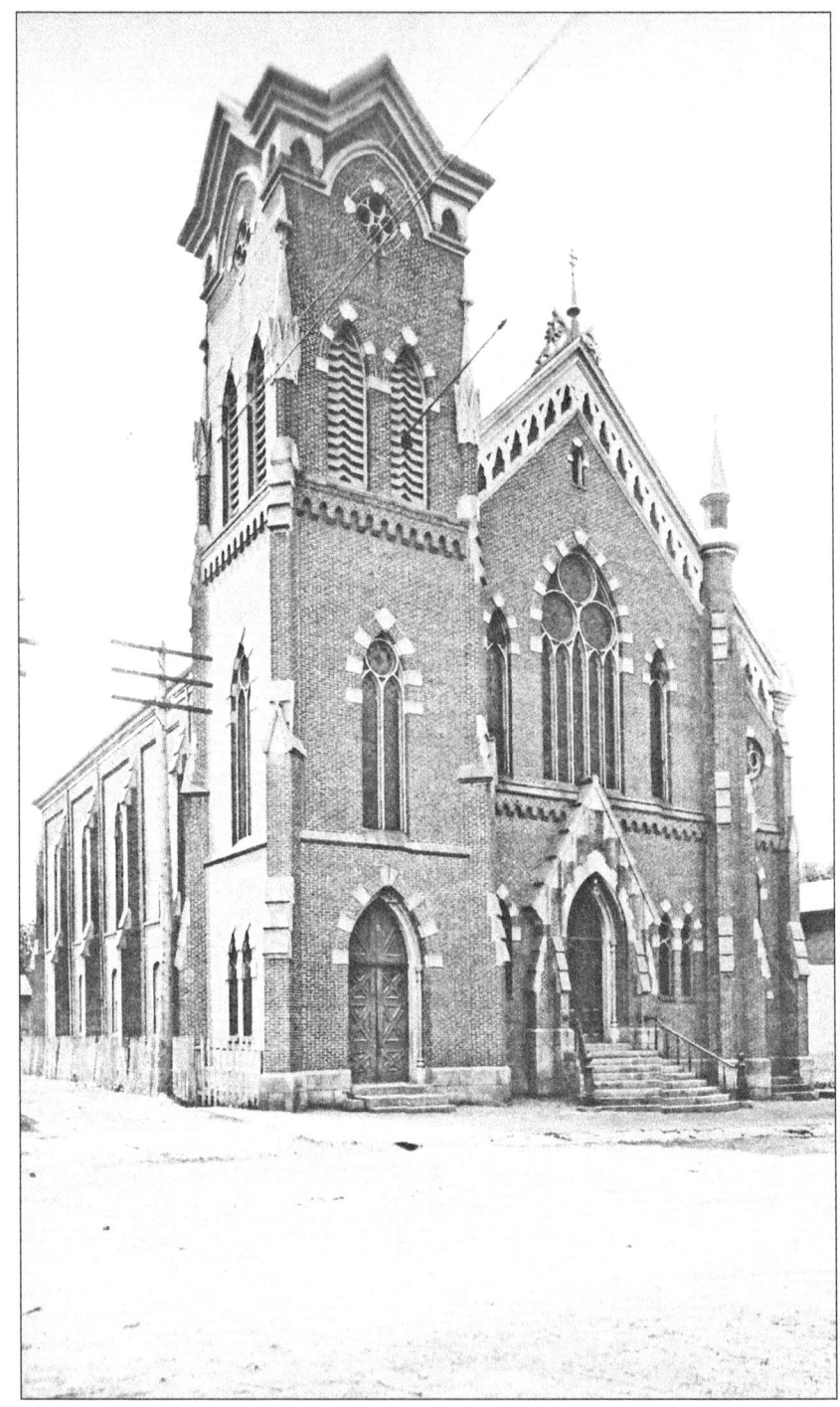

St. Paul's Methodist Episcopal Church holds the distinction of being Seneca County's first organized religious group, founded in 1824. When the congregation's Madison Street church was dedicated in 1884, the ceremony was illuminated by a brass chandelier courtesy of Thomas Edison. The inventor wanted to salute the church's distinction as one of the world's first buildings to be wired at the time of construction.

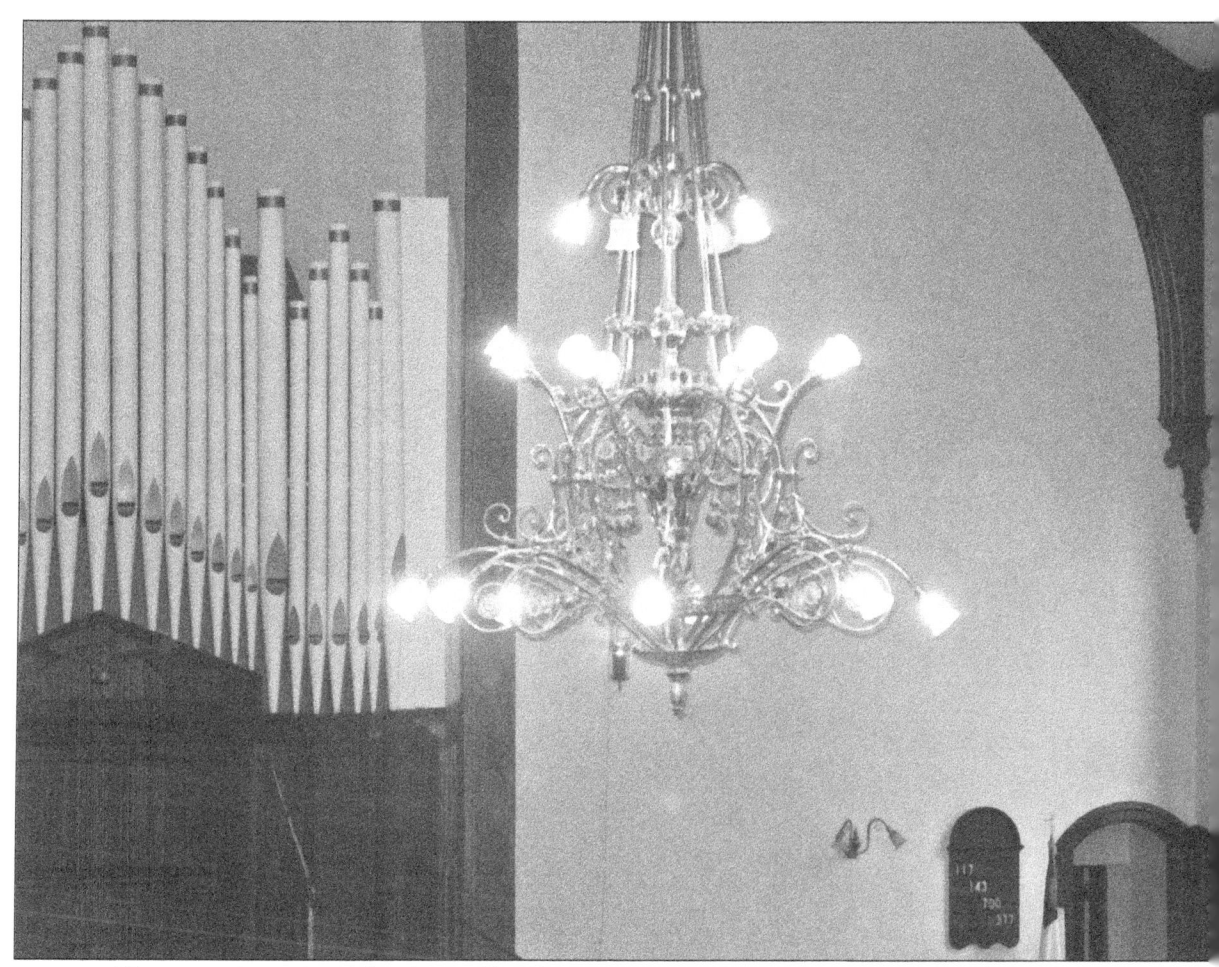

The ornate brass chandelier donated by Thomas Edison to the congregation of St. Paul's Methodist Episcopal Church still hangs in the church today. The Tiffin Edison Electric Illuminating Company, the first central electric power station in Ohio and the 10th in the United States, was built in Tiffin in late 1883. (Authors' collection.)

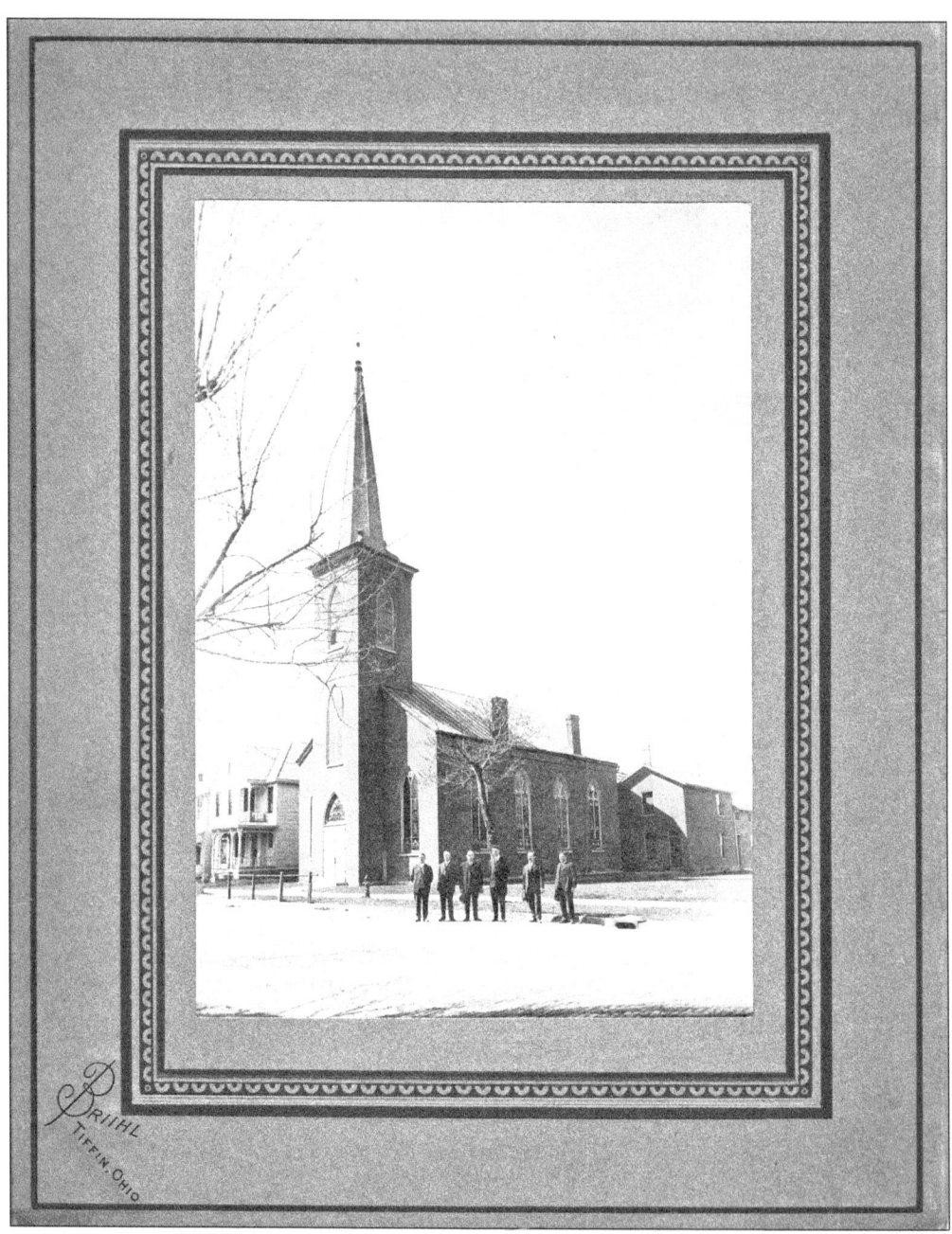

St. John's Evangelical was Tiffin's first Lutheran church, tracing its roots to 1835. This building, erected in 1918, is the third on the site at Jefferson and Main Streets, replacing the original log cabin and an 1857 brick church. Until the World War I era, St. John's services and records were all in German. Today, the congregants are members of St. John's United Church of Christ.

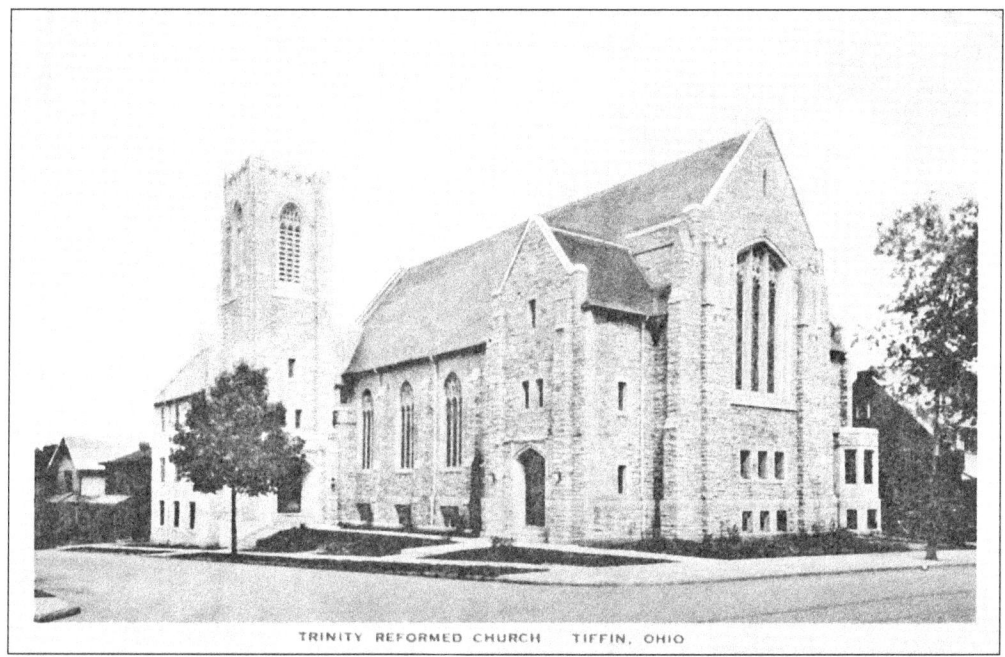

TRINITY REFORMED CHURCH   TIFFIN, OHIO

The 1928 Trinity Reformed church at the corner of Jefferson and East Perry Streets was the result of the merger of two congregations. According to *Seneca County, Ohio History & Families*, "The last service in the old First Church was held on Christmas Eve in 1928. Since chairs would be needed for the Christmas morning service in the new Trinity Church, a procession formed and the march to the new church took place, each person carrying a chair."

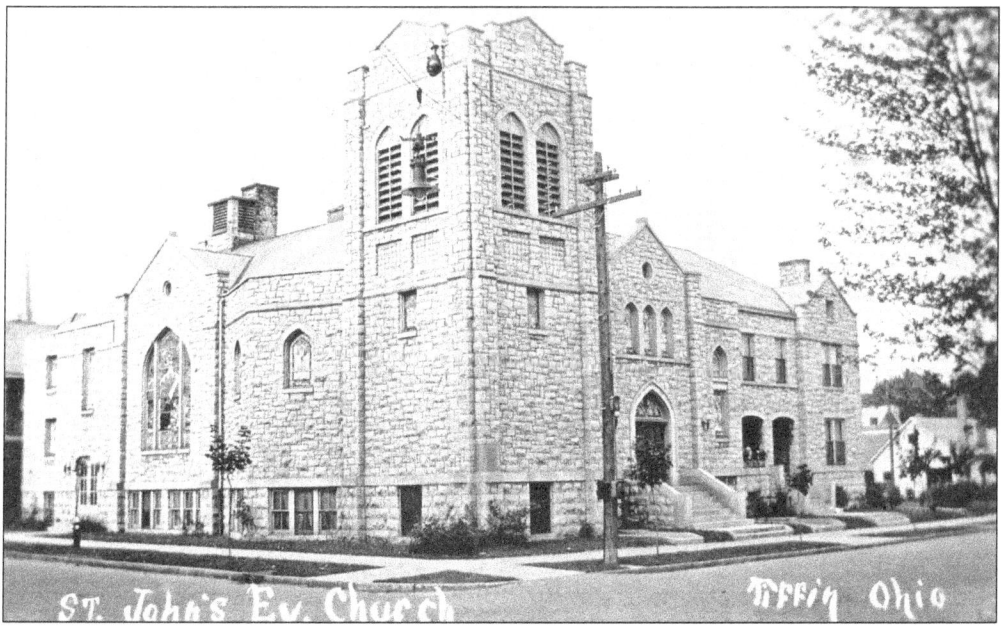

St. John's Ev. Church   Tiffin Ohio

The second St. John's Evangelical Church was a steepled brick building; it replaced the original 24-by-30-foot log cabin. The Lutheran congregation was first known as the Truth's Church, which was easier to remember and say than "the United German Evangelical Lutheran and German Evangelical Reformed St. John's Congregation."

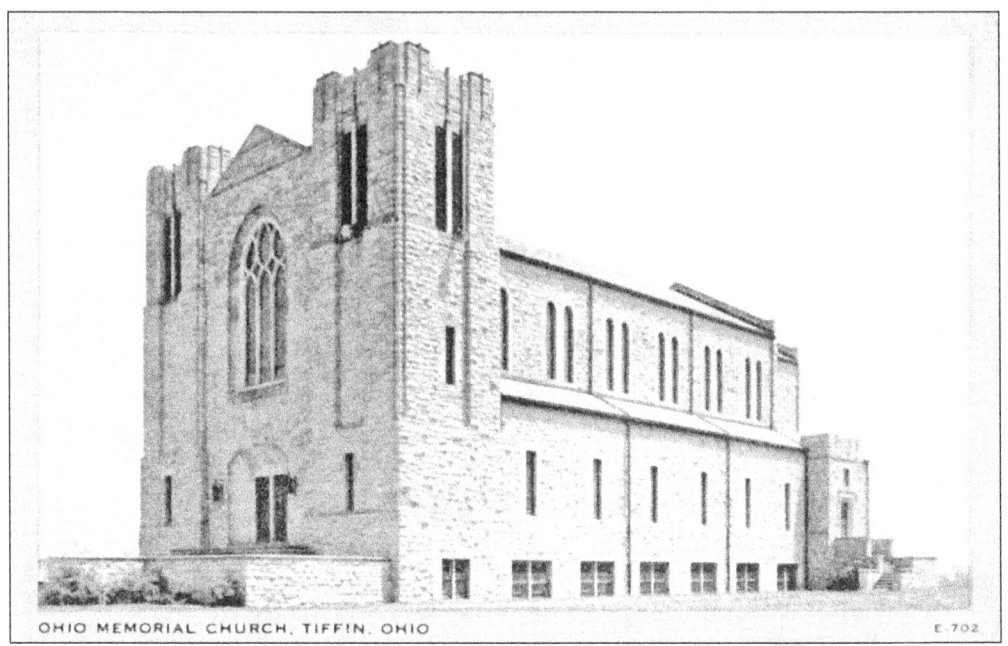

OHIO MEMORIAL CHURCH, TIFFIN, OHIO   E.702

The Ohio Memorial Chapel is a landmark on the grounds of the Tiffin Developmental Center. The church was dedicated in 1928 as part of the Junior Order United American Mechanics campus. A message in the dedication booklet proclaims, "Every tone in the chimes in the tower is a tongue that will ring out to the world every day in the year a message of love and devotion from a thousand children in this home."

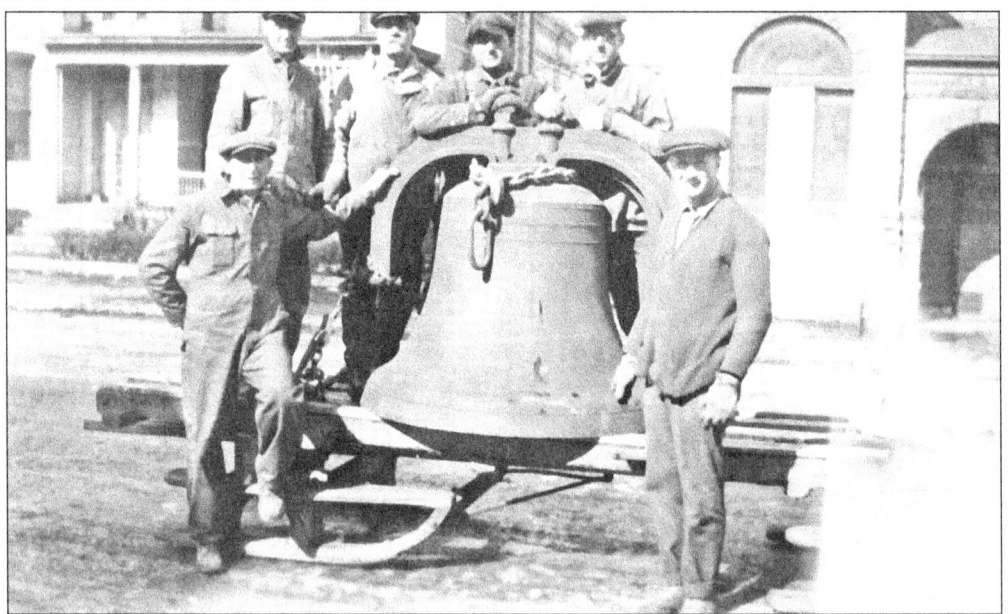

Workers use a sled to maneuver the bell of the Washington Street United Methodist Church to the new church location at 230 South Washington Street. That church, built in 1924, replaced an 1871 building on Market Street (the congregation itself dates to 1829). In 2011, the congregation merged with that of Ebenezer United Methodist Church into the combined Faith UMC, celebrating on North Sandusky Street.

Five

A City Inundated

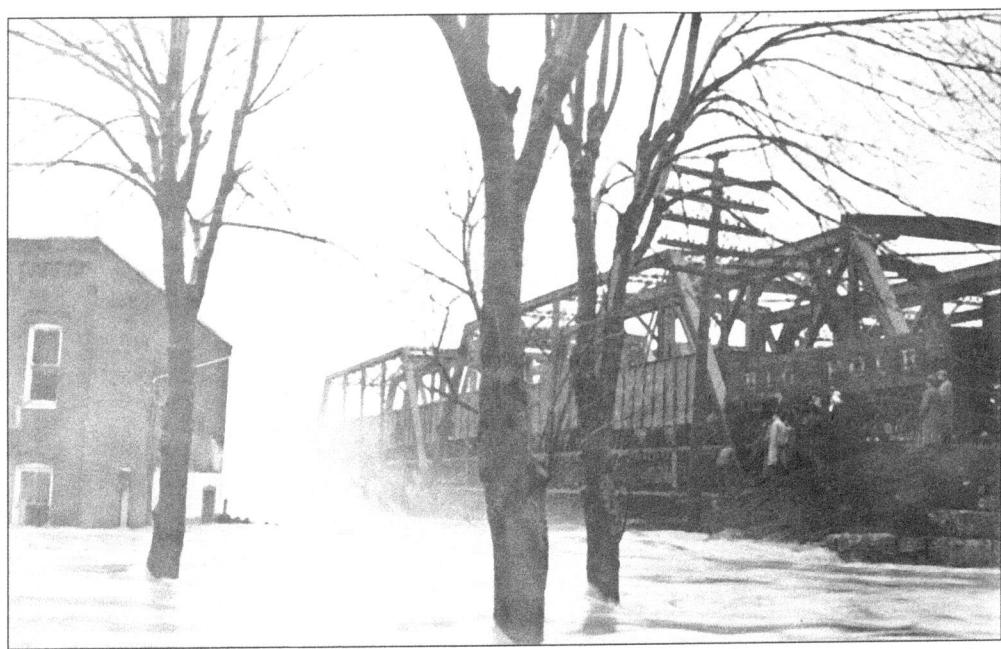

Tiffin residents awaiting rescue stand next to the railroad bridge as the river continues its rise. Thanks to the quick thinking of railroad foreman David Martin, coal cars weigh down the bridge's three trestles, helping them withstand the tide that claimed every other bridge across the Sandusky.

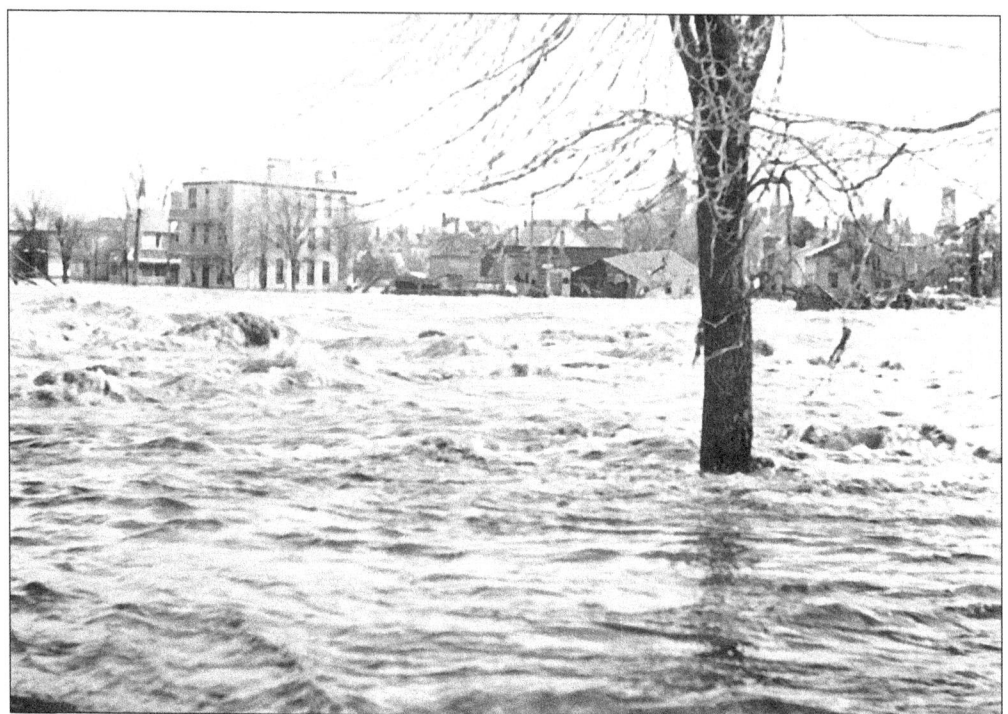

The racing waters of the Sandusky River rush past the VanNette Hotel, situated on Liberty Street near the point where Rock Creek emptied into the Sandusky. The VanNette formerly served as a shoe factory. A total of 16 hotel guests had to be evacuated using baskets.

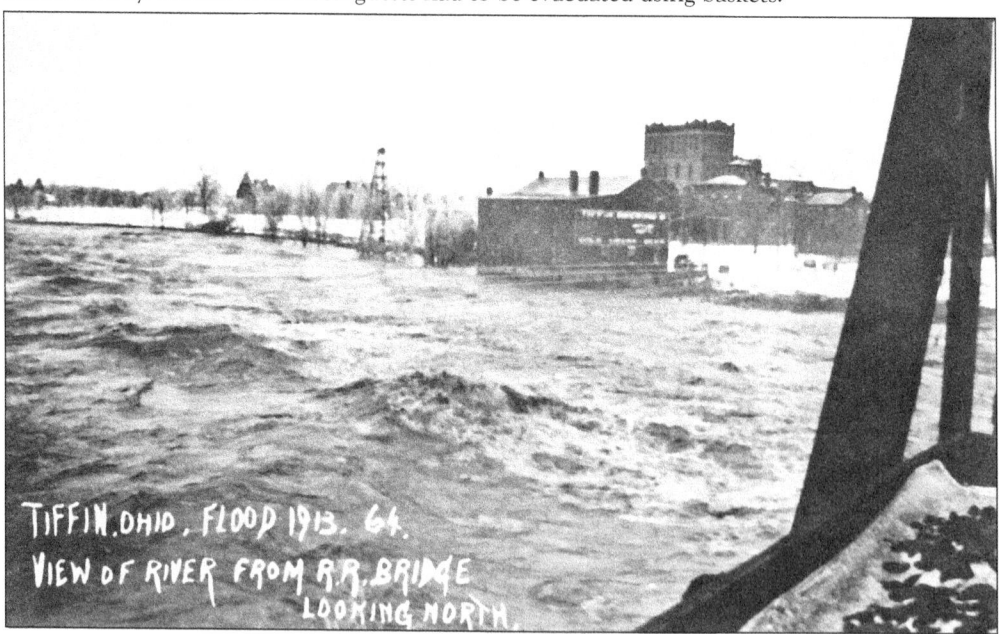

Floodwaters encroach on the plant of the Tiffin Brewing Co. The brewery would survive this round with the Sandusky, though in a weakened state. The 1848 building, constructed along the riverbank, would partially collapse after another round of flooding in 1920. Along with Prohibition, this marked the end of the Tiffin Brewing Co.

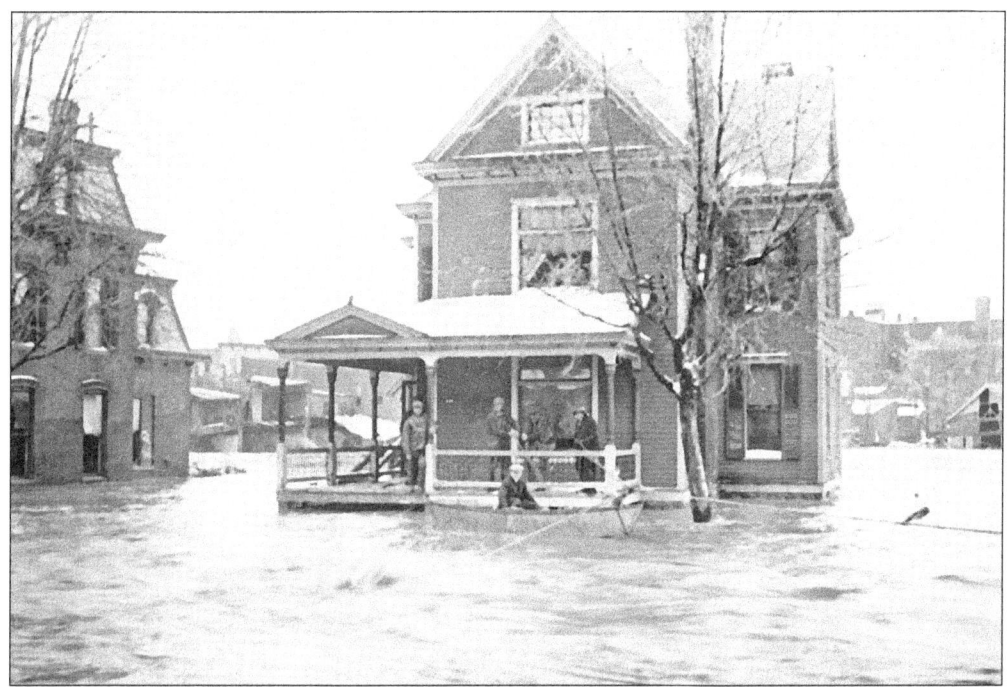

A lone rescuer in a rowboat waits as floodwaters make inroads toward a house along Water Street (present-day Frost Parkway); four people are visible on the porch. The rescuer may be A.A. Weigel, who spent 13 hours clinging to a tree after his boat capsized during a rescue attempt.

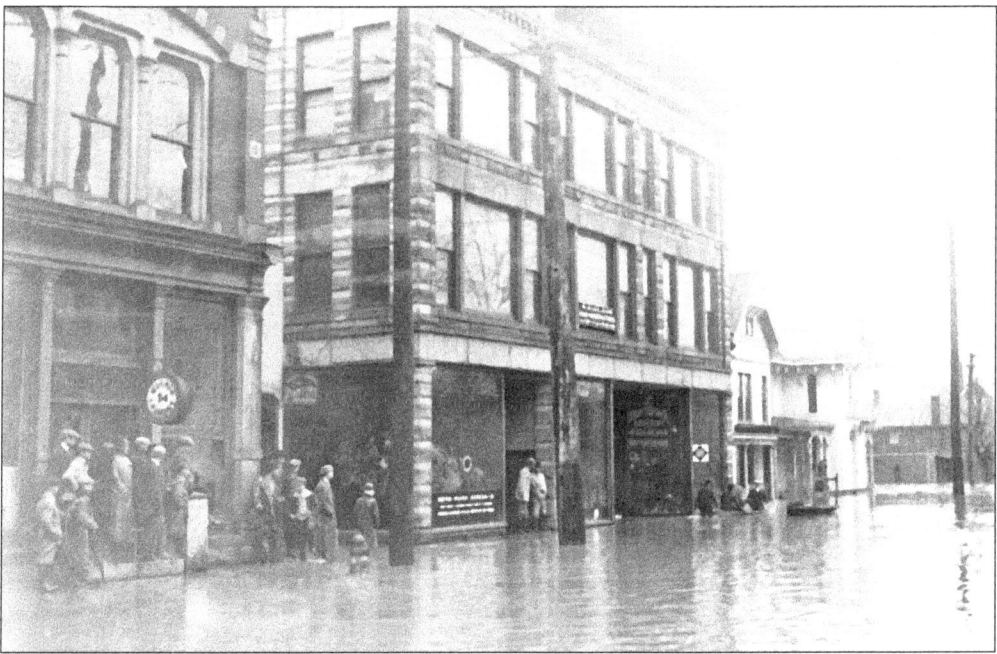

Rescuer A.A. Weigel maneuvers his rowboat in an effort to rescue some of those stranded on Perry Street in front of W.H. Kildow's cigar factory. It was shortly after this photograph was taken that Weigel's boat capsized, leading to his 13-hour fight for his life, clinging to a tree until he himself could be rescued.

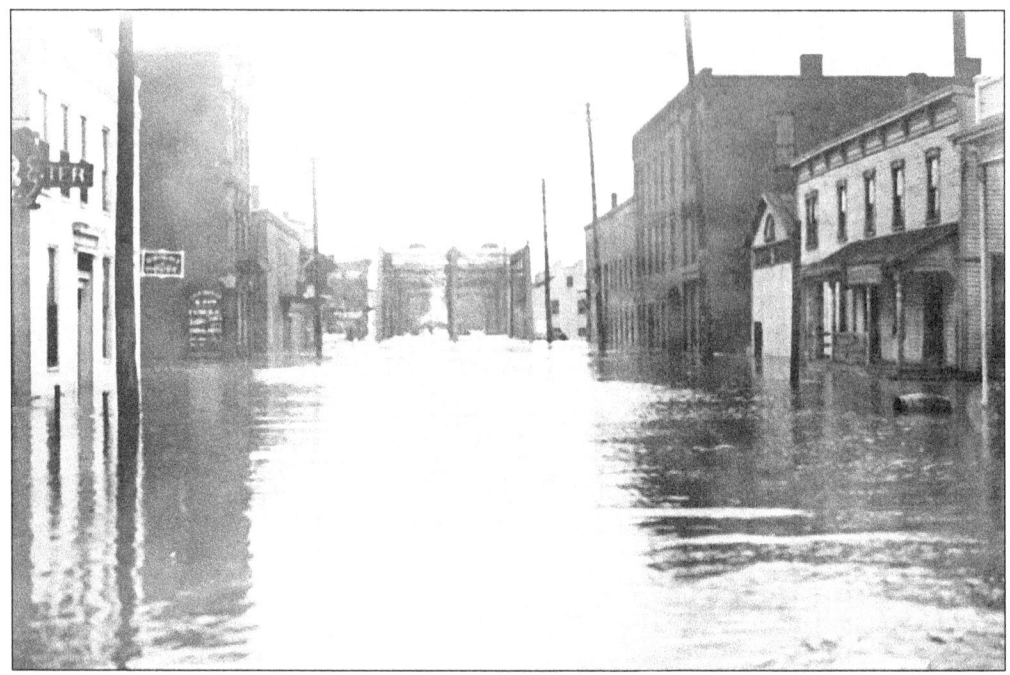

The doomed double spans of the Market Street Bridge stand defiantly against the raging Sandusky. The north-flowing river makes a pair of sharp bends just to the south of Market Street, which speeded the current even further. Note also the proximity of the buildings to the bridge. Construction right up to and over the water's edge further hastened riverbank erosion.

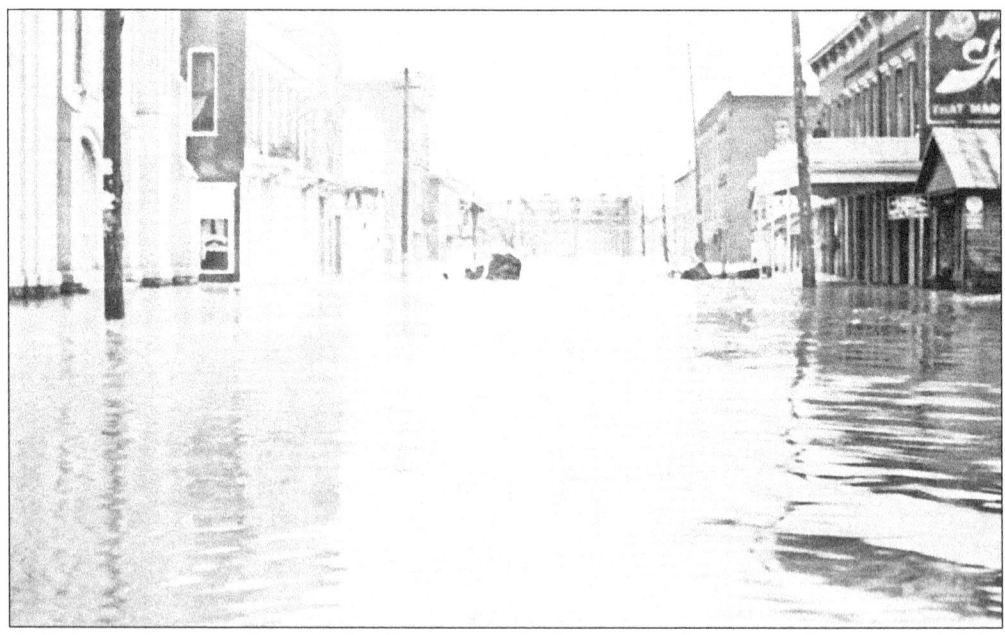

A slightly wider angle of the Market Street scene further reveals the extent of destruction left by the rising floodwaters. The ruins of a horse-drawn wagon and other debris litter the impassible street. Ironically, among the waterlogged businesses is a pump store (second from right).

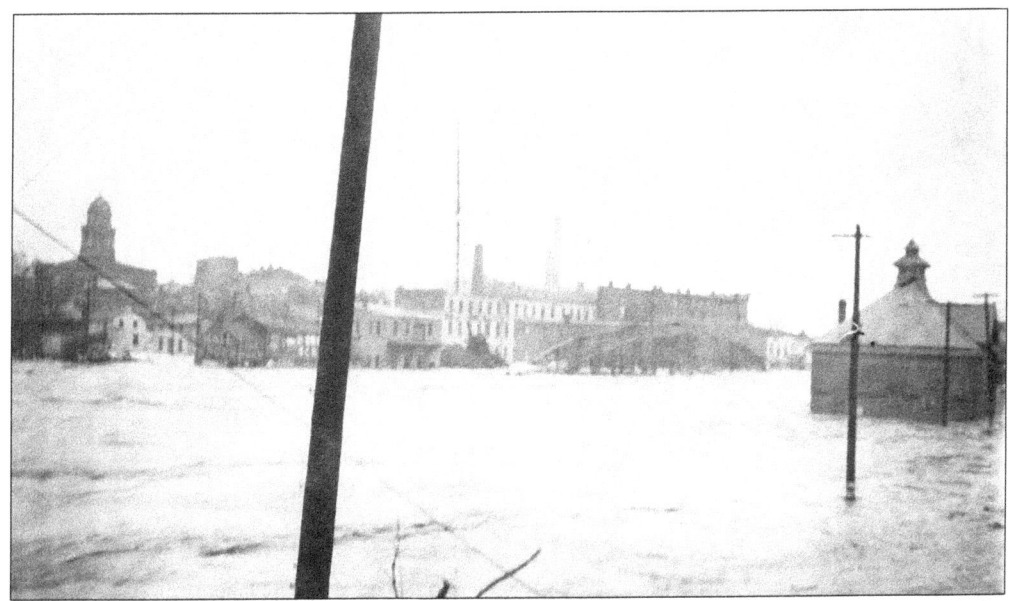

The Monroe Street Bridge is carried away on March 25. Historian Lisa Swickard recorded the recollection of Paul Barnes, who watched the bridge "rise on the waves of the Sandusky, swing around like any ocean-going steamer, and float downstream beautifully. It floated like a great steamship until it met the Washington Street bridge, which it quickly pushed from its resting place."

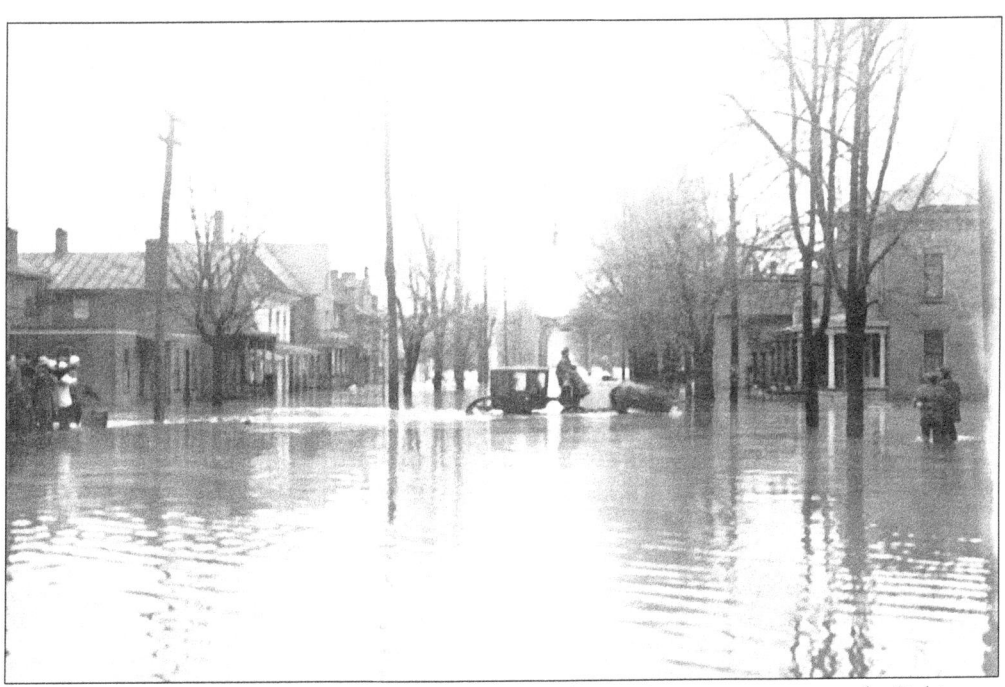

A hack crosses the flooded intersection of Monroe and Perry Streets on its way to the Baltimore & Ohio Railroad station. The Perry Street Bridge still stands in the background, which places the photograph sometime before midday on Tuesday, March 25, when the bridge suddenly broke free of its moorings.

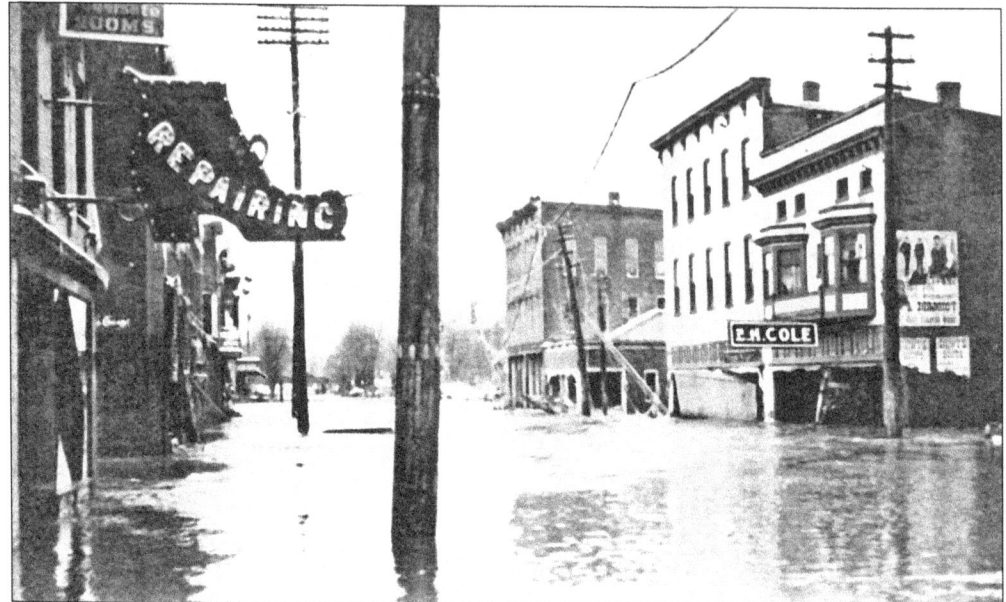

Leland Cole's dry-cleaning shop occupied the first floor at 19–21 South Washington Street; the Cole family lived in the apartment above the business. The Coles were rescued when a firefighter got a ladder to the back balcony and the family scrambled across the ladder on hands and knees.

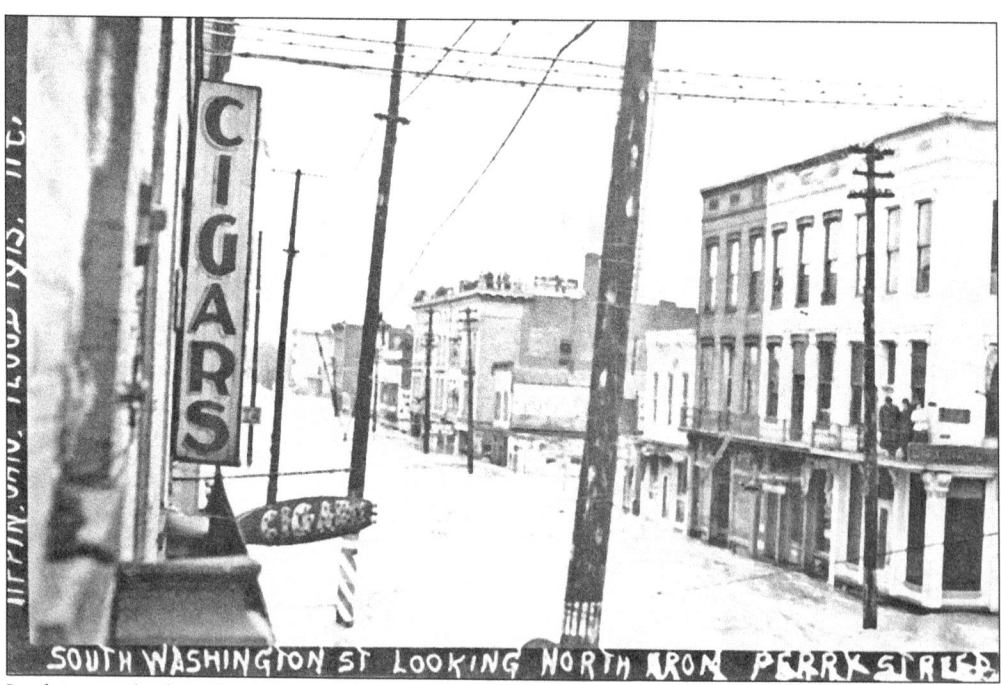

In this view looking back toward the river, the businesses of Washington Street have water rather than customers at their doors. Among the waterlogged businesses visible on the left is the Mystic Theater. On the east side of the street are a dentist, a restaurant, a livery, a dry goods store, and the woolen mills. Note also the many onlookers on the rooftops.

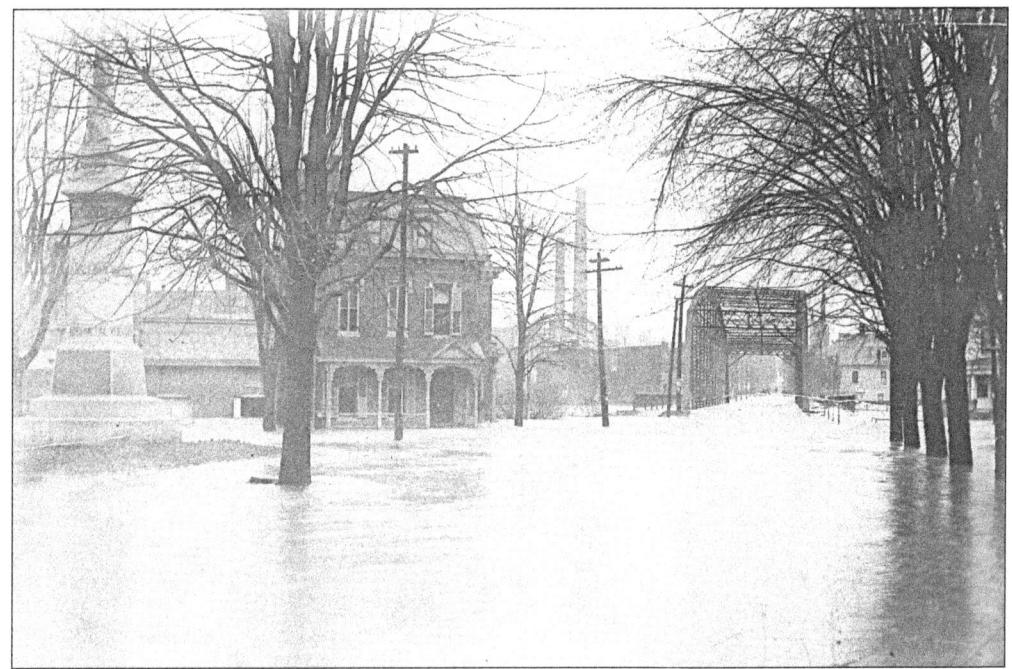

The Monroe Street Bridge has yet to succumb to the water's wrath at the time of this photograph. To the left, the Soldiers and Sailors Monument keeps watch over the unfolding horror. The camelback Monroe Street Bridge was the only one not replaced during the city's rebuilding efforts.

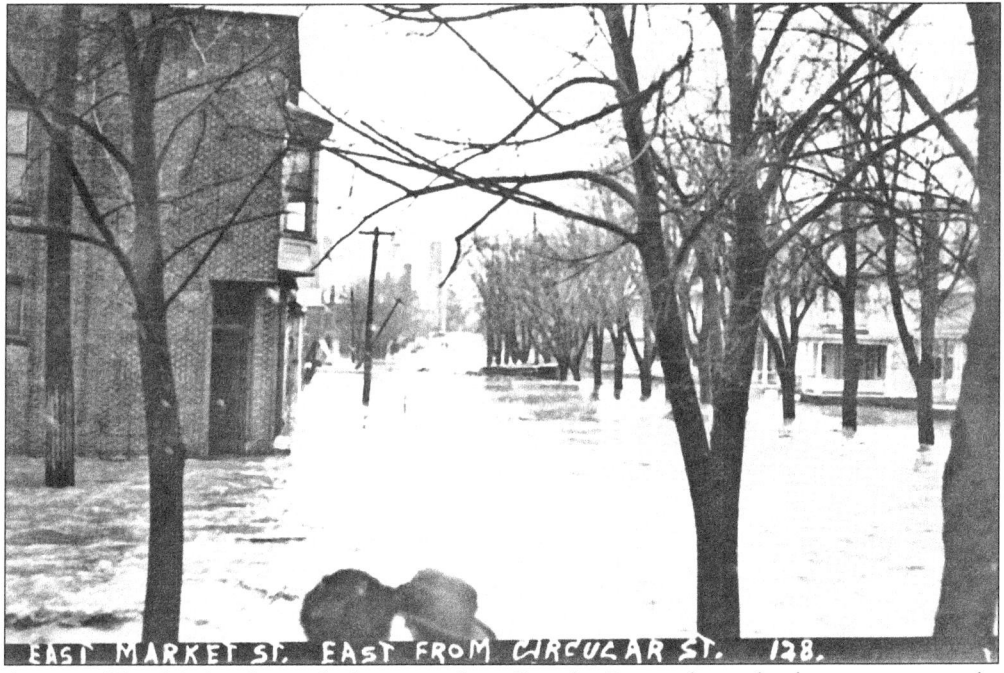

A view of East Market Street, looking east from Circular Street, shows the devastation wrought by Rock Creek as it also overflowed its banks. "There was a great lake of water on College Hill, between Market, Greenfield and Main Streets," Myron Barnes recalls. But no bridges were lost to the floodwaters of Rock Creek.

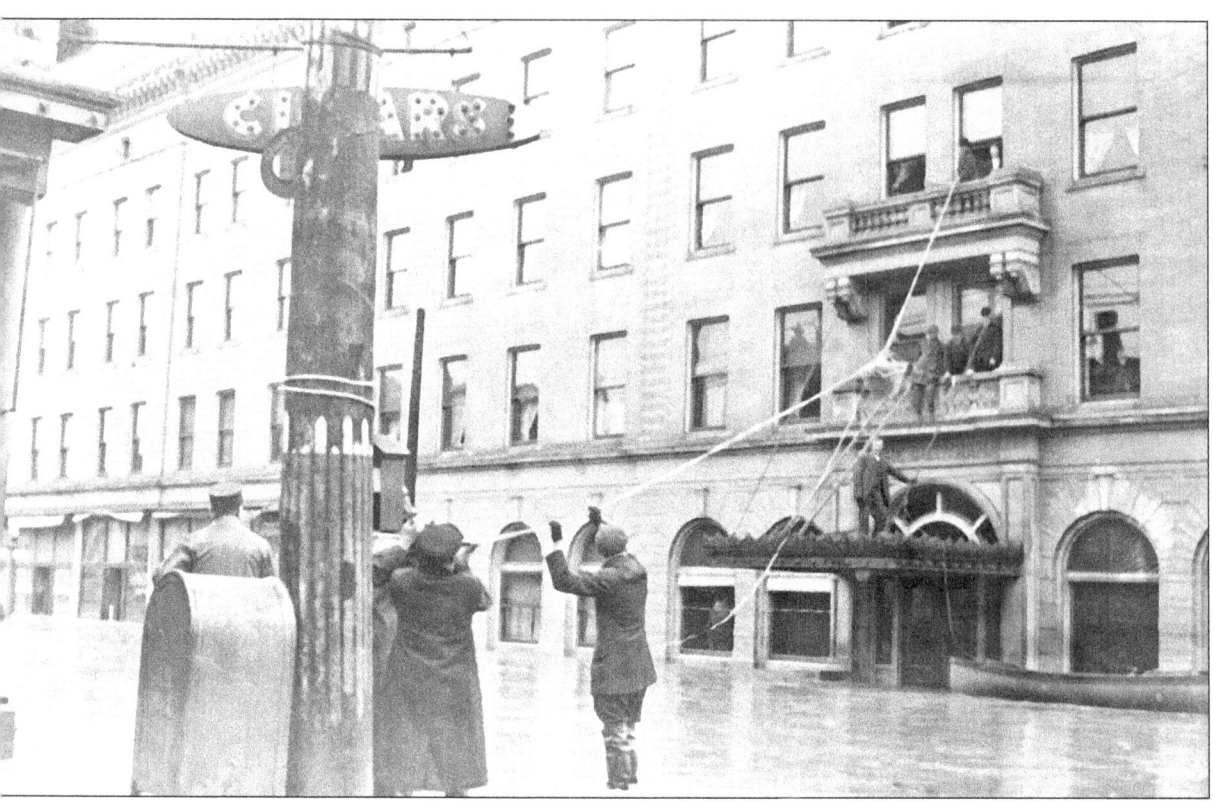

Rescue scenes, such as this at the southeast entrance of the Shawhan Hotel, quickly became commonplace as the Sandusky River rose. One man stands atop the first floor overhang; others watch as a basket is relayed down from the third floor to street level.

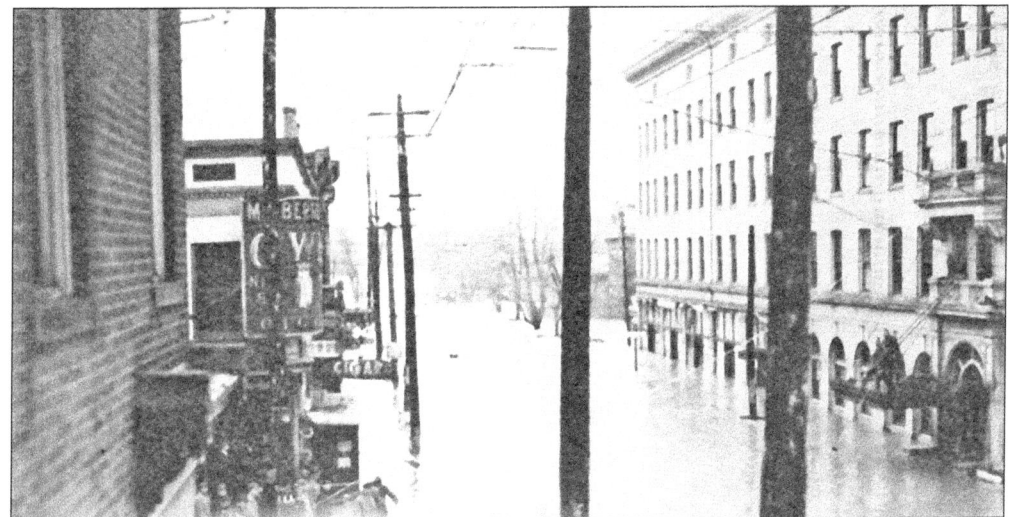

The Perry Street Bridge has been swept away in this view looking west from the intersection with Washington Street. The Shawhan rescue rope has been put in place, secured by the hotel's third-floor balcony and a telephone pole on the opposite side of Perry, in front of the cigar store.

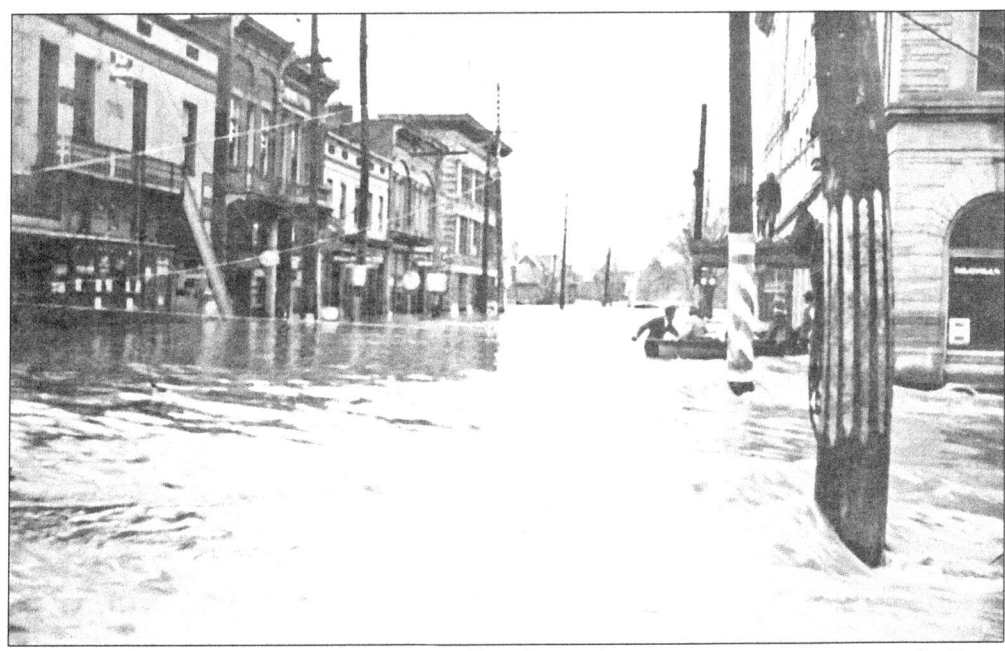

A closer view of the same Shawhan rescue effort shows a boat evacuation in progress at the Perry Street entrance. The fast-moving water is more than knee deep as those stranded at the hotel are guided into a boat.

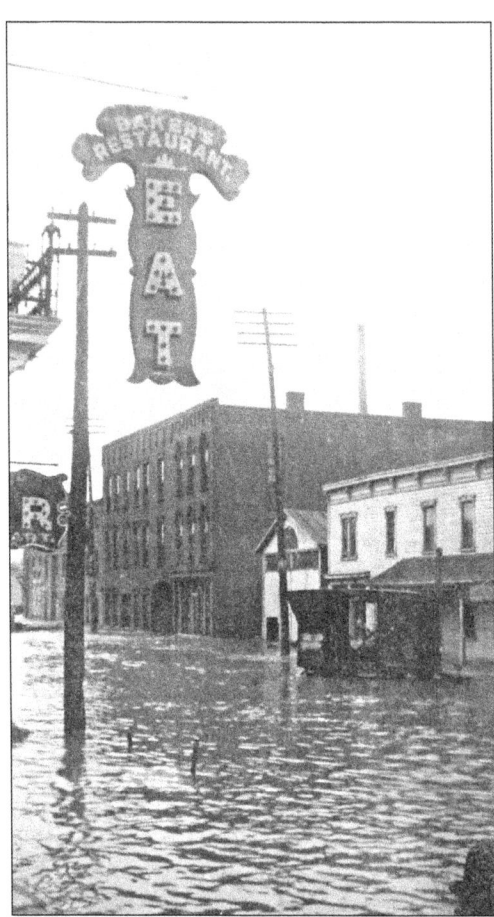

Baker's Restaurant and its beckoning "Eat" sign stand in contrast to the slate-gray sky that produced the epochal rains and resulting floodwater. Between March 23 and March 26, Tiffin absorbed seven inches of rainfall.

A group of boys stands in the ankle-deep water across from the Presbyterian church at the southwest corner of Monroe and Market Streets. Church officials reported $600 in flood-related damage sustained to the building and its contents.

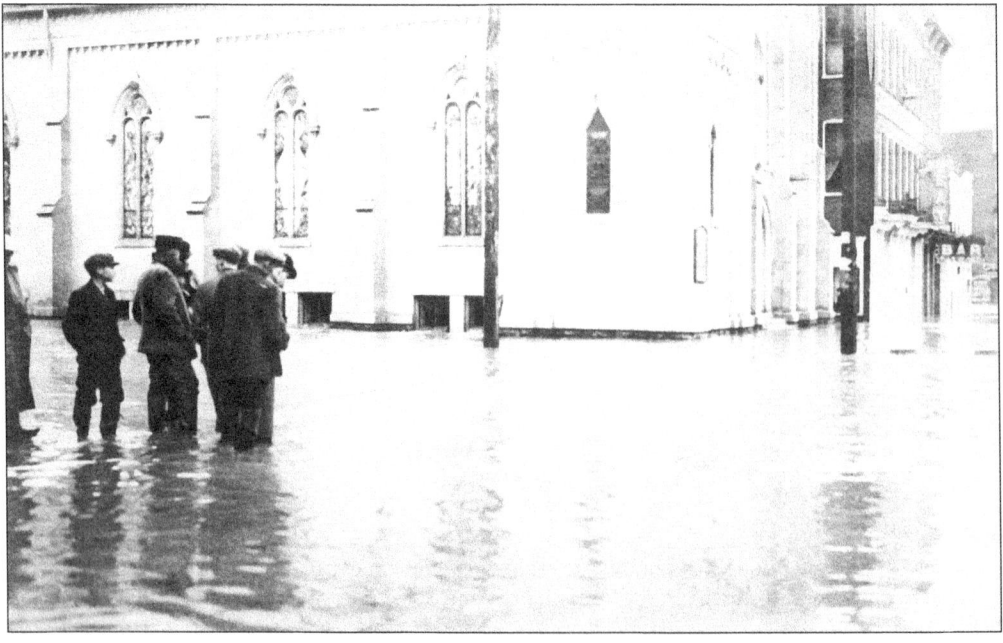

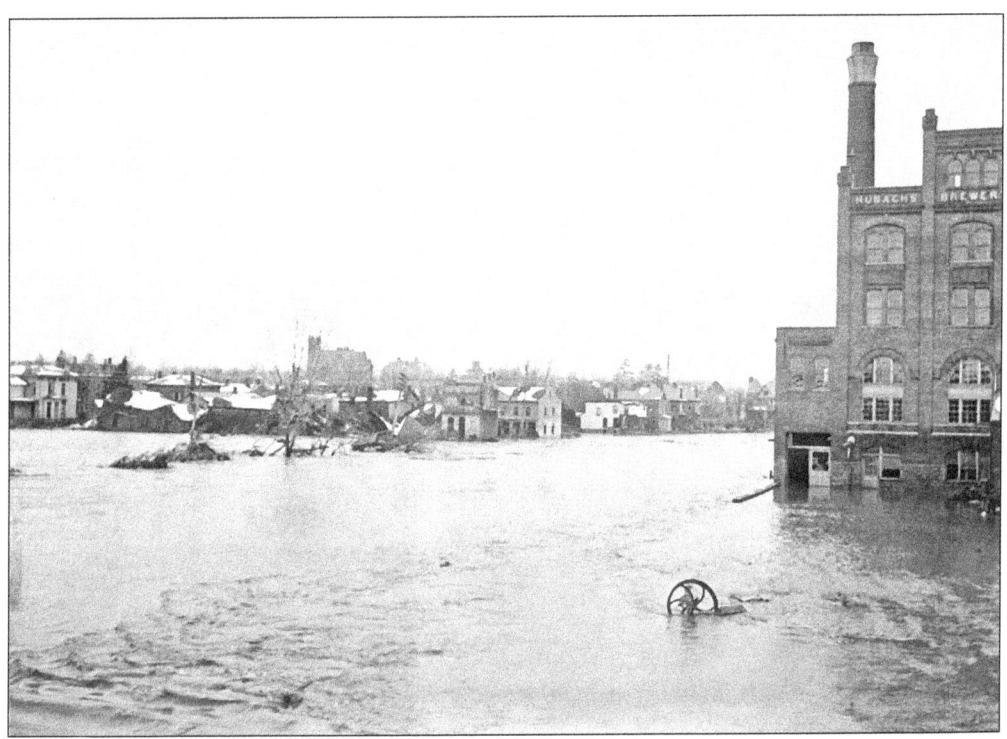

Hubach's Brewery, at the foot of Madison Street and at the end of the Sandusky's pair of sharp bends, was the high point for Tiffin's flooding. There, the Sandusky reached 28.9 feet, 10 feet above any previous reading. Brewery owner Henry Hubach estimated his flood-related losses at $10,000, among the greatest listed by any individual claimant.

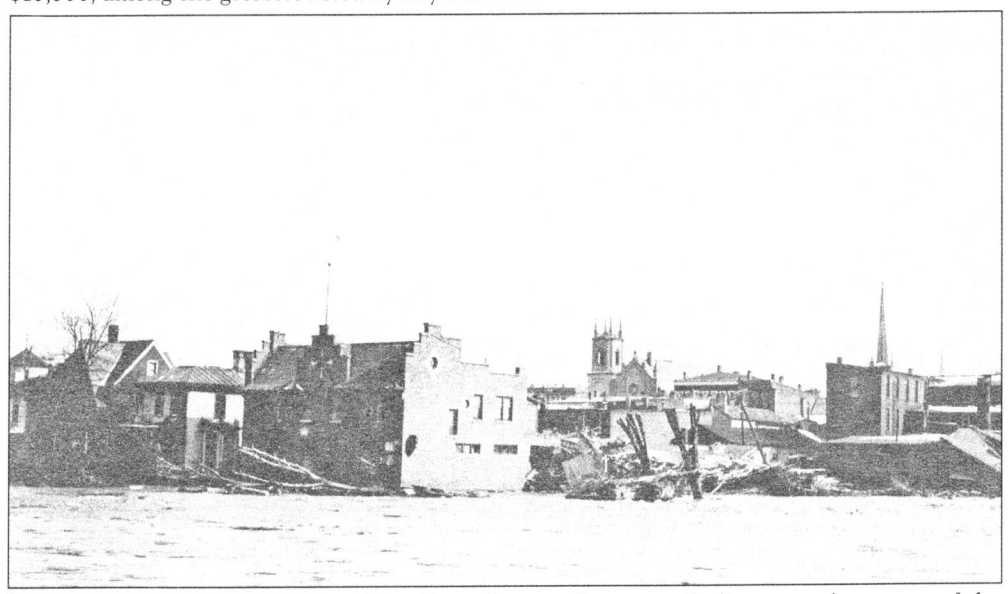

The view across the river toward East Perry Street offers a small glimpse at the extent of the flood-wrought devastation, yet church steeples continue to rise hopefully. The Standard Garage building, with its distinctive stepped facade and round side window, remains in use a century after being battered by the storms.

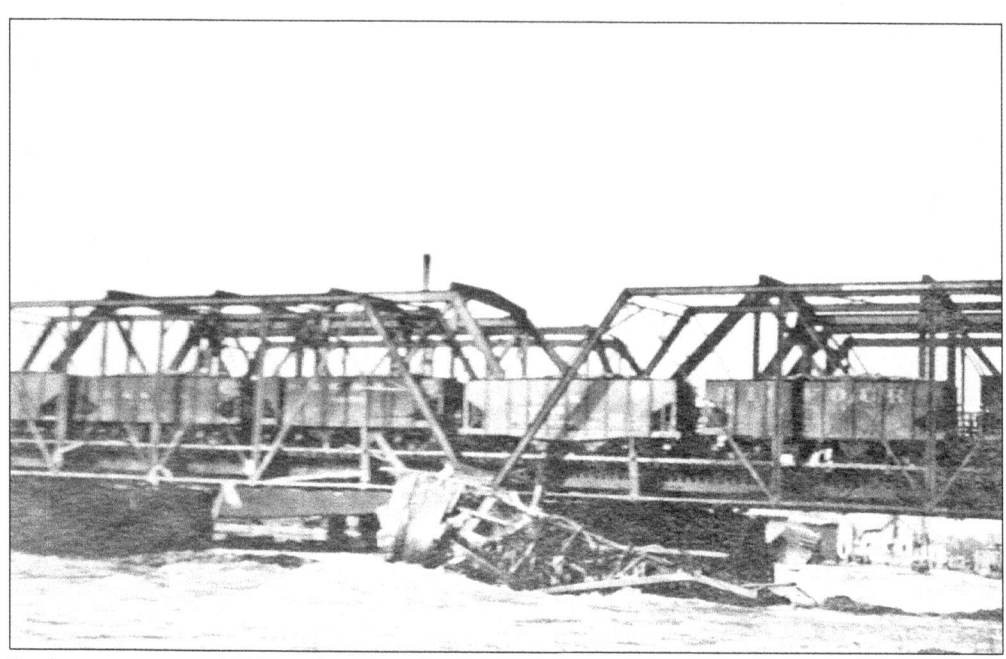

In this image, two of Tiffin's three weighted railroad bridges are visible. A considerable amount of debris already has accumulated around the bridge pier, while in the background a riverside neighborhood does its best to withstand the raging waters.

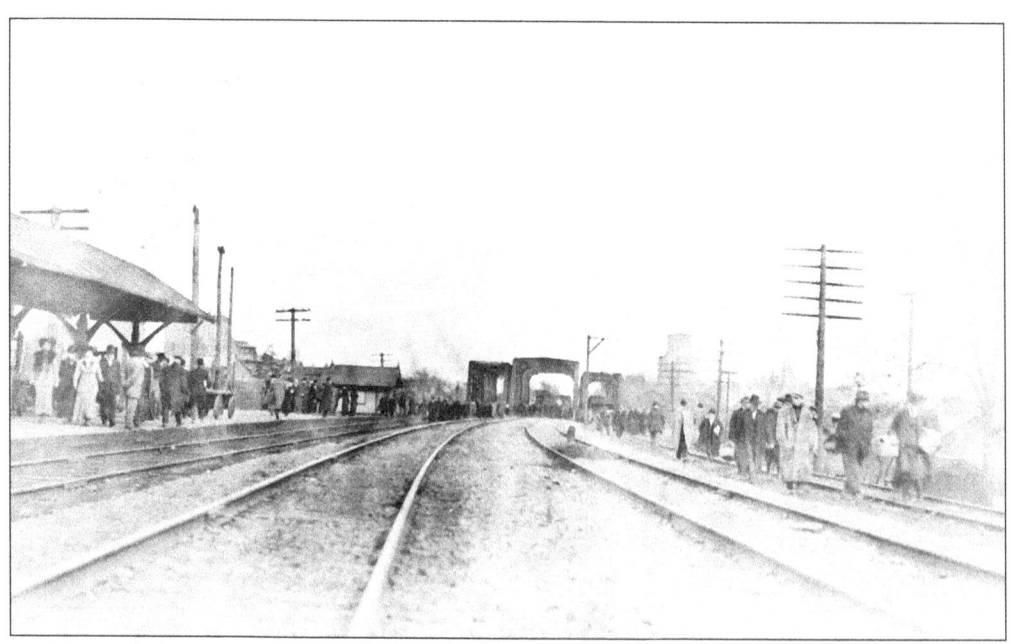

Until completion of a temporary bridge, those who needed to cross the Sandusky River in the days after Tiffin's flood were forced to walk across the railroad bridges. The Pennsylvania Railroad station is on the left in this photograph.

Six

A CITY CHALLENGED

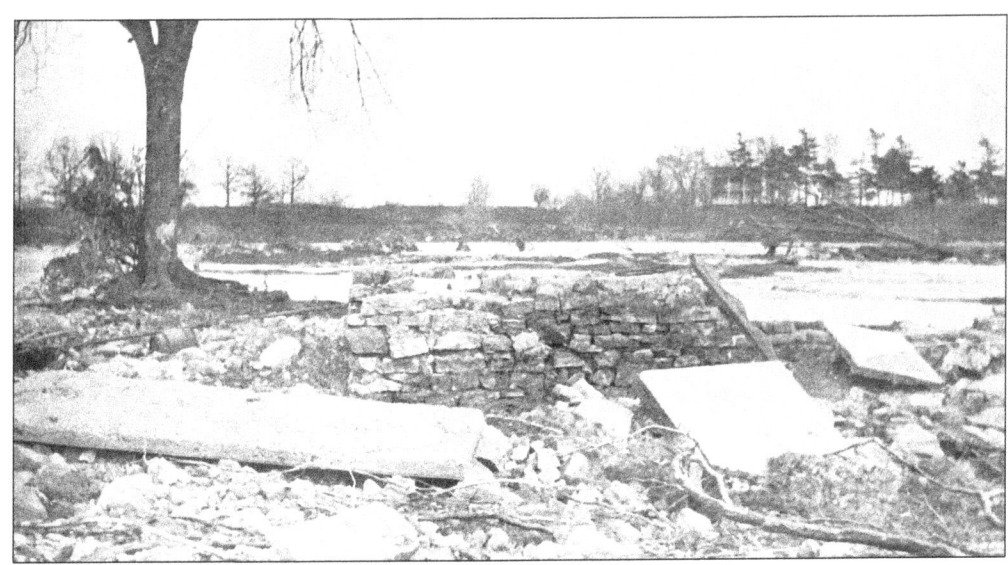

The foundation is all that remains of the Klingshirn home, which was swept from its location at 256 East Davis Street on March 25. Onlookers conducted an hours-long vigil as fast-moving currents prevented rescuers from reaching the house. Around 11:00 p.m., the house finally gave way, and 10 family members were dashed to their deaths.

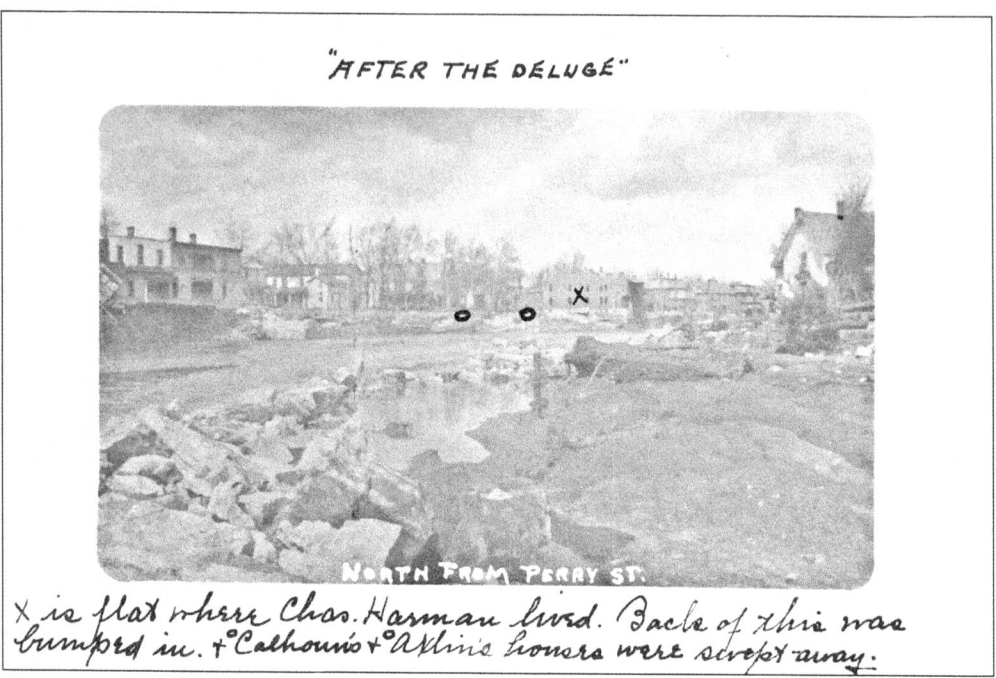

"AFTER THE DELUGE"

NORTH FROM PERRY ST.

X is flat where Chas. Harman lived. Back of this was bumped in. + Calhoun's + Axlin's houses were swept away.

A view northward from Perry Street reveals the devastation where the Axline and Calhoun homes stood along Water Street on the Sandusky's far bank until March 25, 1913. William and Addline Axline lost their lives, while Charles and Mabel Calhoun merely lost all of their possessions.

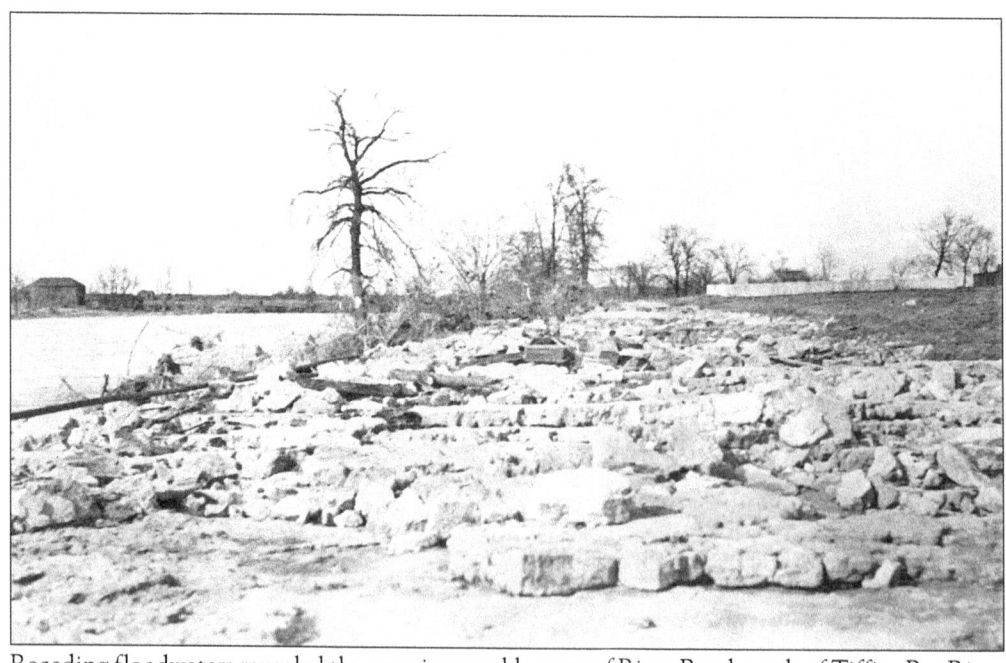

Receding floodwaters revealed the near-impassable mess of River Road north of Tiffin. But River Road quickly became an essential artery in the city's healing, if not its actual recovery, from the flood. The majority of the bodies of the 19 people killed had been carried upstream.

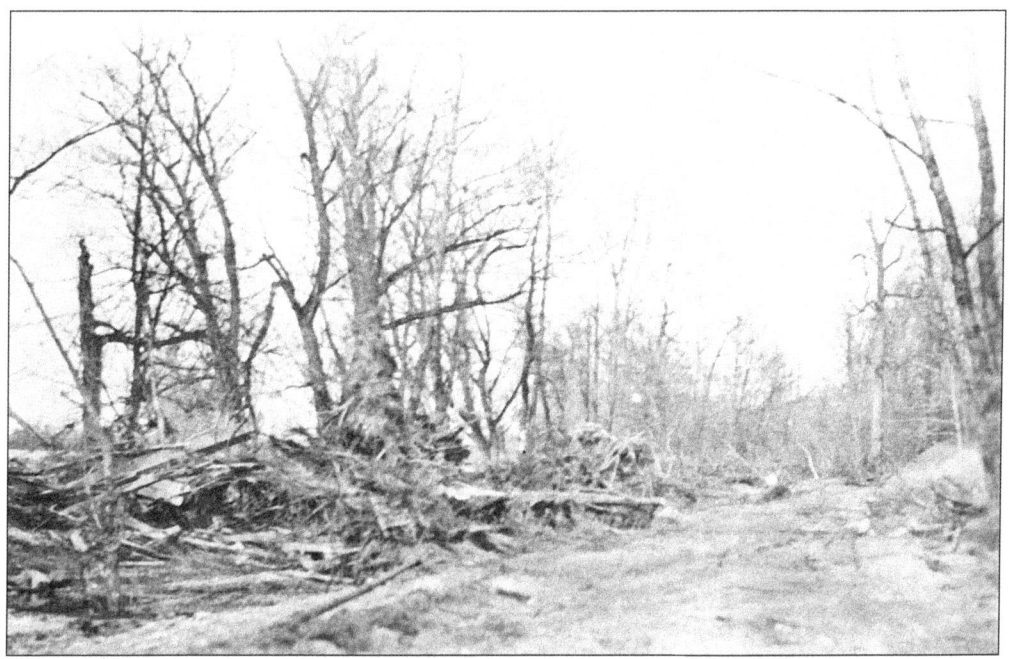

Another view of the River Road shows the task facing Tiffin residents in the ongoing recovery and cleanup effort. Trees uprooted by the water are strewn haphazardly across the mud of the unpaved road.

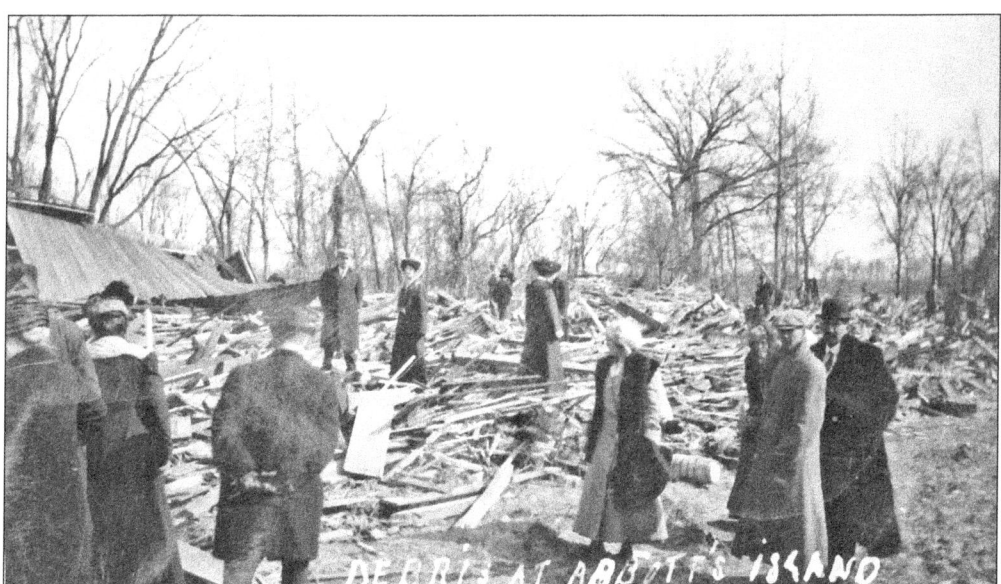

Detritus from the flood is strewn about Abbott's Island about six miles north of the city. A *Tiffin Tribune* report describes the debris pile as "several feet deep, 40-feet wide and one-quarter of a mile long." More gruesome discoveries awaited—the bodies of most of the flood victims would be discovered on Abbott's Island.

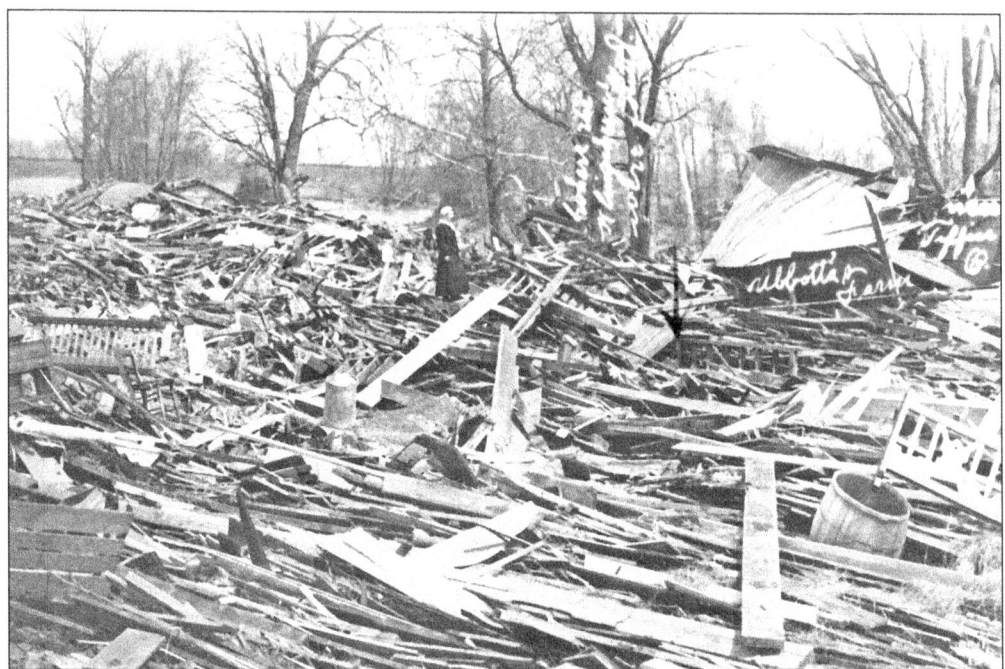

A closer view of the Abbott's Island debris reflects the arbitrary nature of the flood's destruction. Intact barrels and bedsteads sit strewn among the splintered remains of buildings and barns.

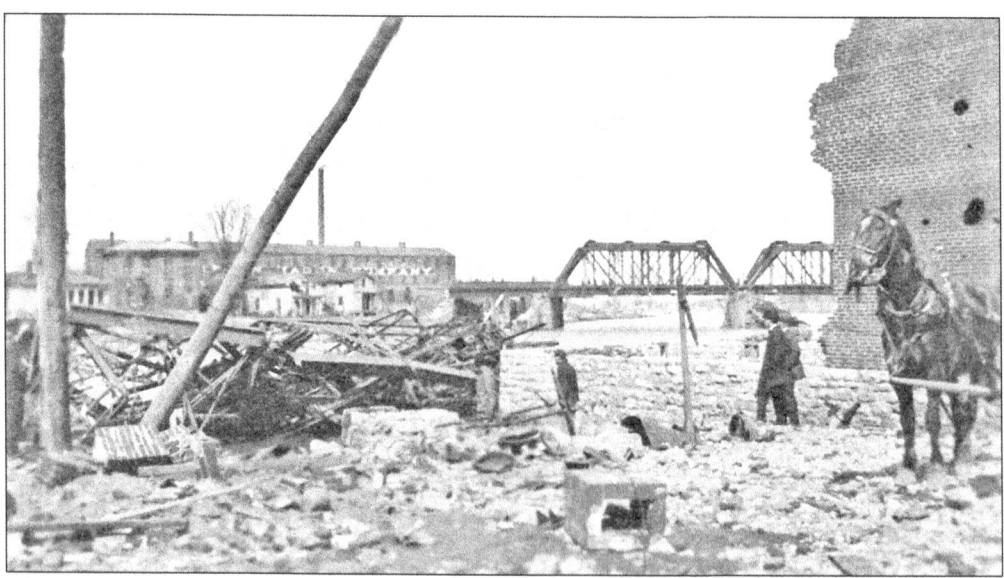

The intact railroad bridges offer some semblance of normalcy as cleanup efforts get under way at riverside businesses. To the left of the bridge sits the Tiffin Wagon Company plant, one of the businesses hardest hit by the flooding. Entire sheds were swept away, and company officials estimated their total losses at $80,000.

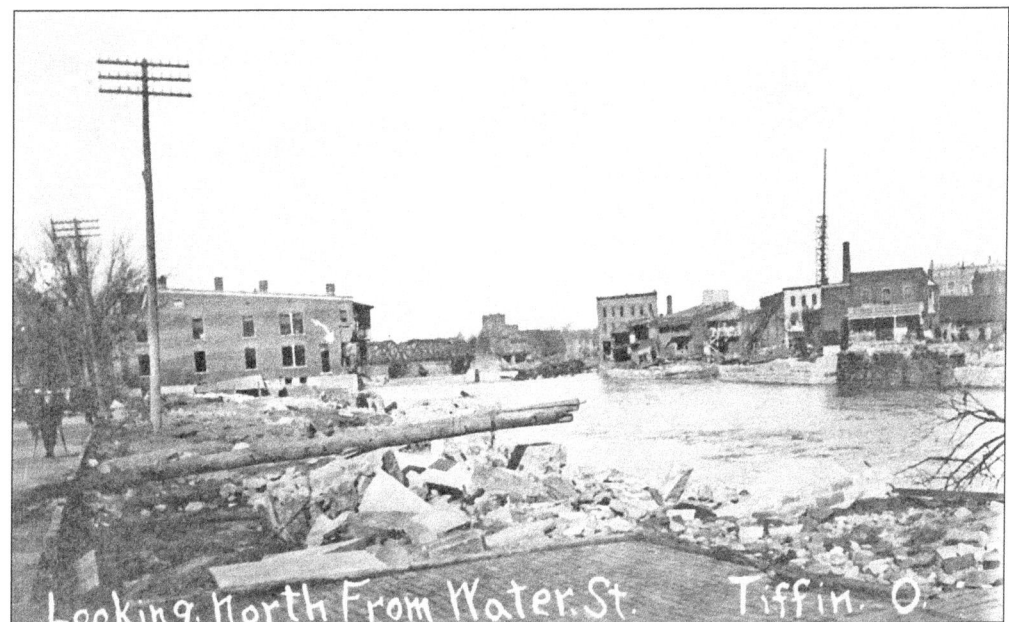

Looking North From Water St. Tiffin. O.

As the Sandusky retreats to its banks, the view from the point at Water Street where the Axline and Calhoun houses were swept away reveals the extent of the rebuilding effort facing Tiffin. A wider river channel and high retaining walls, as well as more restrictive building requirements, were among the solutions to prevent the disaster from visiting some future generation.

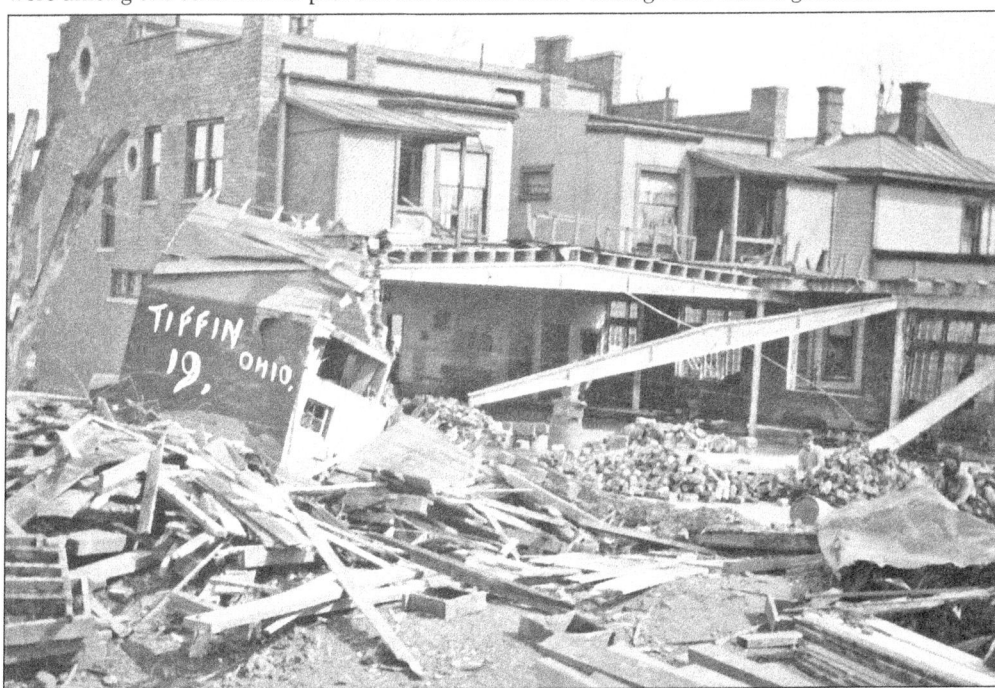

TIFFIN OHIO. 19,

The rear of the Standard Garage, at the river's edge at 14 East Perry Street, shows the beating absorbed by the brick building. At the height of the flood, a basket rescue had been needed to retrieve a pair of families stranded in second-floor apartments. Garage proprietors reported a total of $4,500 in flood-related damage.

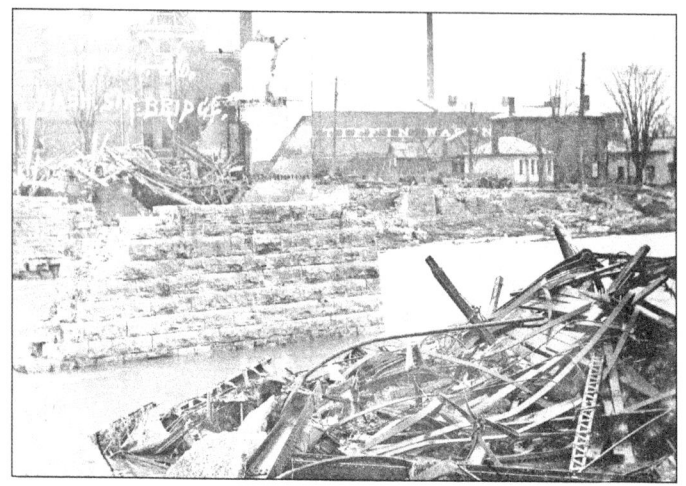

The exposed pier of the Washington Street Bridge is all that remains in the flood's wake. The *Tiffin Tribune* attempted to describe the indescribable, the three hours between the first and the final spans coming unmoored: "The intervals between the crashing of the bridges was filled with the roar and crushing of houses and buildings which were carried downstream in the mad current."

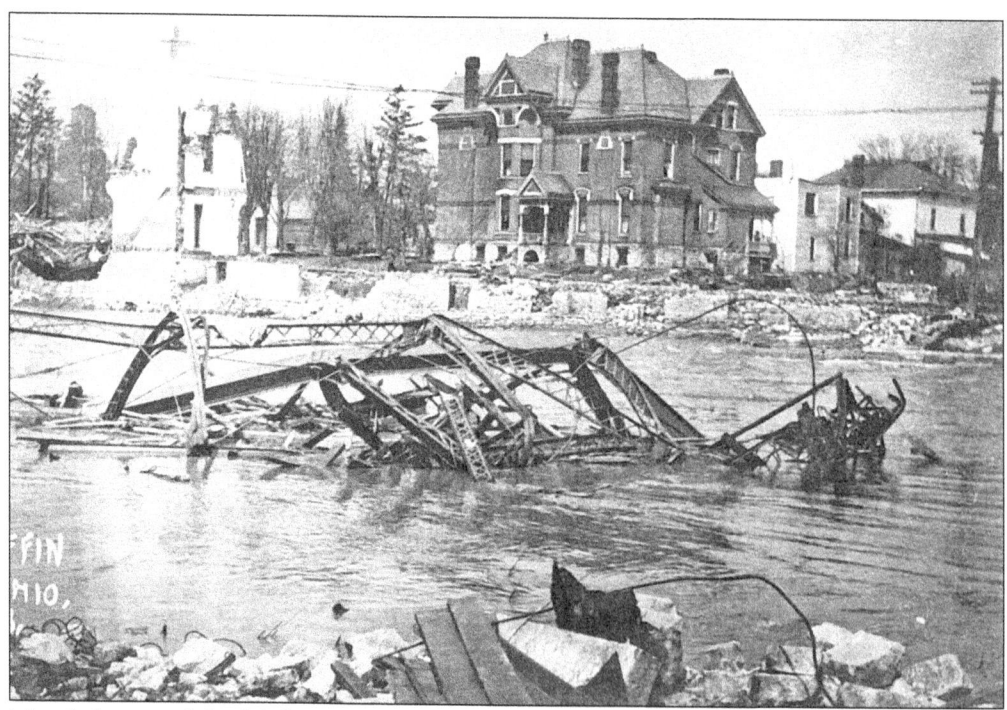

Mangled ruins of the Madison Street Bridge are all that remain at the site of the Washington Street structure. Overlooking the scene is the home of the late Warren P. Noble, attorney, state representative, congressman, Ohio State University trustee, and bank founder. Noble's widow, as well as several others living in the home, had to be rescued as the floodwaters rose.

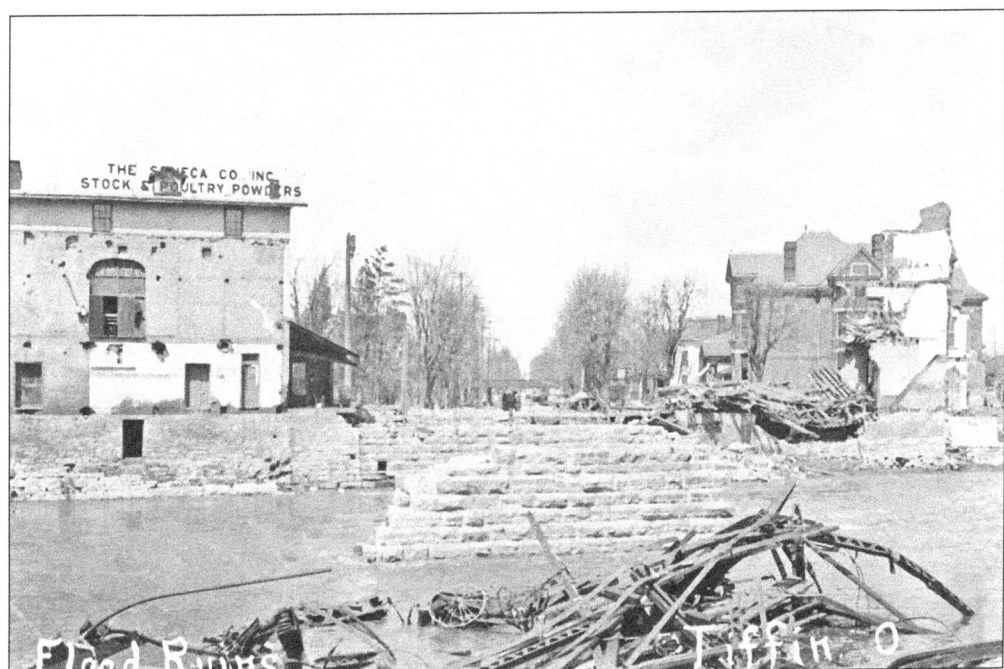

This view looking northward across the river toward the railroad viaduct on North Washington Street offers a hint of the task ahead in preventing another devastating flood. Note the debris in the foreground, resting on the riverbed. Deepening the Sandusky's channel through the city center would be a key to flood prevention.

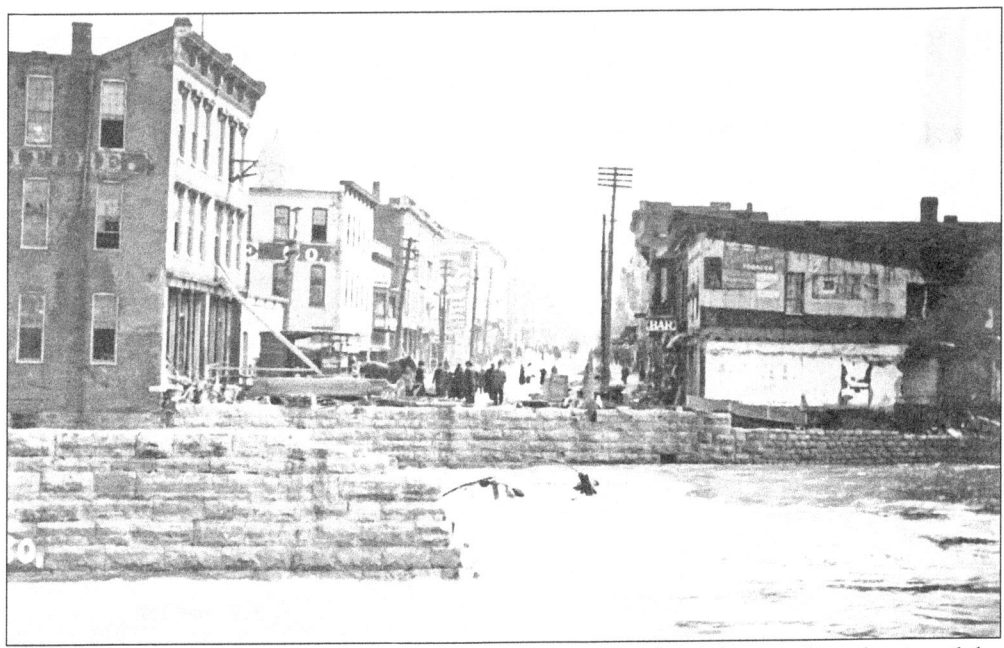

Onlookers contemplate the Sandusky's might as they survey flood damage from the site of the washed-out Washington Street Bridge. Rising over the scene in the left background is the dome of the Seneca County Courthouse.

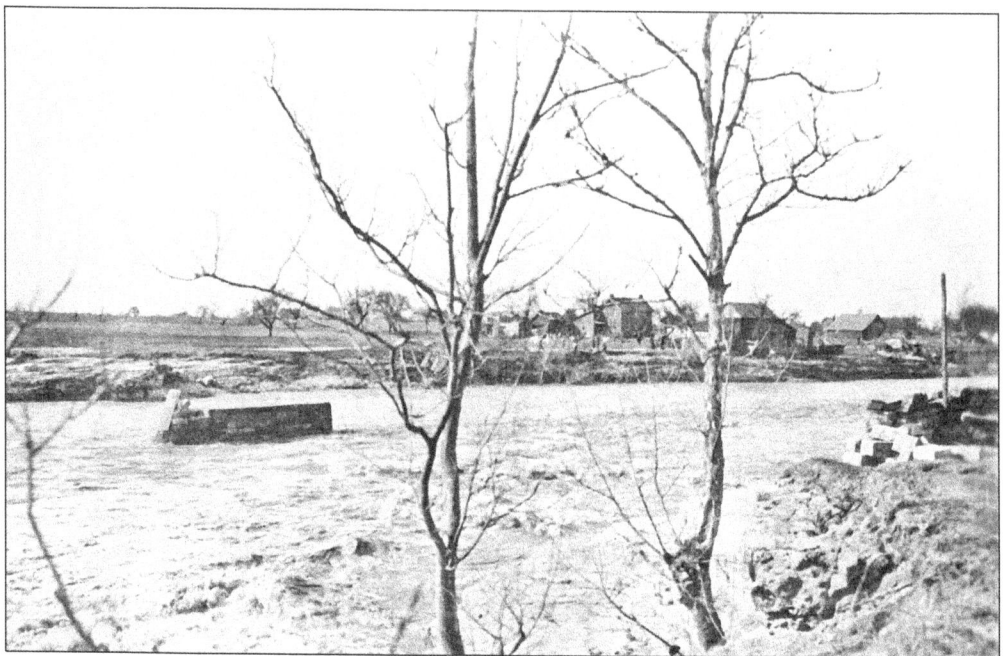

The Huss Street Bridge provided the northernmost link between Tiffin's two sides of the Sandusky River. It was here that four of the 19 flood victims met their end after the Davis Street home of Jacob Knecht was swept away and carried upriver.

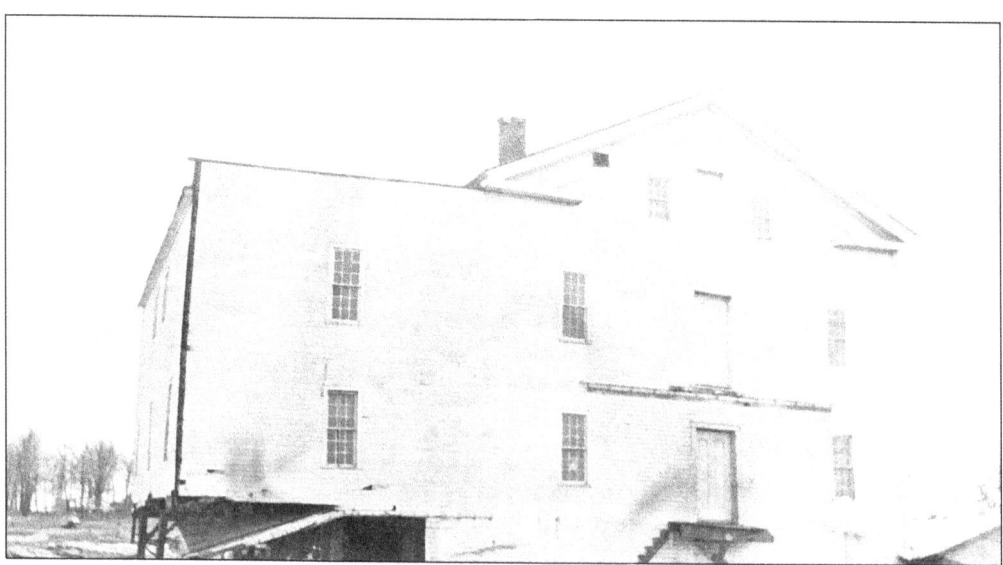

Speck's Mill would return to production for more than two decades after post-flood repairs were made, closing for good in October 1940. Mill owner Harry Speck claimed $3,000 in flood-related losses to the 1846 structure.

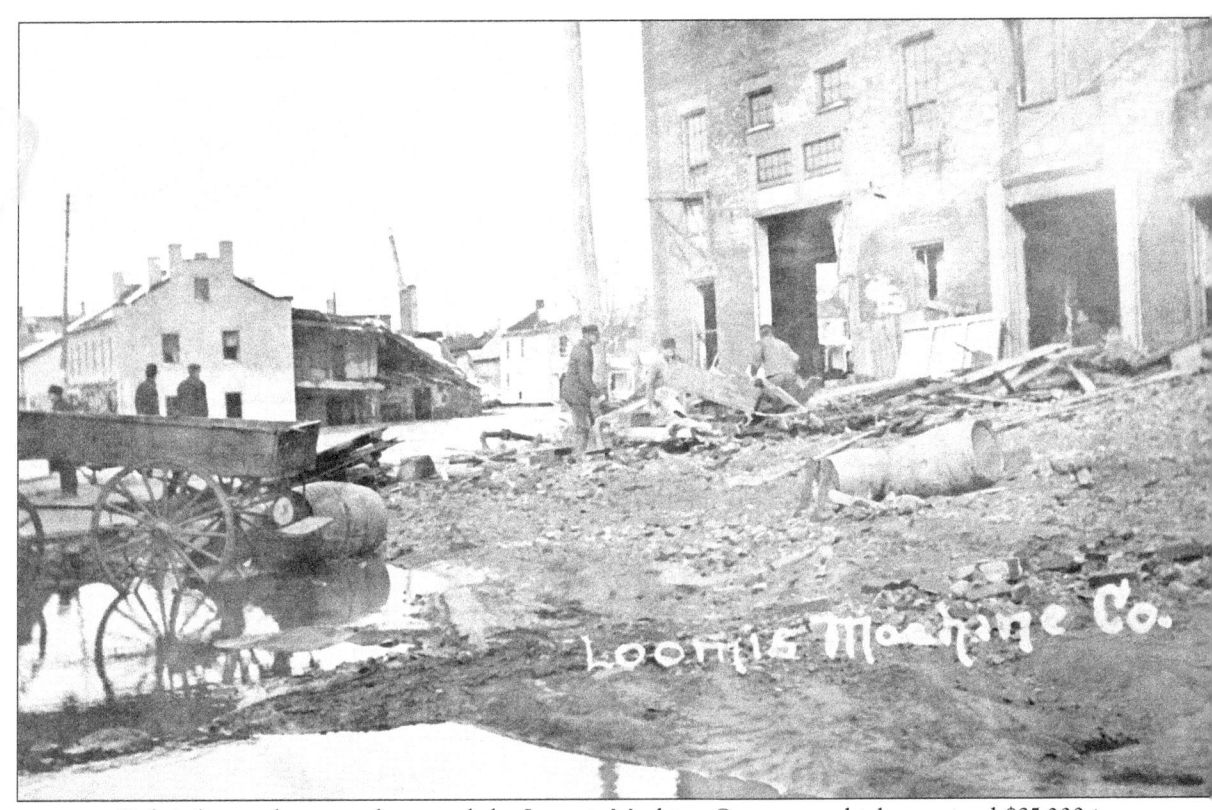

Debris litters the grounds around the Loomis Machine Company, which sustained $35,000 in damage from the flood. Loomis remained in business into the 1950s, manufacturing oil-drilling equipment that went into use all across the country.

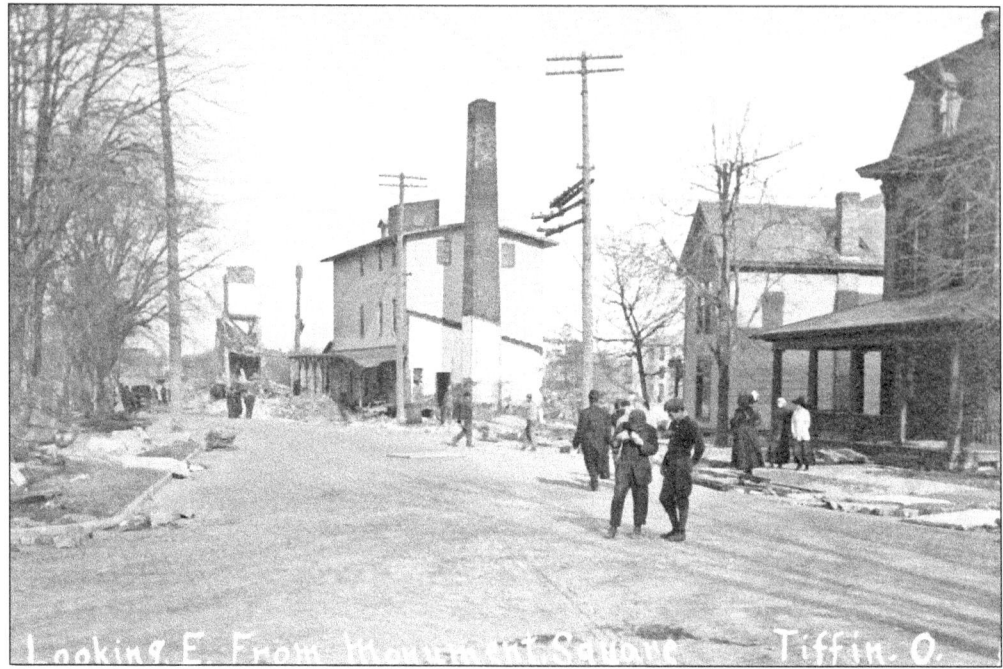

The Seneca Stock Food Company (center) was among numerous properties condemned as the city acquired land for the widening of the Sandusky River. Two years after the flood, company officials sold the land to the city for $7,000 and the right to dismantle the building for salvage. It finally came down in March 1916.

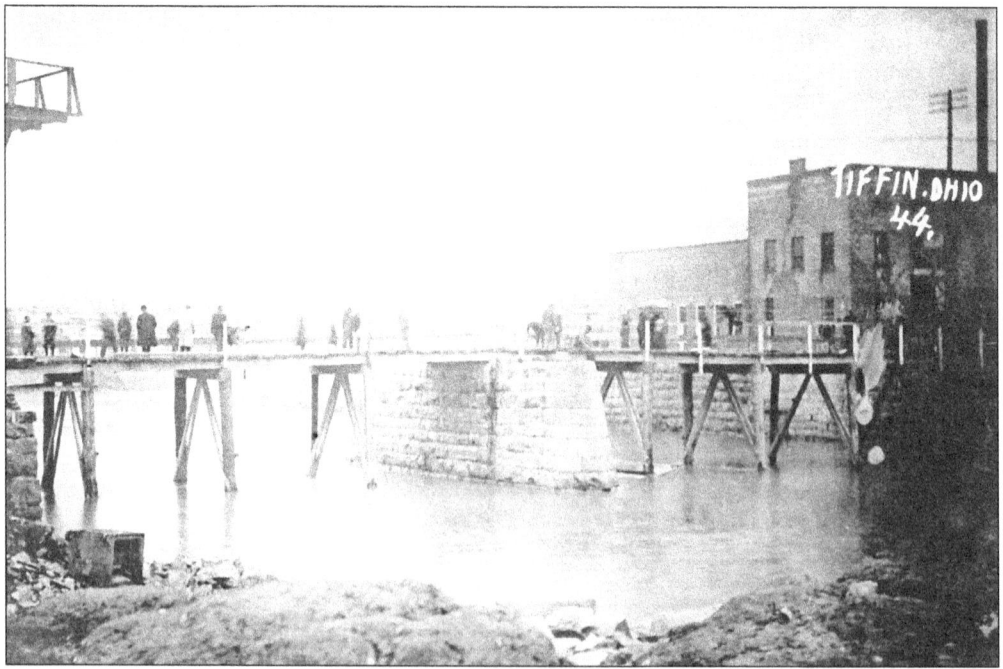

Completion of a temporary footbridge at the Market Street crossing was an early sign of Tiffin's flood recovery. The bridge was erected at a cost of about $1,000, and the first day subscriptions were offered, locals donated a total of $735, according to the *Tiffin Tribune*.

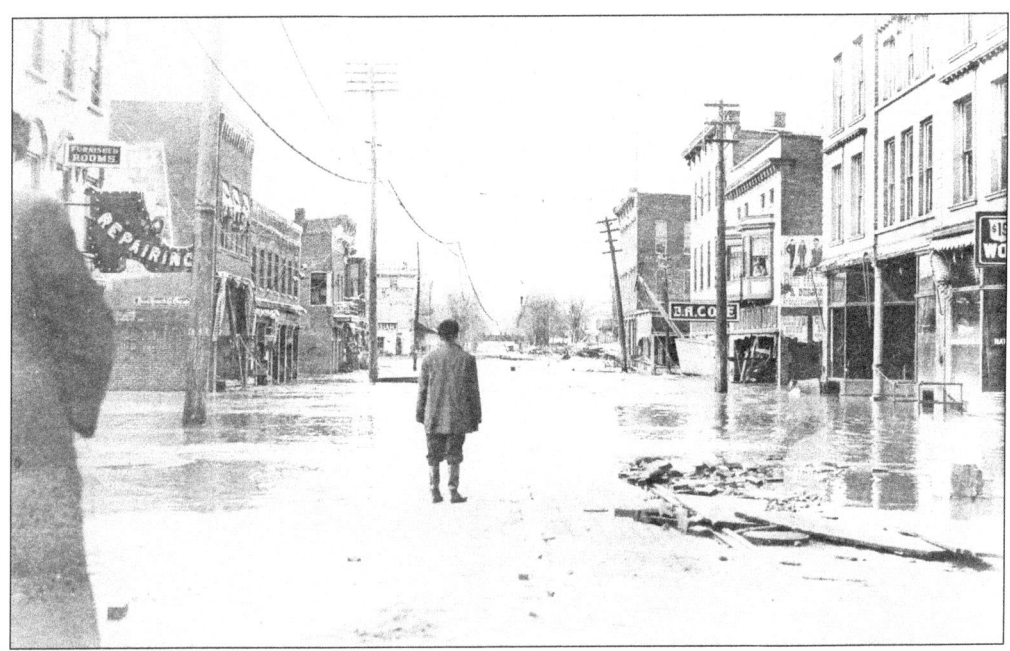

A lone boy contemplates the extent of the devastation as he surveys Washington Street from the south side of the washed-out bridge. A man is visible in the window of the apartment above Leland Cole's dry-cleaning store, from which the Cole family had been evacuated at the height of the flood.

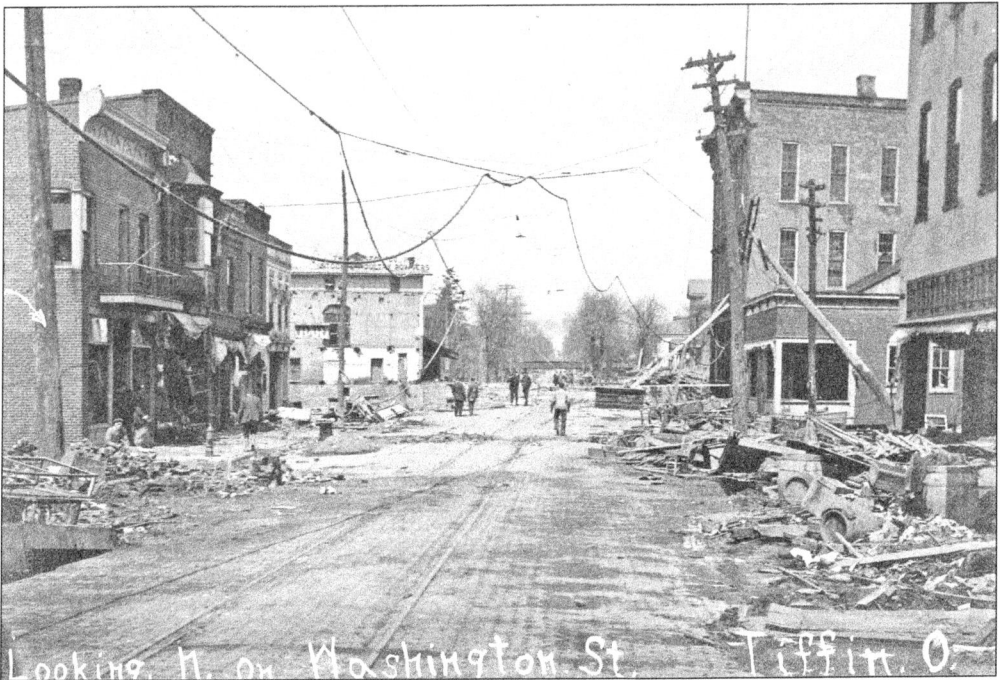

Looking N. on Washington St. Tiffin. O.

In a later view of the same scene, the Sandusky has retreated completely into its banks, revealing the jumbled mess left behind, both at ground level and among the wires strung above. Boxes and barrels are among the few recognizable pieces of debris left by the floodwaters.

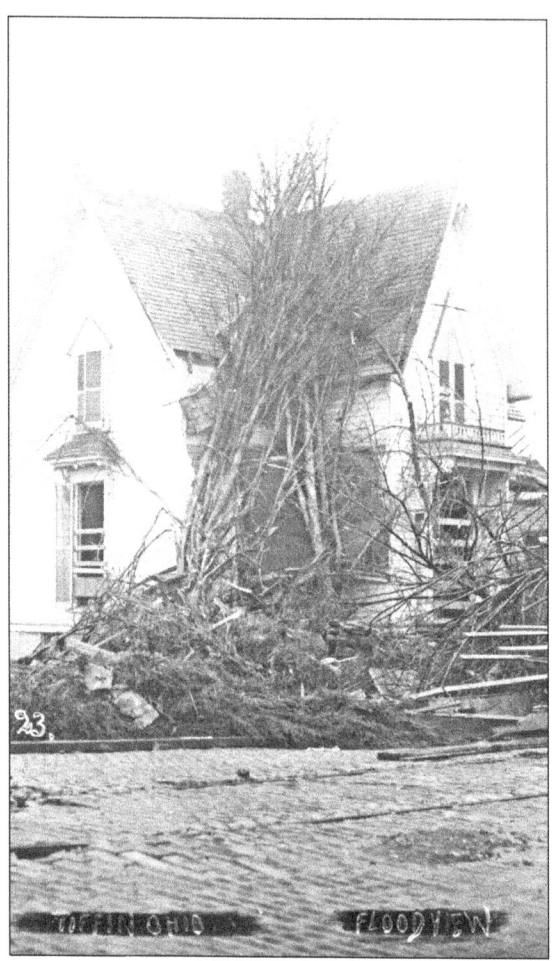

A corner of the Bertschey home became a repository for wreckage churned up by the raging Sandusky floodwaters. The house itself was razed in the effort to prevent future Tiffin flooding.

The Washington Street Bridge, the gateway to Tiffin's downtown, was the first to be replaced. A three-arch concrete span was constructed at a cost of $49,000. The initial attempt to cast the first concrete arch ended in a weight-related collapse, with one worker suffering an ankle injury.

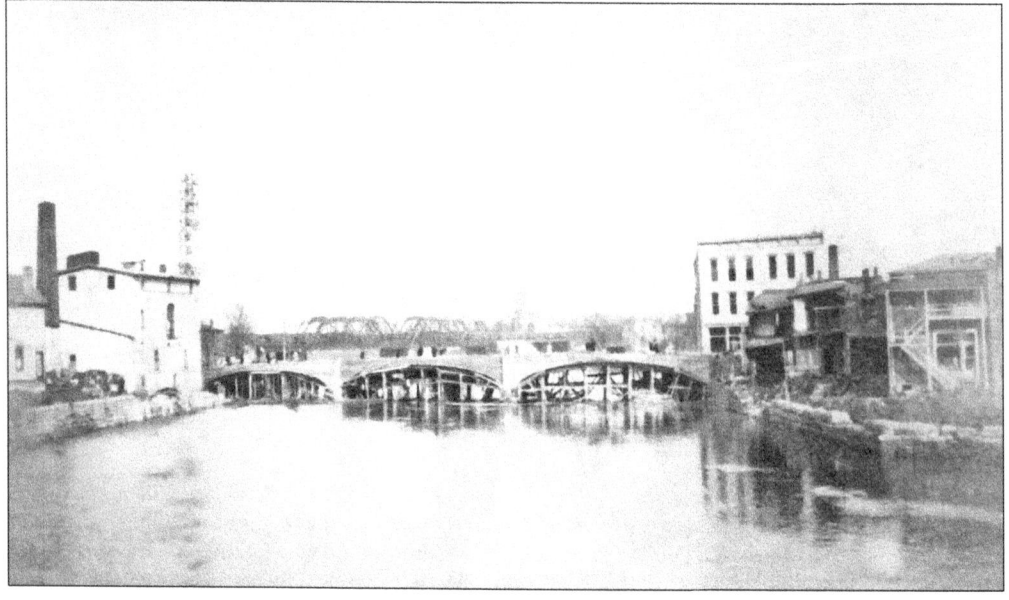

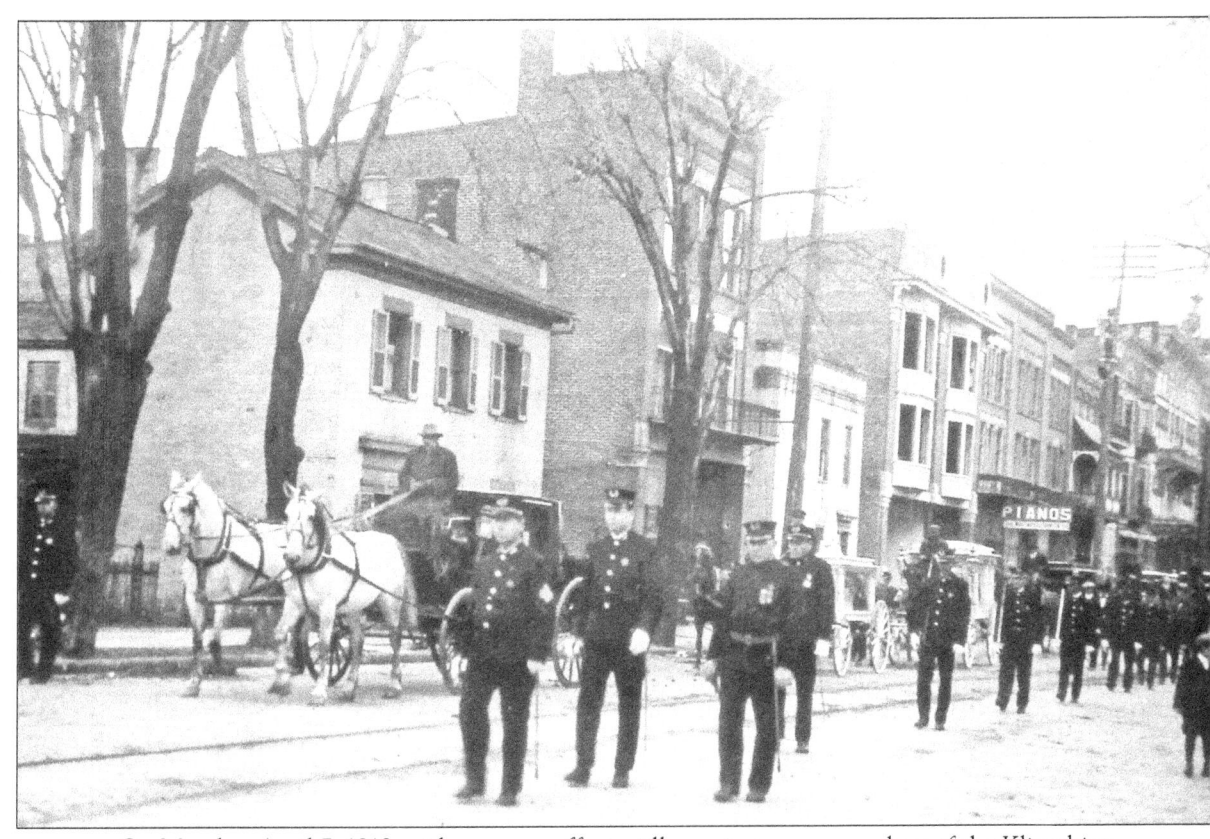

On Monday, April 7, 1913, with recovery efforts still ongoing, seven members of the Klingshirn family were laid to rest following a funeral service at St. Joseph's Catholic Church. The horse-drawn hearses of five of the Klingshirn children (along with the husband of one) and their mother then made a solemn parade to St. Joseph's cemetery.

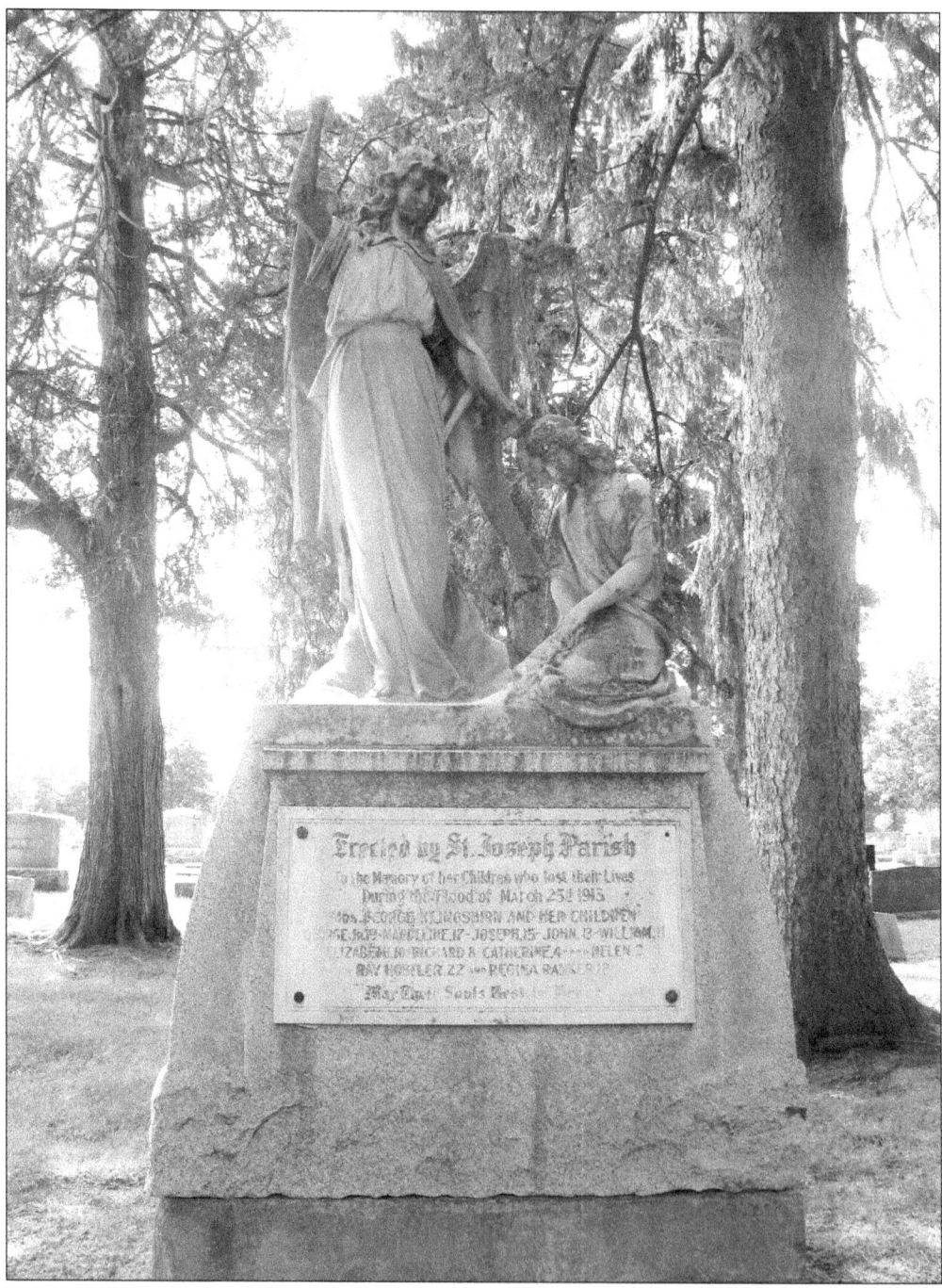

In March 1914, St. Joseph's parishioners dedicated a monument to their 12 fellow congregants who had not survived the previous year's flood. The *Tiffin Tribune* described the monument: "The base . . . is of extra white North Carolina granite, upon which the statue of Carrara marble rests. There are two figures, one representing Faith and the other Hope, carved from a single block of white marble." (Authors' collection)

Seven

A CITY OF LEARNING

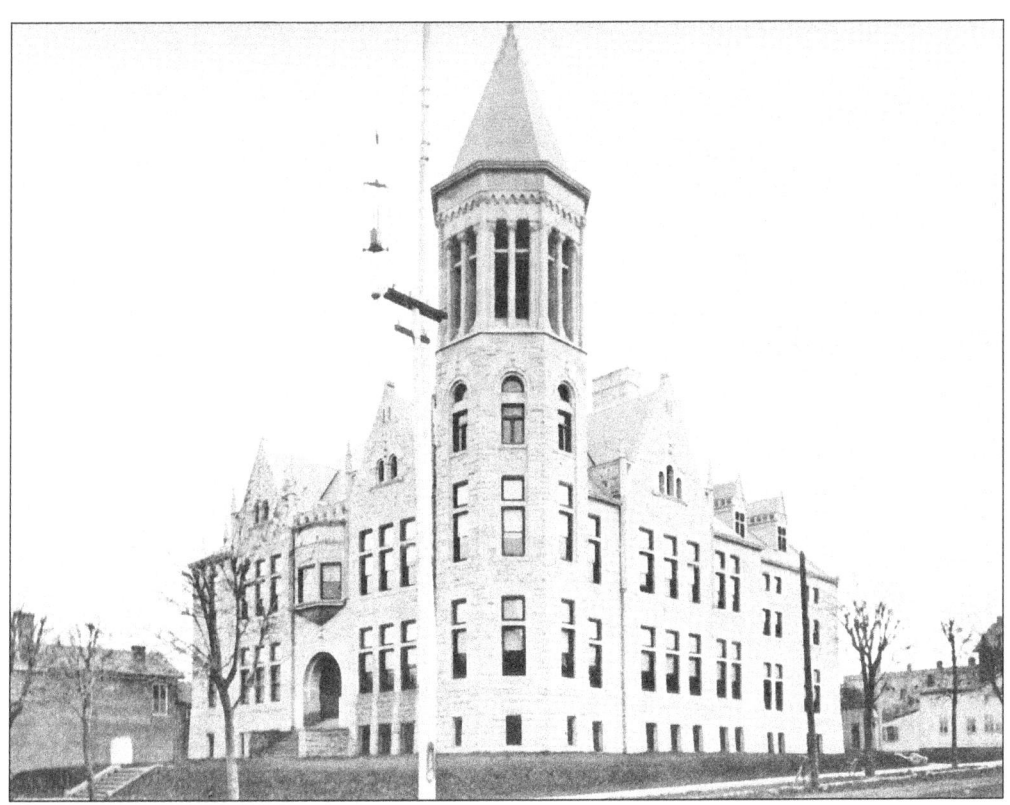

Columbian High School was named in commemoration of Chicago's World's Columbian Exposition of 1893. This building went up the year after the world's fair, at the intersection of East Market and Jefferson Streets and at a cost of $75,000. Expanded in 1931, the building became East Junior High when a new Columbian opened in 1961. Abandoned after Tiffin Middle School opened in 2003, the addition has been torn down.

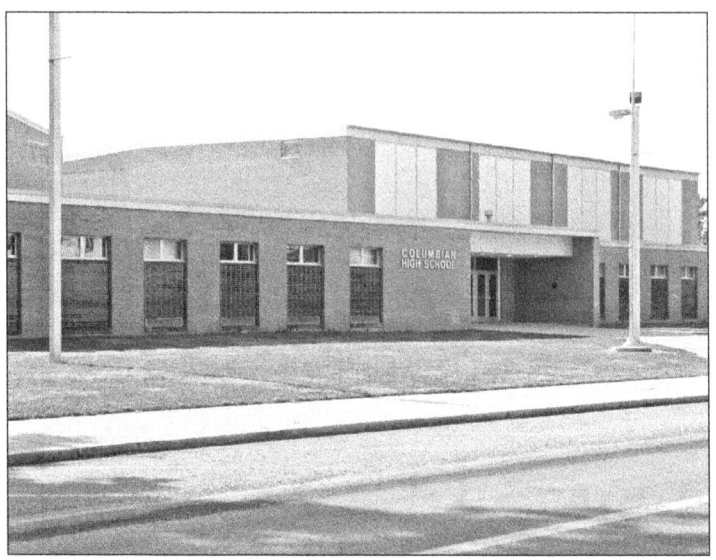

The present-day Columbian High School was dedicated on February 19, 1961, at 300 South Monroe Street (though the school was in use for the entirety of the 1960–1961 school year). Among its features is a planetarium, which would have been much in demand at the height of the space race during the building's early years. Construction costs totaled nearly $1.9 million. (Authors' collection.)

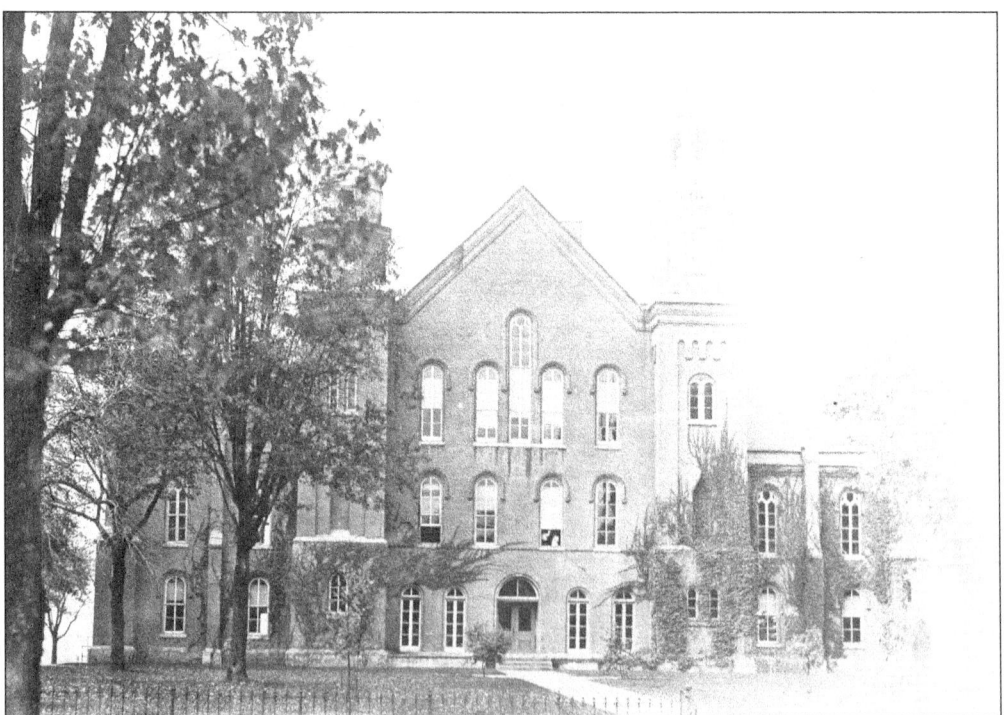

The Union School was completed in 1856 to serve the needs of the recently combined communities of Tiffin and Fort Ball. The Monroe Street campus covered 2.5 acres, with construction costs of $45,000. Tiffin's high school students met on the third floor until growing class sizes resulted in construction of the first Columbian High School. Union School was torn down in the late 1950s to make space for the present-day Columbian.

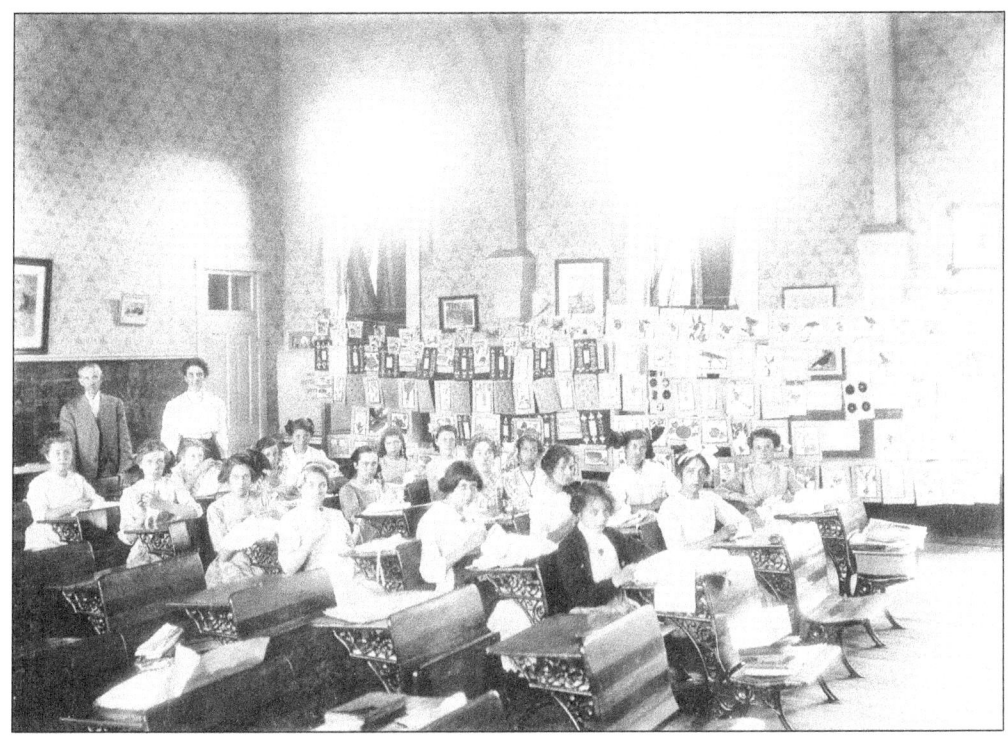

The members of Theresa Pittenger's sewing class are seen in their Union School classroom in this 1906 photograph. Also standing in the back of the room is Superintendent Charles Allen Krout, for whom one of Tiffin's elementary schools would later be named. A wide array of the girls' sewing projects is on display across the side of the room.

A centennial first grade class of the Union Street School, under the direction of teacher Janet Martin, poses for a photograph during individual and group reading time. A 1956 centennial pamphlet notes the building's impending replacement: "This school, which has served from the day of man and brute power of the atom, has reached the point of inadequacy, and can no longer meet the demands of a new world."

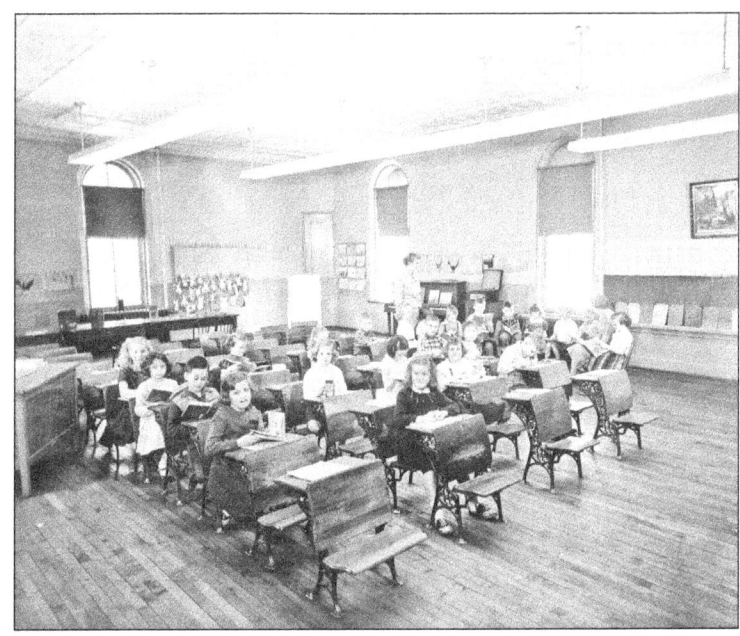

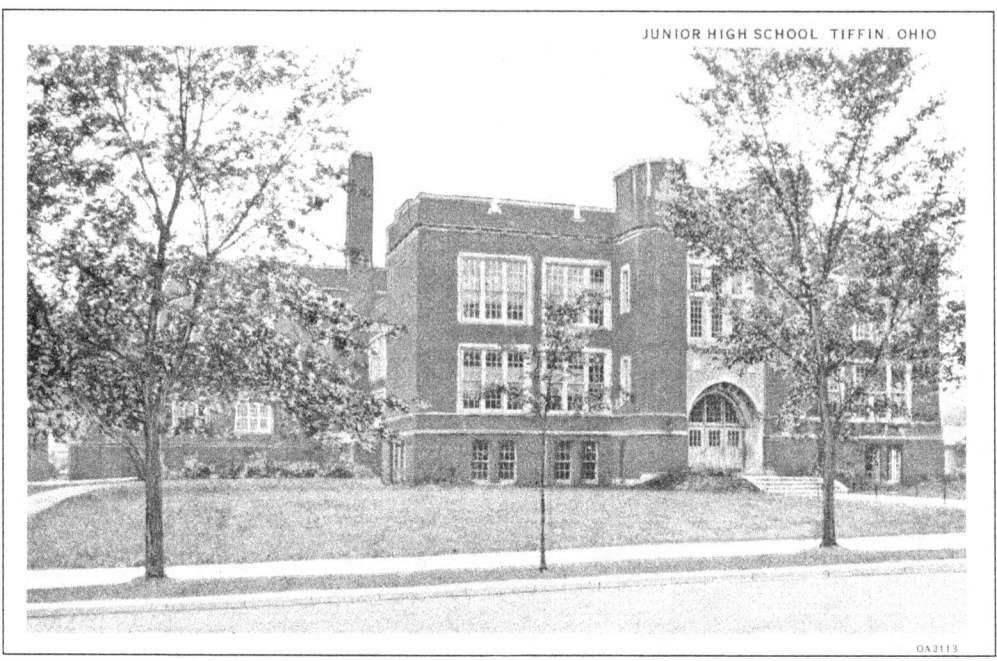

Constructed in 1924, this building on West Market Street served as Tiffin Schools' sole junior high school until growing enrollment merited the construction of a new high school and the conversion of the former Columbian into East Junior High. This building became West Junior High. The rival schools served until the opening of the Tiffin Middle School in 2003. The West building has since been razed.

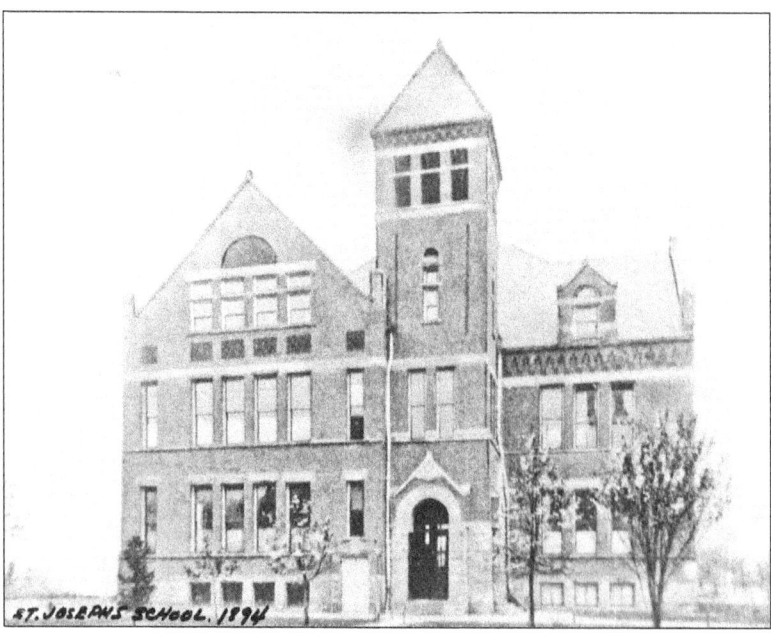

The second St. Joseph School was built in 1894 to the south of the church, and it replaced the building that had served first as the congregation's temporary church in 1855. As with the St. Mary's School on South Sandusky Street, St. Joseph serves students through grade eight. They then have the option of attending Calvert High School.

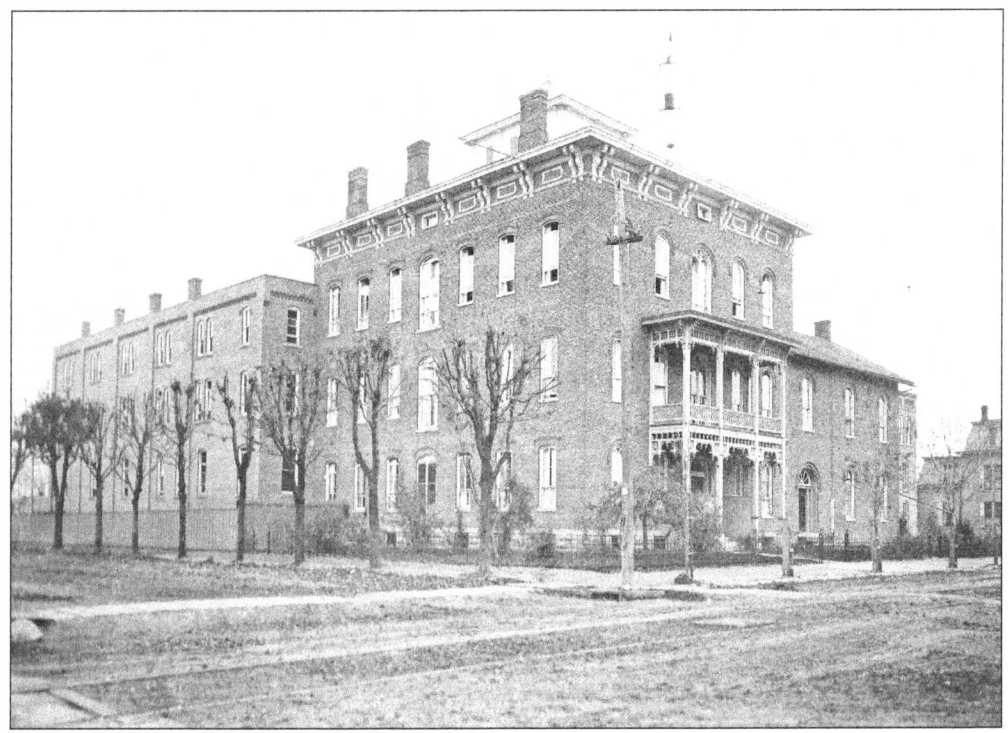

Pictured here is Tiffin's Ursuline convent. Constructed in 1863 on Jefferson Street (between Madison and Tiffin Streets), the three-story brick building served as a boarding school for girls. That school included the city's first kindergarten, which was coed. Formally known as the College of the Ursuline Sisters, the school gained a reputation for its music department. The building was torn down in 1975.

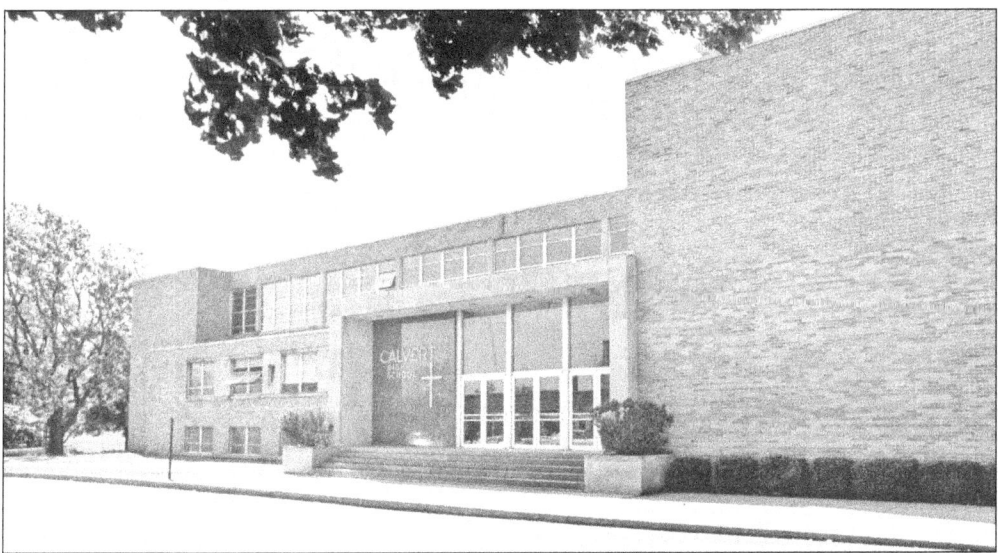

Calvert High School, located at 152 Madison Street, is a product of the Ursulines' girls' high school going coed in 1923. The private high school, affiliated with the Toledo Roman Catholic Diocese, houses students in grades 7 through 12. The Senecas' football and golf teams each have produced state champions—the football team won back-to-back titles in 1980 and 1981.

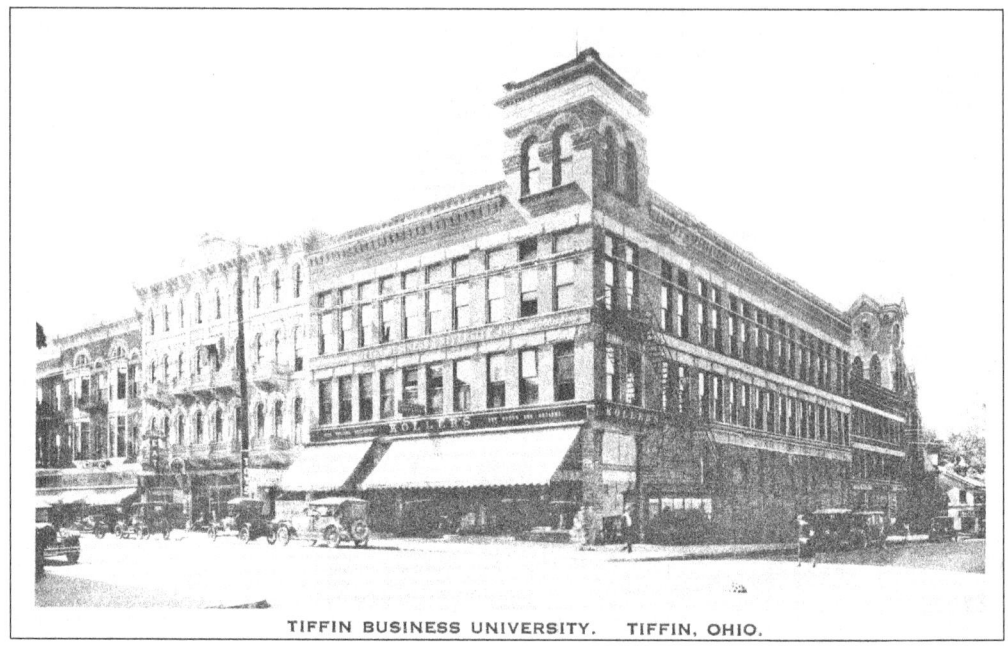

TIFFIN BUSINESS UNIVERSITY.   TIFFIN, OHIO.

The upper floors of the Remmele Building, at the southwest corner of South Washington and Madison Streets, were home to Tiffin University from 1918 to 1956. The university, founded in 1888 as Tiffin Business University (the name was shortened in 1939), moved to its present location after purchasing the former Miami Street School. Campus expansion has led to beautification of long stretches of Miami Street, including a former junkyard.

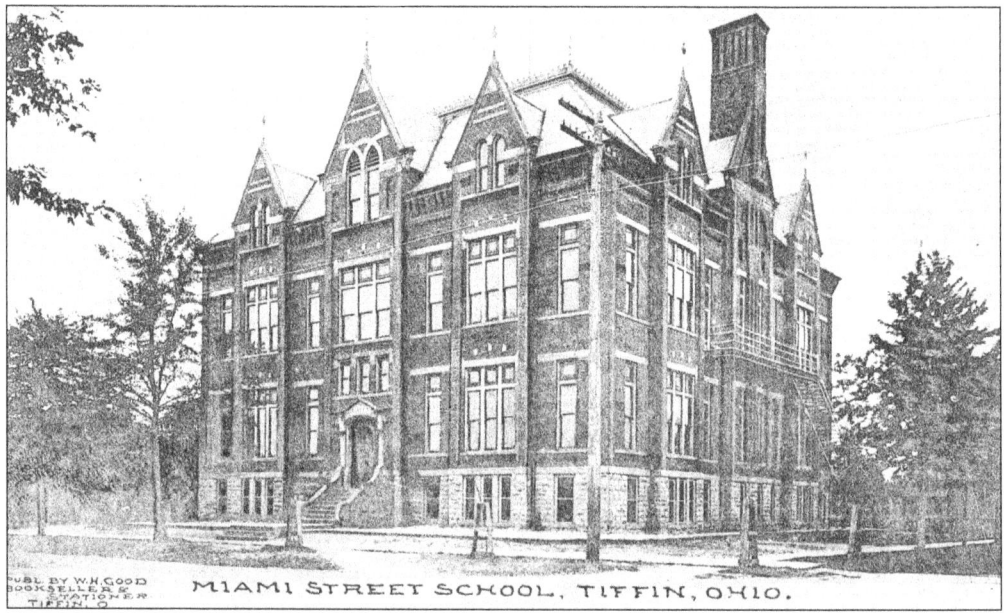

MIAMI STREET SCHOOL, TIFFIN, OHIO.

The former Miami Street School now serves as one of the main classroom buildings for Tiffin University. Over the years, the school's degree offerings have expanded to include education and law enforcement. Today, TU boasts one of the nation's top degrees in homeland security and terrorism. In addition to a growing main campus, Tiffin University now has seven branch campuses across the state of Ohio.

Heidelberg's University Hall is pictured here on a vintage postcard. Today, the building houses the president's office, several administrative departments, Rickly Chapel, and the Heidelberg archives. "Tiffin has always been generous in its financial support of the college," writes historian Myron Barnes, "and these investments have paid the community handsome dividends."

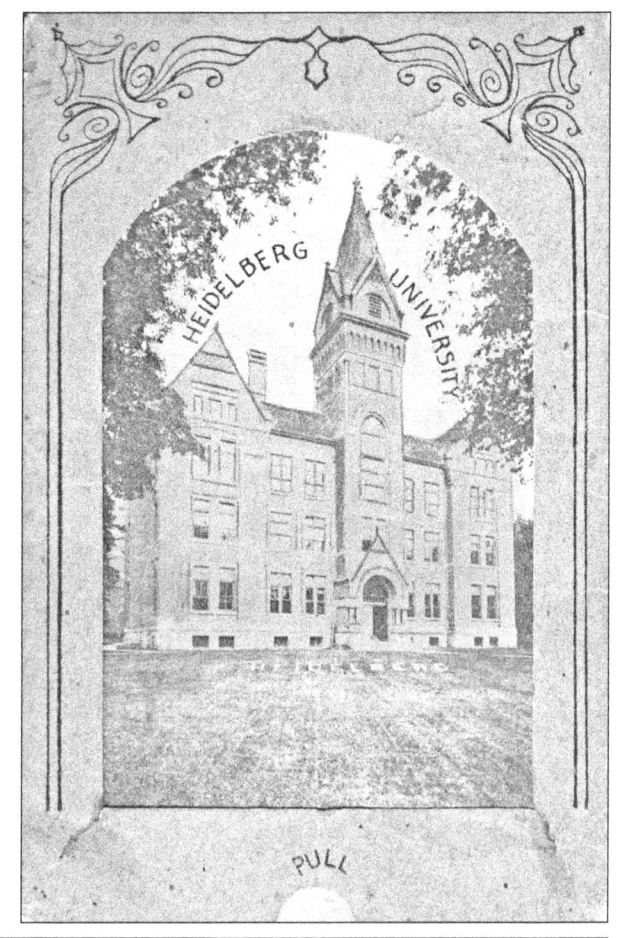

Heidelberg College's Williard Hall was named in honor of the school's fourth president, George Williard. Williard opened as a dormitory for women in 1907, and renowned sociologist Jane Addams spoke at the dedication. Williard, located on the eastern edge of the campus along Greenfield Street, was destroyed in a fire in January 2000 and subsequently replaced.

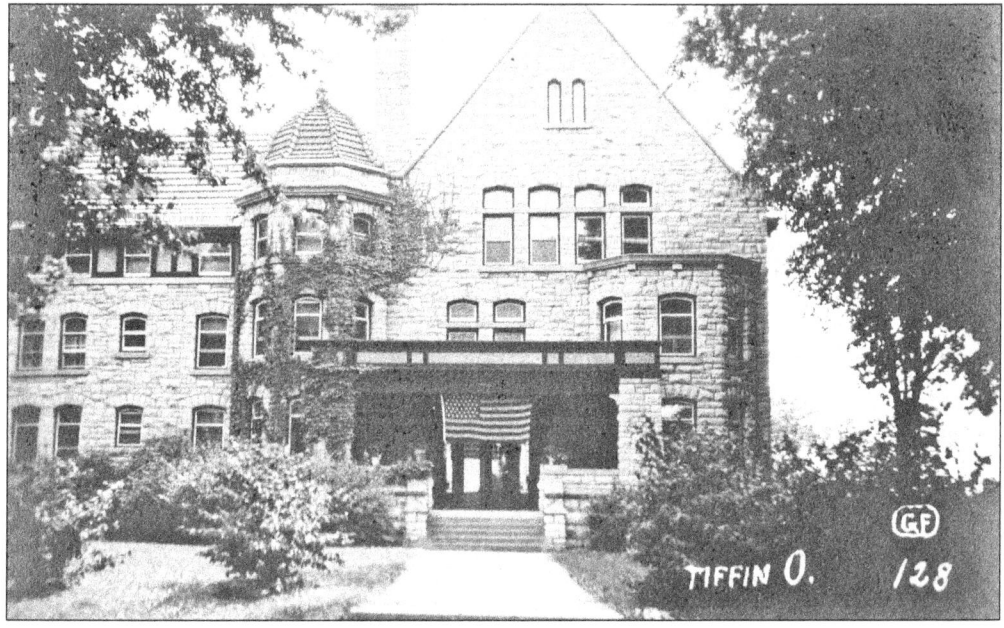

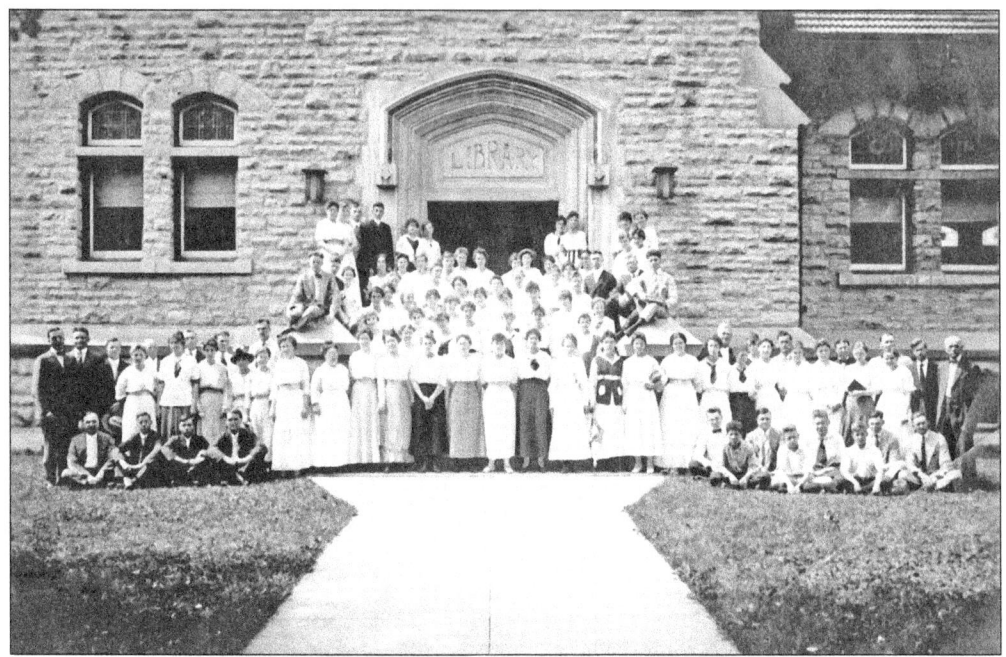

Summer school students pose outside the Heidelberg College library in 1916. In 1967, the catalog was moved to Beeghly Library; Beegly's circular shape and concrete construction cast it as a distinctive Tiffin landmark.

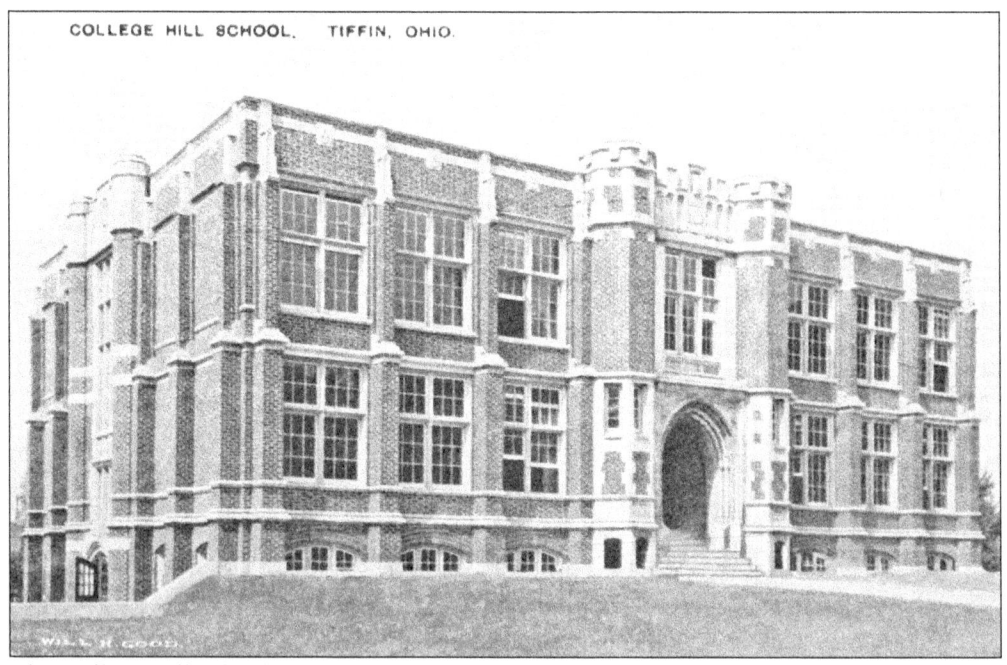

The College Hill School is now known as Heidelberg's Aigler Alumni Hall. It is home to the university's graduate studies, as well as the anthropology, psychology, and political science departments. Heidelberg is renowned for its mineral collection and its Conservatory of Music, as well as its annual presentation of Handel's *Messiah*—a recognition of the community's and the college's German roots.

Eight

A CITY ON THE MOVE

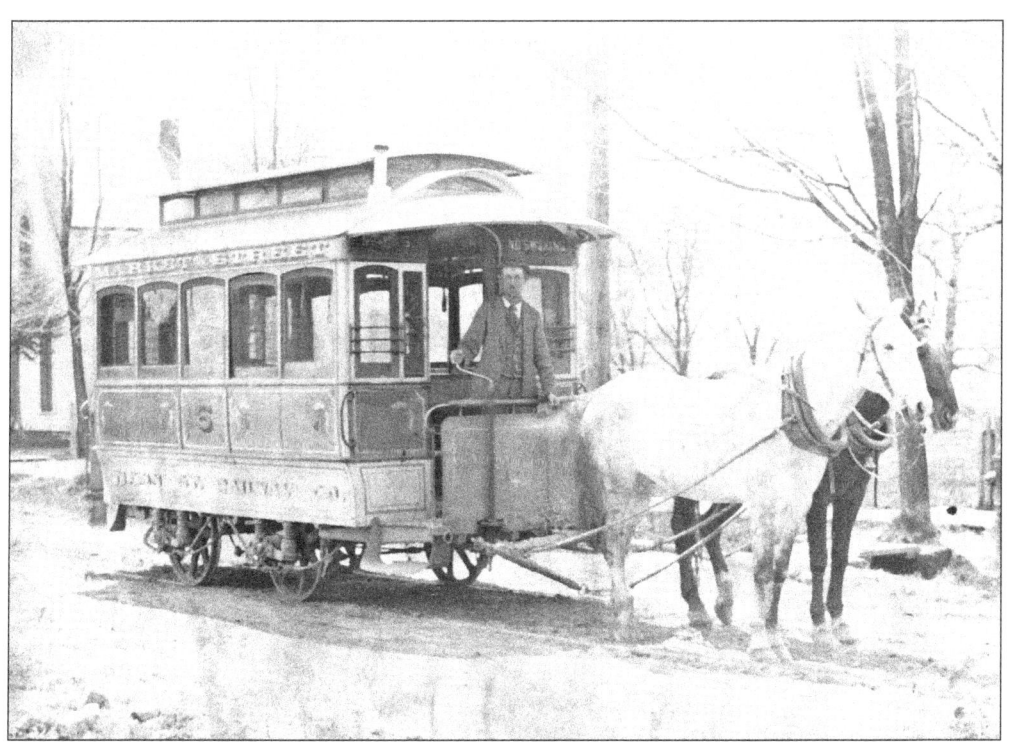

The driver of a Market Street car of the Tiffin Street Railway Company poses with his pair of horses. The railway went into operation on July 3, 1888, and quickly gained popularity among groups of ladies who used it to travel from St. Joseph's Church to the new Highland Park. "This resulted in a brisk business for the Tiffin Street Railway," reports historian Myron Barnes.

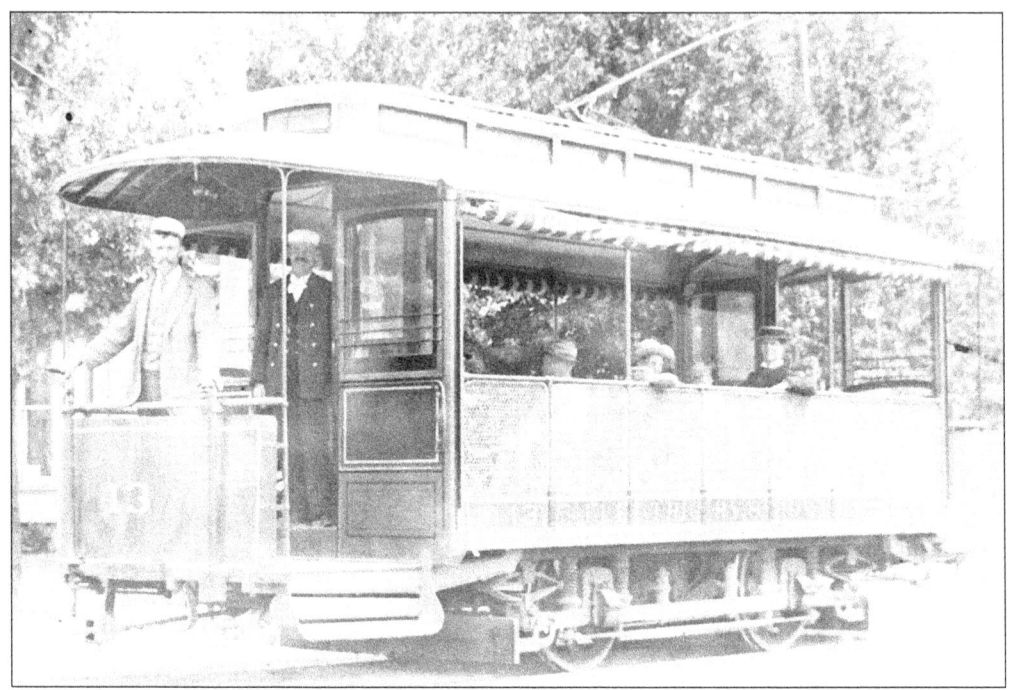

Horse-drawn streetcars gave way to electrified trolleys in the 1890s. Such transportation proved essential as Tiffin industrialized, bringing employees to factories such as National Machinery, Brewer Pottery, and Beatty (Tiffin) Glass being built on the outskirts of the rapidly expanding town. In the days before paved streets, changing lines proved easier as track was simply taken up and relaid where needed.

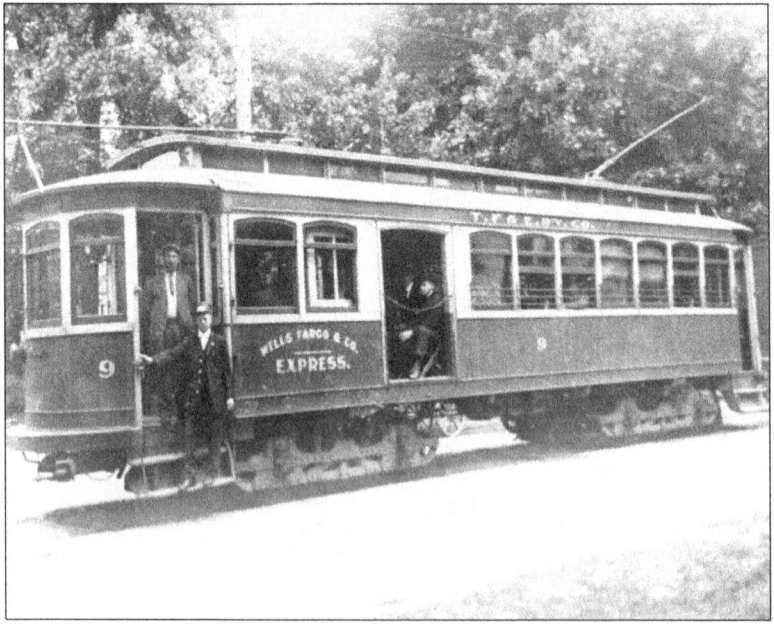

Conductor Lester R. Caldwell and motorman James Hoffman stand in front of the Wells Fargo Express car of the Tiffin, Fostoria, & Eastern interurban railway. The popularity of the interurban declined in direct proportion to the rise in affordability and convenience of the automobile. This particular line ceased operation on October 1, 1930.

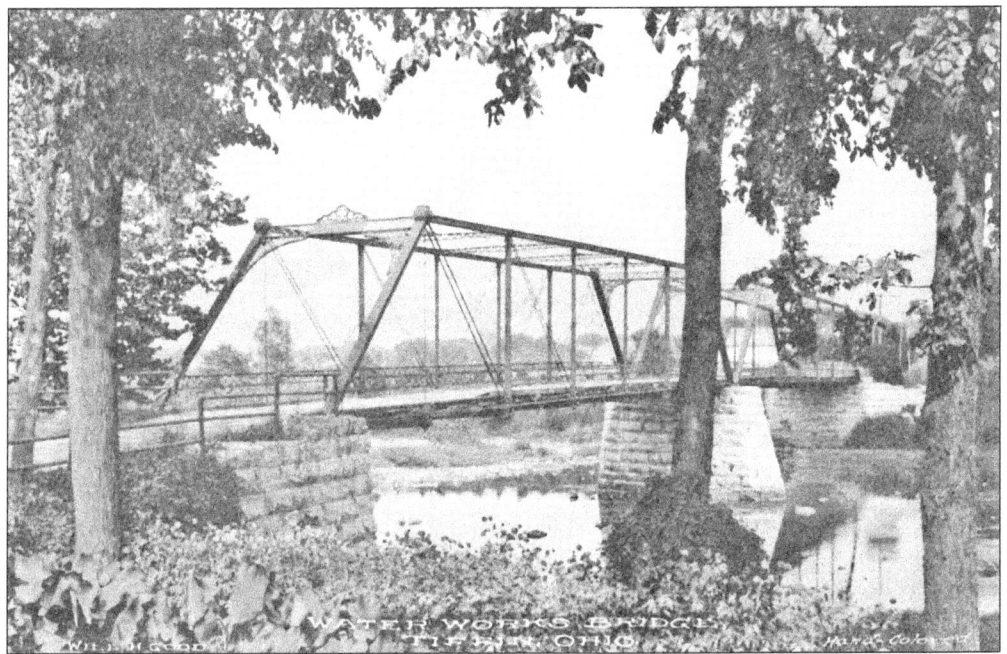

The Water Works Bridge was the pre–Flood of 1913 forerunner of the Ella Street Bridge. The double-span iron bridge, which rested atop a stone pier and abutments, made a picturesque accompaniment to the redbrick Tiffin Water Works plant just to the north. The waterworks itself is on the site of the former Lugenbeel Mill.

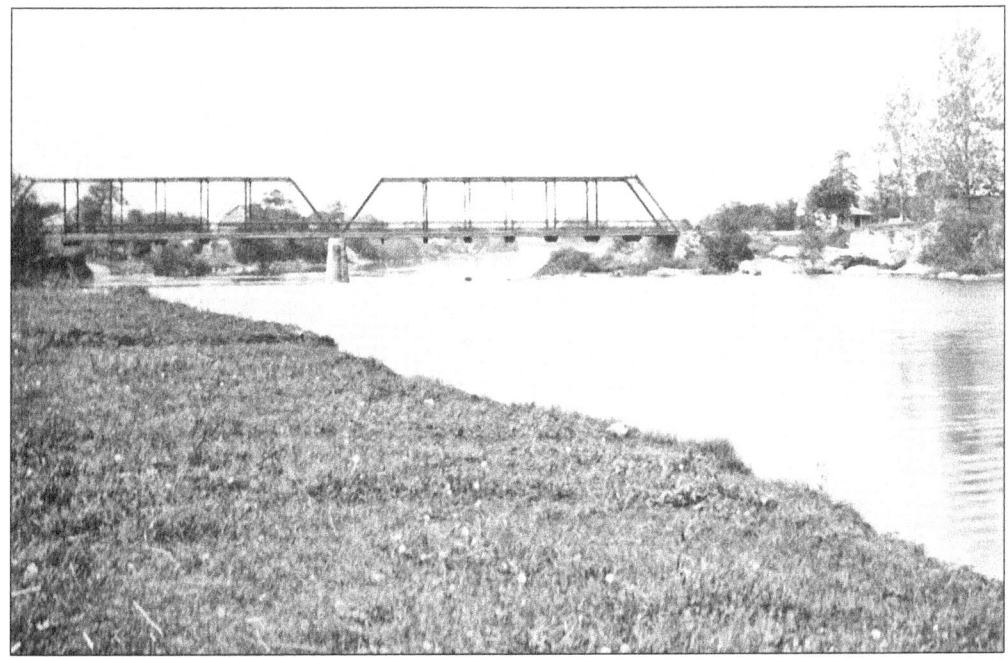

A pre-flood view of the Huss Street Bridge shows one route by which visitors would have reached Riverview Park, out of view to the right. It also shows a serene Sandusky River, uncontained in any way and lapping right up to its banks. The scene would be much different after the devastation of 1913.

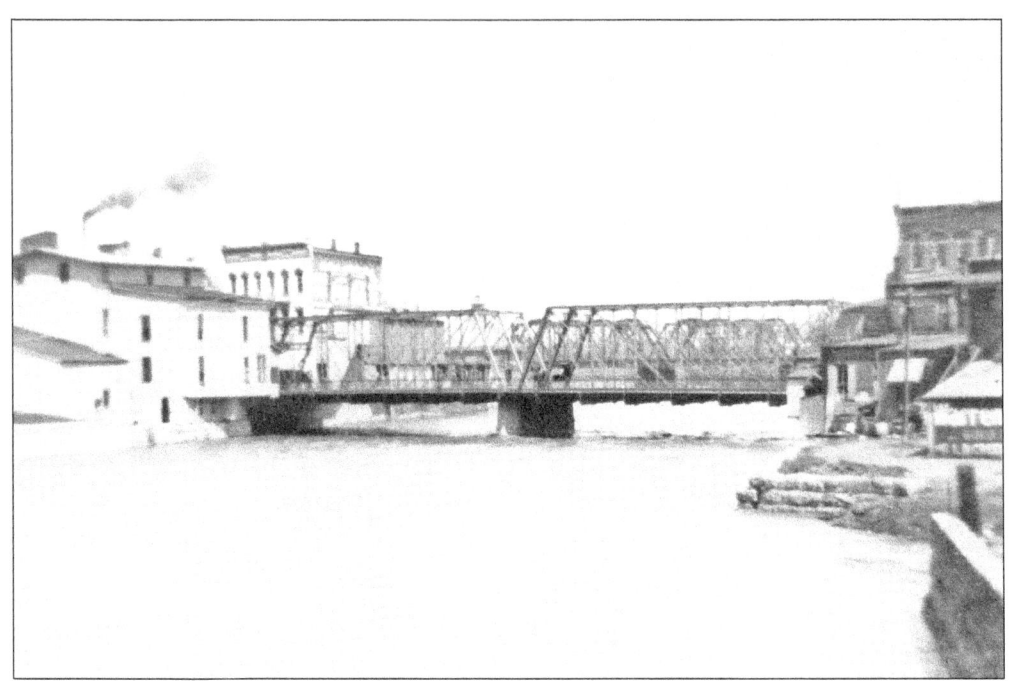

A pre-1913 view of the Washington Street Bridge and the railroad bridges beyond it reflects just how urban and industrialized Tiffin's business center had become. Note especially the building at left, which projects far out over the waters of the Sandusky River. Tiffin was soon to learn a dear lesson about the cost of haphazardness.

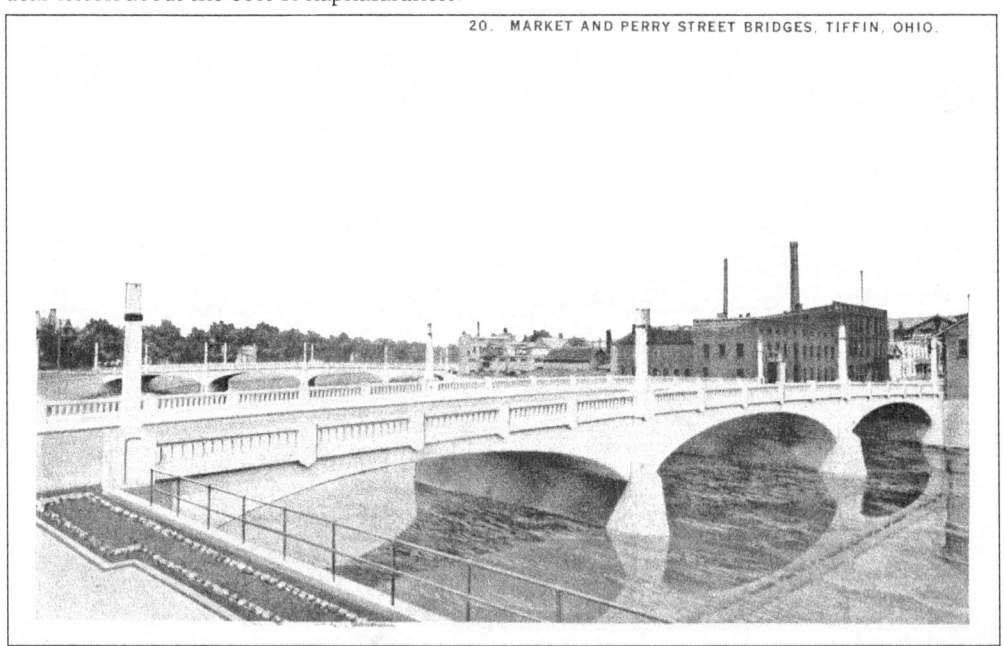

20. MARKET AND PERRY STREET BRIDGES, TIFFIN, OHIO.

The post-flood decision to recast all of Tiffin's bridges in concrete resulted in a much sturdier and cleaner look, even though they are not ideal for a postcard view. This view shows the Market (foreground) and Perry Street Bridges, with the Washington Street Bridge barely visible beyond. The bridge at Monroe Street was not replaced.

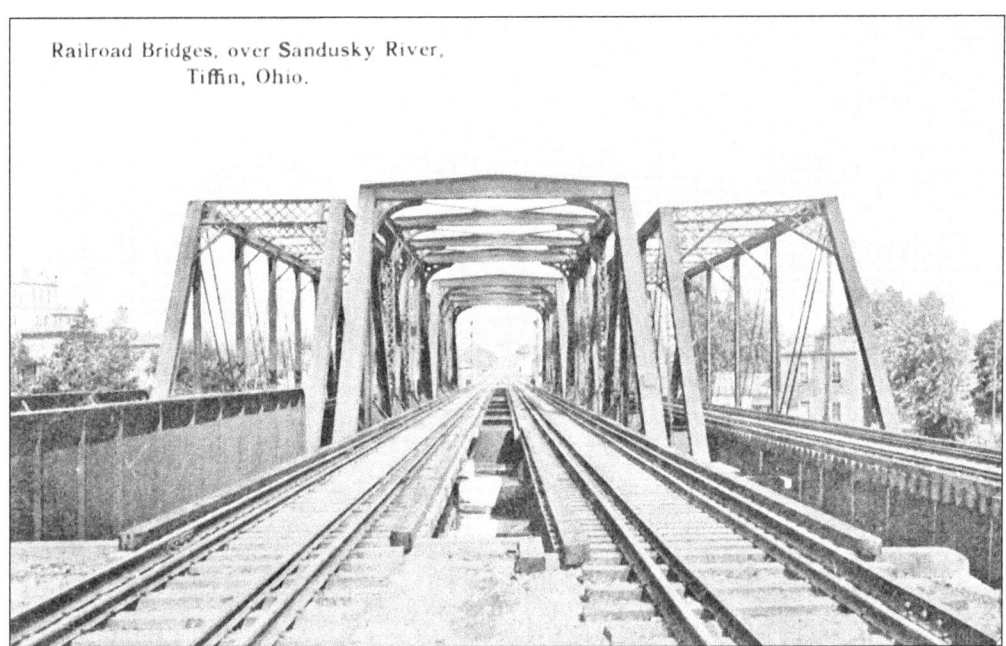

Railroad Bridges, over Sandusky River,
Tiffin, Ohio.

A turn-of-the-20th-century postcard shows a through view of Tiffin's trio of railroad bridges. The massive iron structures conveyed a sense of both importance and permanence. Indeed, they were Tiffin's only spans of the Sandusky River to withstand the fury of the Flood of 1913.

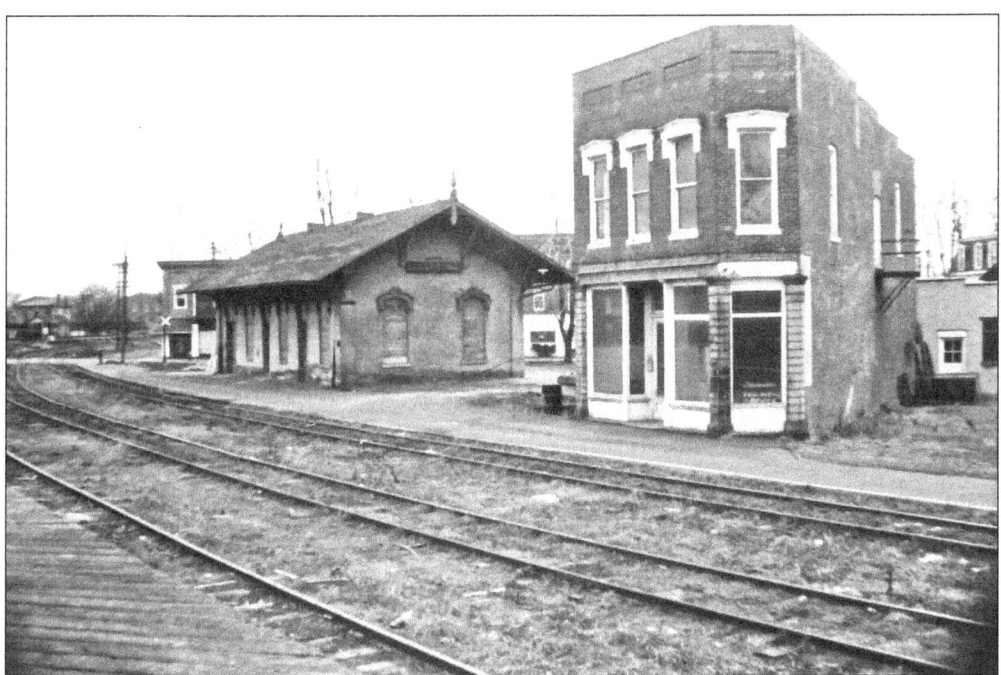

The Tiffin passenger depot was built in 1862 by the Sandusky Dayton Cincinnati Railroad Company. It was one of six rail depots in the Tiffin area and served until July 1938. Community programs now take place in the restored depot, which also features landscaped grounds with a rock garden, waterfall, and grotto.

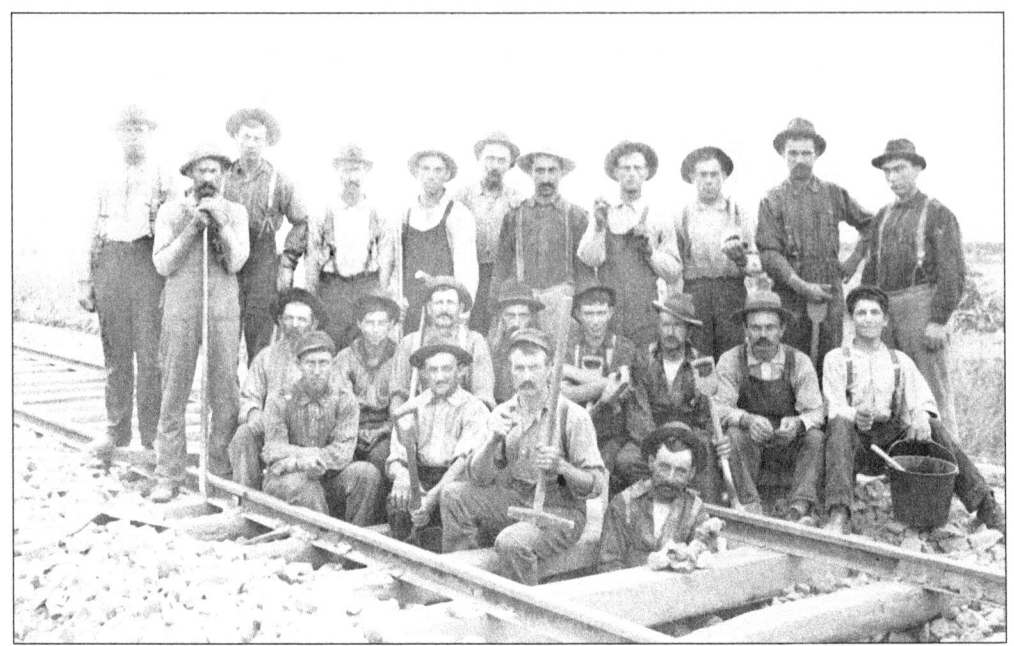

Construction workers pause for a photograph while working on the tracks of the Toledo, Tiffin & Eastern Railroad, about 1873. Note especially the young water boy at the right end of the second row and the two men in the foreground who are in a hole beneath the track bed. The railway itself eventually became part of the Pennsylvania Railroad network.

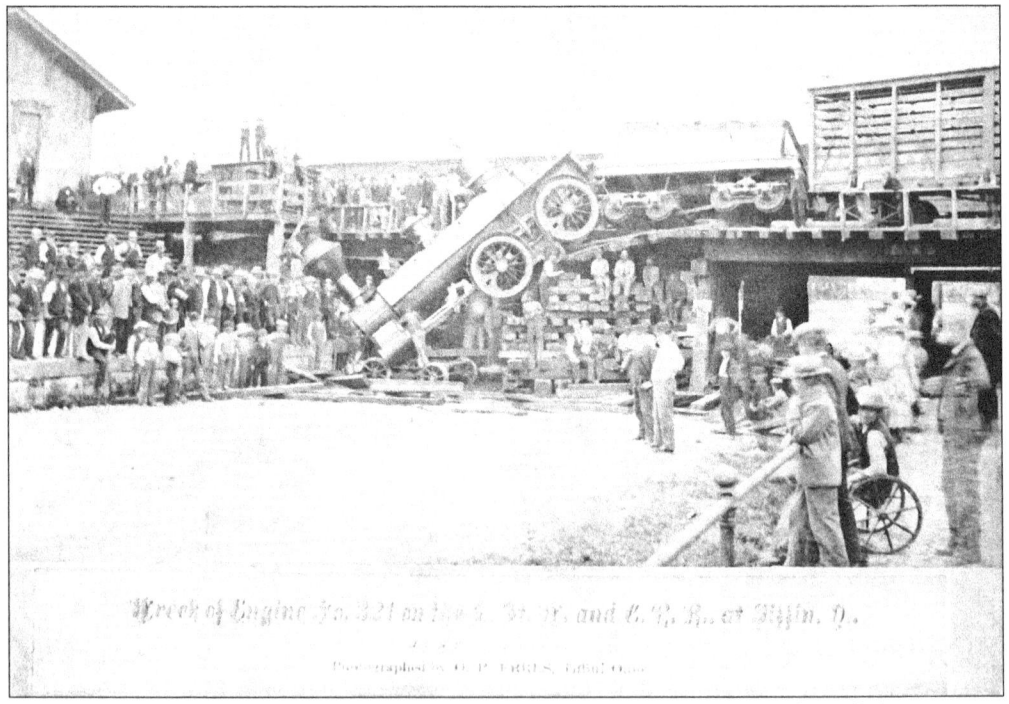

A locomotive of the Pittsburgh, Fort Wayne and Chicago Railroad dangles off the overpass following this wreck at Tiffin on June 29, 1881. The derailment drew a large crowd of spectators, including a man in a wheelchair, as workers attempted to stabilize the scene.

Carts stand at the ready at Tiffin's Pennsylvania Railroad depot. Built in the early 1870s, the depot was first built by the Toledo, Tiffin & Eastern Railroad. This was among the lines absorbed as the Pennsylvania expanded. The acquisition allowed Tiffin locals and the products they produced faster access to urban centers such as Pittsburgh, Philadelphia, and New York.

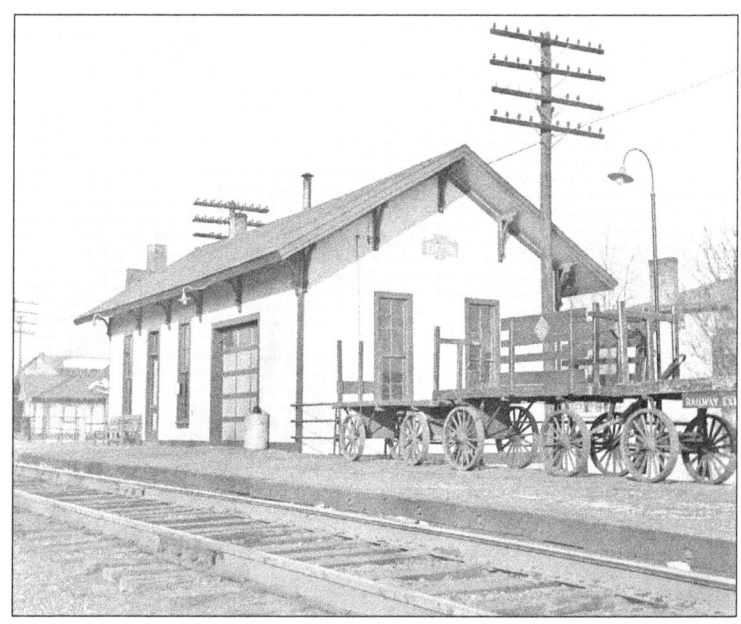

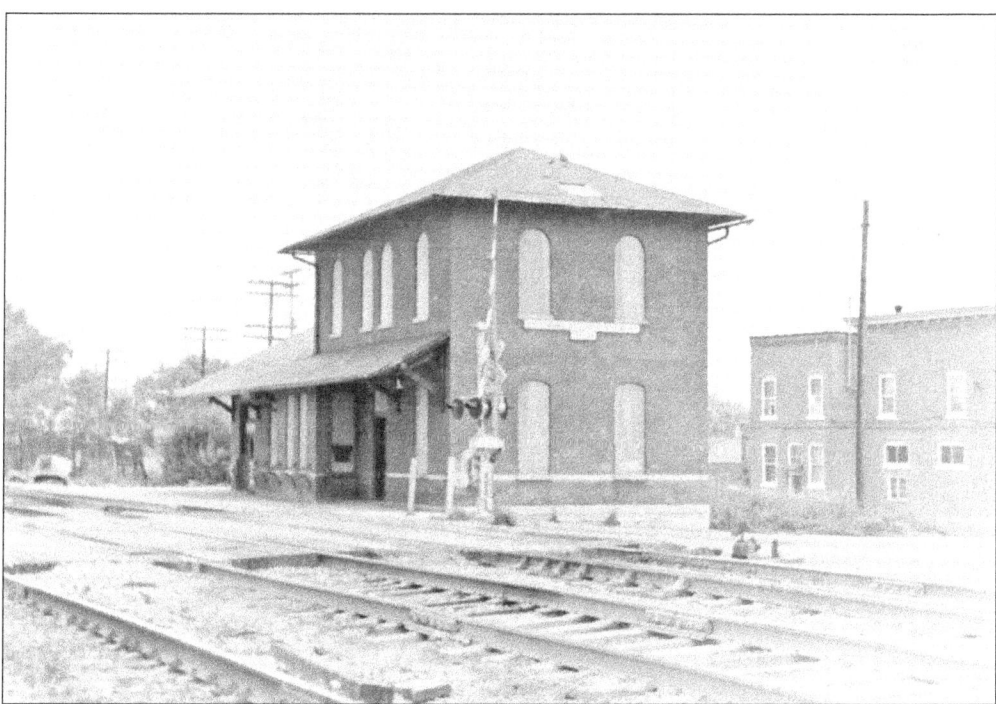

The Baltimore & Ohio passenger station sat across the railroad tracks from the Pennsylvania depot. This line helped open the way west toward Chicago. William Lang's *History of Seneca County* refers to the B&O's iron bridge over the Sandusky River as "decidedly the best railroad bridge in the county."

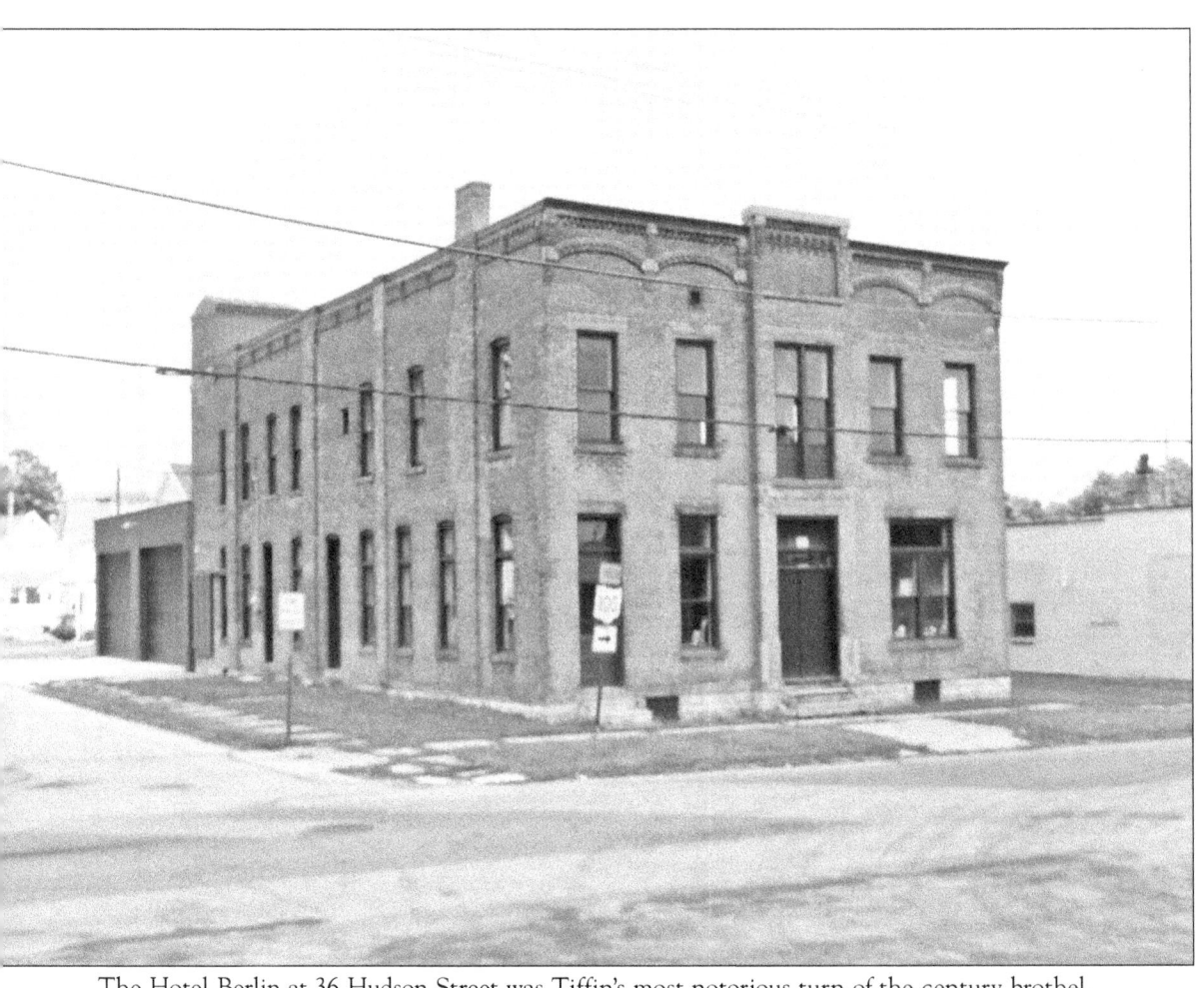

The Hotel Berlin at 36 Hudson Street was Tiffin's most notorious turn-of-the-century brothel. Mattie Nisonger, with her daughter Dora Willis Hasson, ran the house along the railroad tracks after commissioning the building around 1890. Mattie was active in the business until her death at the Hotel Berlin in 1922, at age 76. (Authors' collection.)

Nine

A City of Place

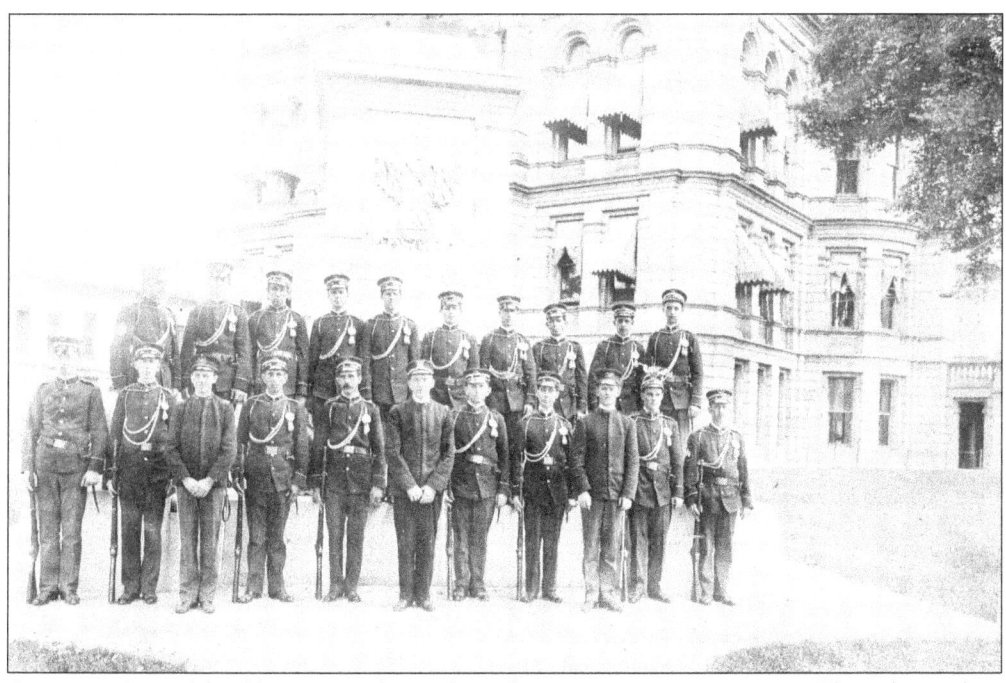

Company No. 1 of the Ohio National Guard stands at attention in 1909 or 1910. The only members of the ornately clad unit identified are Frank Guss, at center, and Officer Clarence C. Mann, front right. They stand in front of the Gibson Monument at the Seneca County Courthouse, which was only a few years old at the time (it was dedicated in 1906).

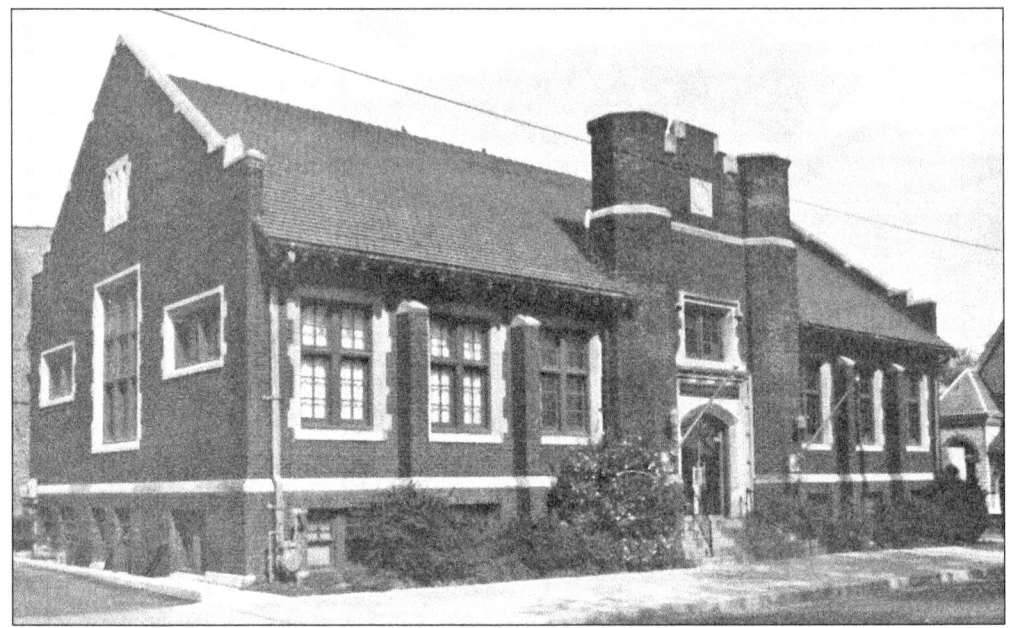

Tiffin's Carnegie library, built with a $25,000 grant, was housed in this English Tudor–style building on Jefferson Street, across from Columbian/East Junior High, from 1913 to 1976. Its circulation expanded to include all of Seneca County in 1936, and its stock had reached 66,000 volumes before the decision for new construction was made. Today, the building is home to Seneca County's juvenile justice facilities.

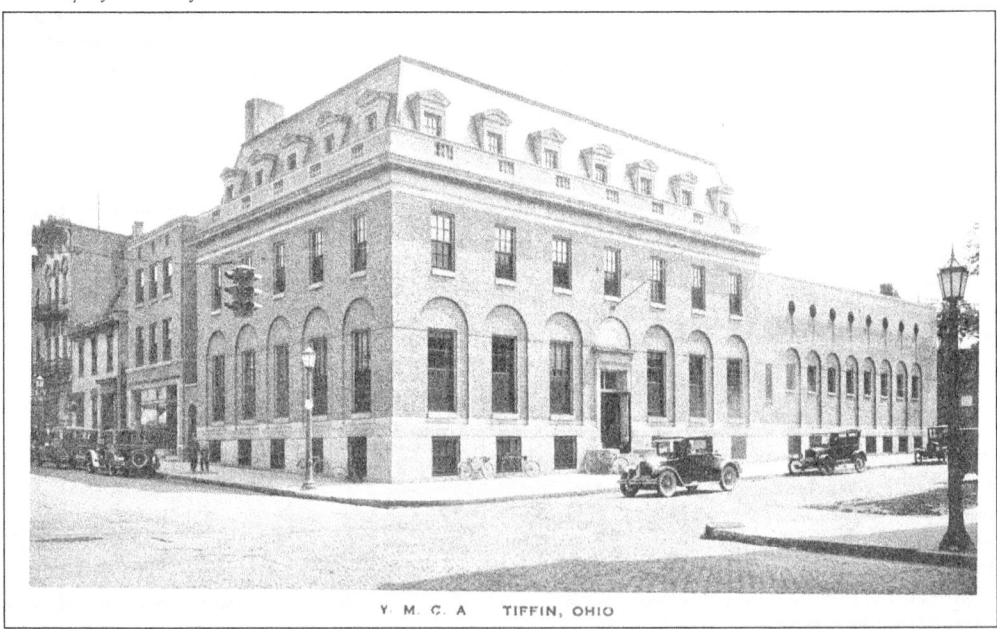

Tiffin's YMCA is the result of the generosity and efforts of Della Shawhan Laird, widow of Rezin Shawhan. The building she commissioned at the corner of Monroe and East Market Streets (opposite city hall) opened fully equipped in 1924 at a cost of more than $250,000. It was outfitted with a gymnasium and swimming pool as well as men's dormitories. A replacement building at Hedges-Boyer Park opened in 1980.

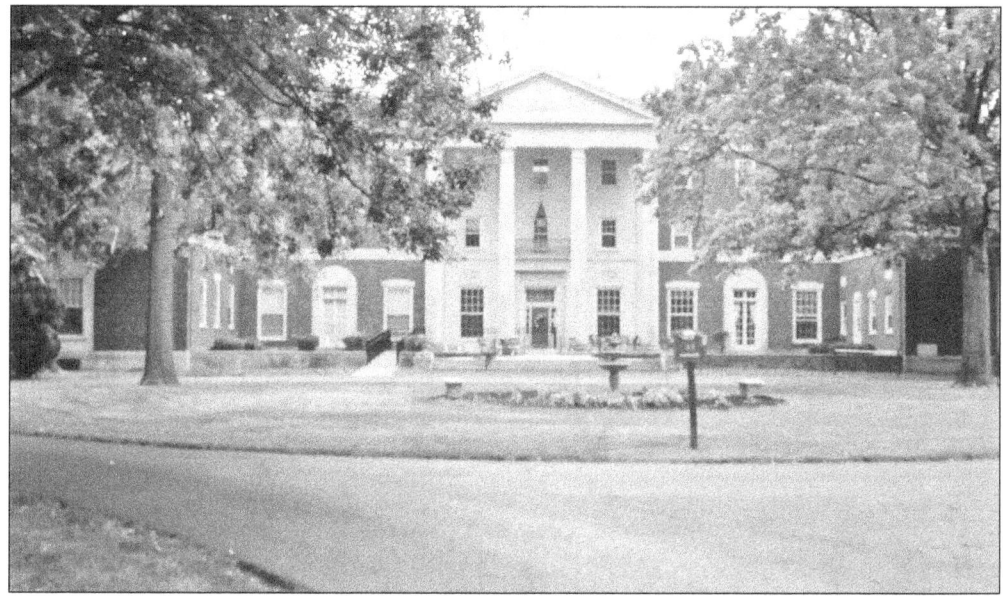

The Daughters of America was an auxiliary of the Junior Order of American United Mechanics. The group's national home for its elderly and ailing members was run at 652 North Sandusky Street from 1930 until 1989. The Georgian building had private accommodations for 66 women. It became known for its impressive wrought-iron entranceway and well-tended grounds. (Authors' collection.)

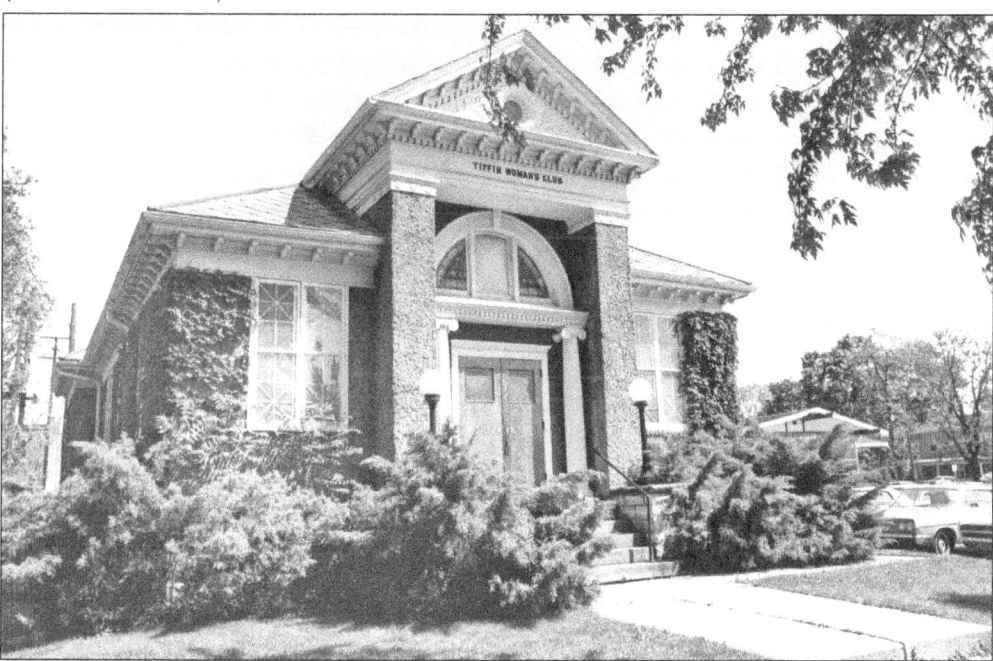

The Tiffin Woman's Club was headquartered in this building on Frost Parkway from the time the club purchased the building in 1920. The club's aims, historian Myron Barnes reports, "stressed the promoting of public welfare and good citizenship, a united effort for the general improvement of humanity, as well as the objective of assisting in the higher development and broader culture of its members."

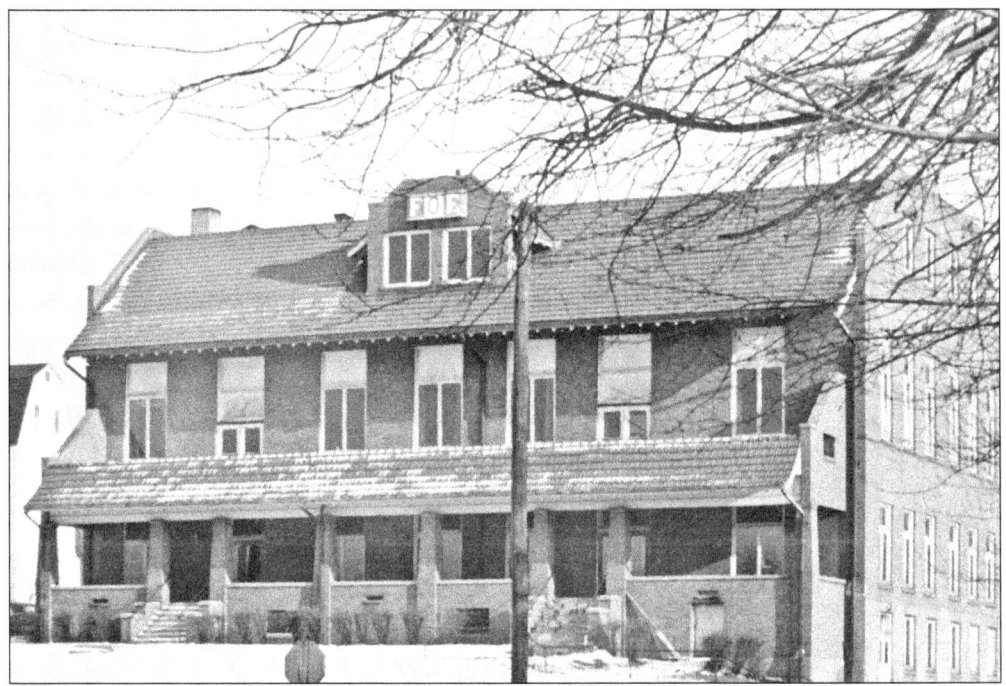

Tiffin's Fraternal Order of Eagles aerie has its lodge at 68 Riverside Drive. Nationally, the Eagles support diabetes, spina bifida, and cancer research. The Eagles, headquartered in Grove City, Ohio, also offer services to the families of active military members. The national organization was founded in Seattle in 1898 and now boasts an international membership of more than 800,000.

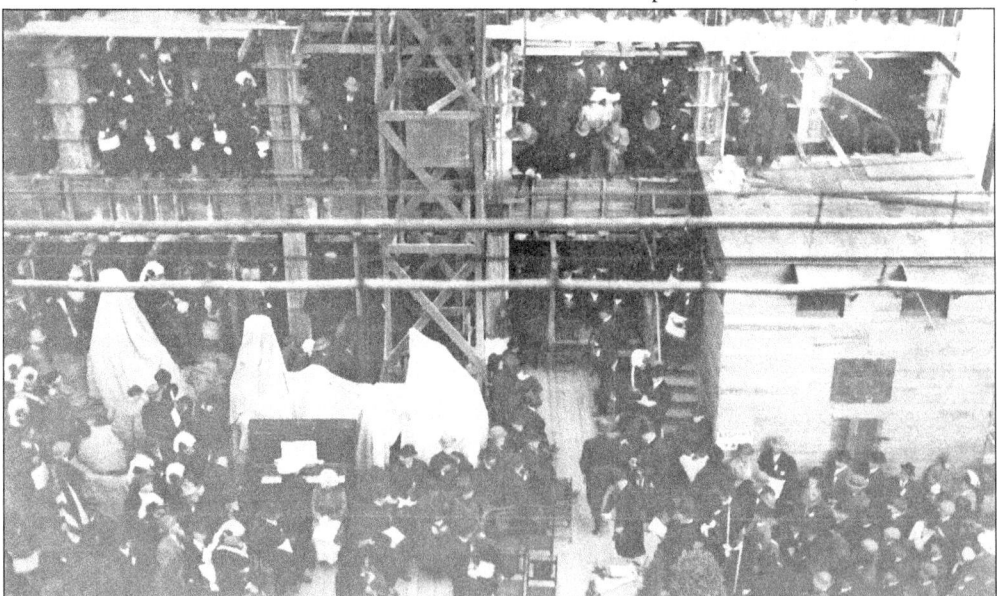

The cornerstone for Tiffin's Masonic Temple, at 179 South Washington Street, was laid in 1913. The event drew nearly 1,000 Masons and friends, including the entire complement of Ohio Grand Lodge officers. Construction was completed in 1915, and the temple remains in use today. Among its features are a ballroom, dining facilities complete with a kitchen, club area, and dedicated meeting rooms.

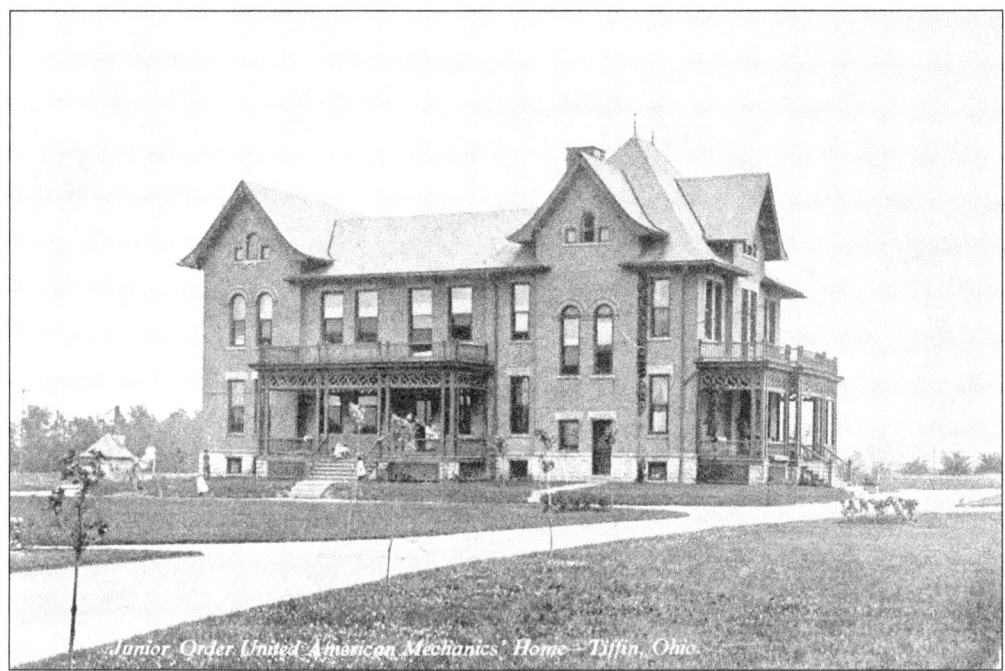

The Junior Order of United American Mechanics operated an orphanage in northeast Tiffin starting in 1896. Charles H. "Dad" Kernan (himself an orphan twice over) oversaw its growth and assimilation into the community. The self-sufficient campus eventually came to house more than 30 buildings. The home's peak enrollment was 1,105 children in 1935. After its 1945 closing, the campus was sold to the State of Ohio to be used as a mental hospital.

The Betty Jane Memorial Center was the legacy of National Machinery president and chairman of the board John H. Friedman. The rehabilitation facility was a tribute to the Friedmans' daughter, who had died in 1935. The St. Francis Avenue campus was the Betty Jane Center's second home; it was originally run out of the Friedmans' former home at 235 North Sandusky Street.

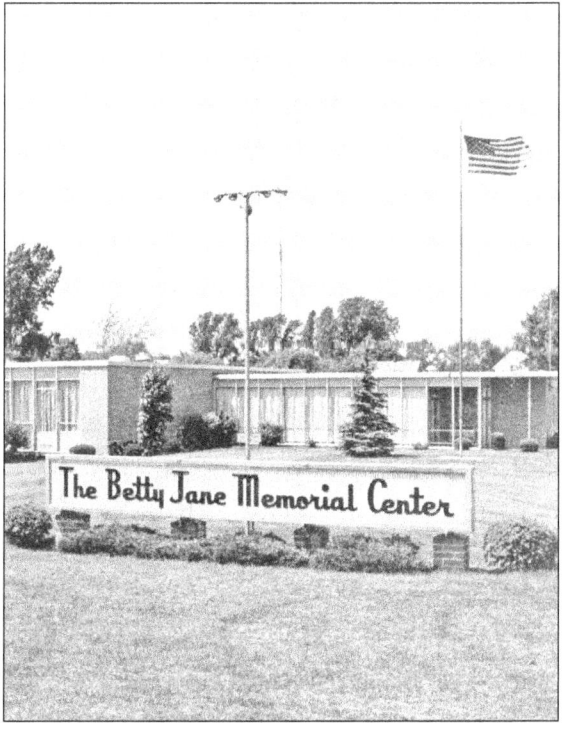

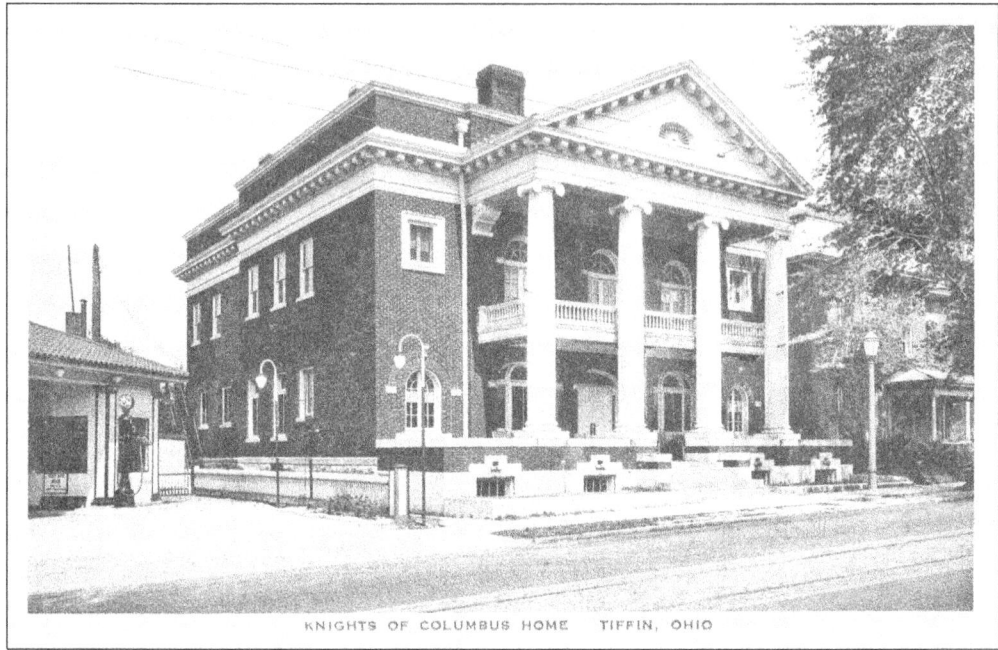

KNIGHTS OF COLUMBUS HOME   TIFFIN, OHIO

Tiffin's Knights of Columbus home stands at 49 East Perry Street. The national Catholic fraternal benefits organization was founded in New Haven, Connecticut, in 1882. Its focus is on educational, charitable, religious, social welfare, war relief, and public relief works. The K of C also has helped families achieve economic security and stability through its life insurance, annuity, and long-term care programs.

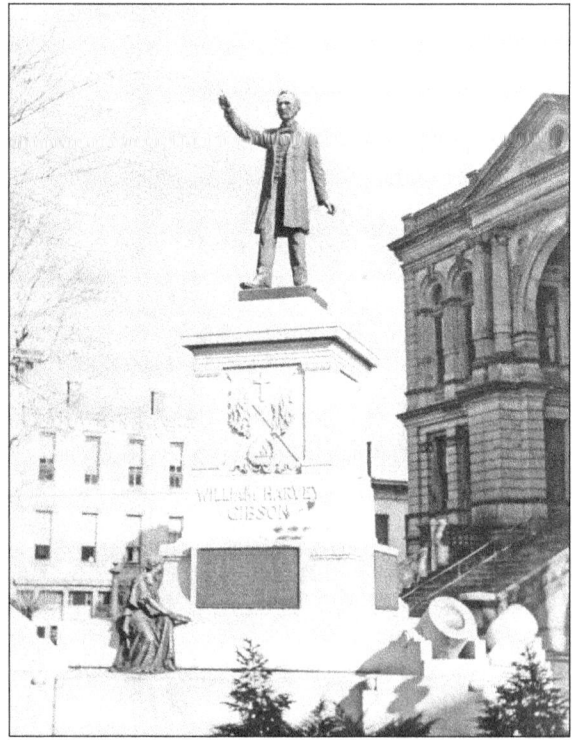

This statue of noted Tiffin resident William Harvey Gibson has anchored the southwest corner of the courthouse square since its dedication in 1906. Gibson's distinguished career included tenures as Ohio state treasurer and a Civil War general. In his later years, Gibson, an attorney by trade, was much in demand as a speaker on Independence Day and at other patriotic celebrations.

Springdale, at 318 Sycamore Street, was built in 1853 by William Harvey Gibson, who lived there until moving into town in 1880. The Gothic Revival residence was later home to cigar maker W.H. Killdow. In addition to his military, legal, political, and oratorical careers, Gibson was an organizer of Tiffin's first volunteer fire brigade and the Ohio Republican Party. (Authors' collection.)

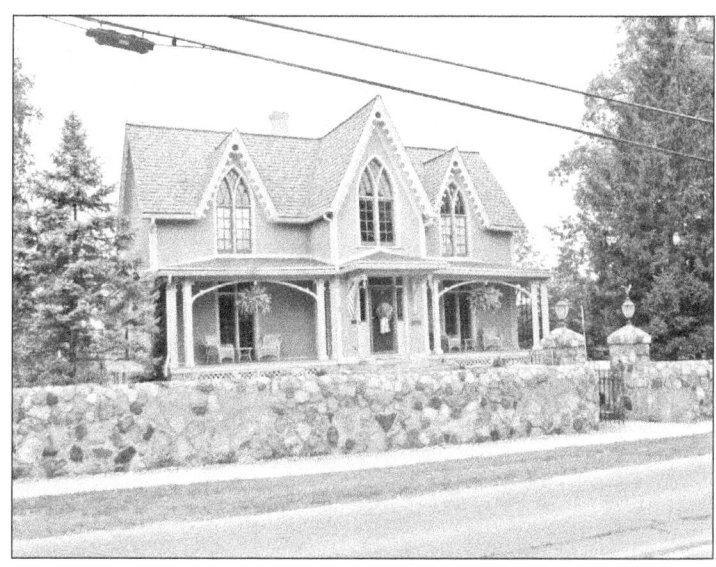

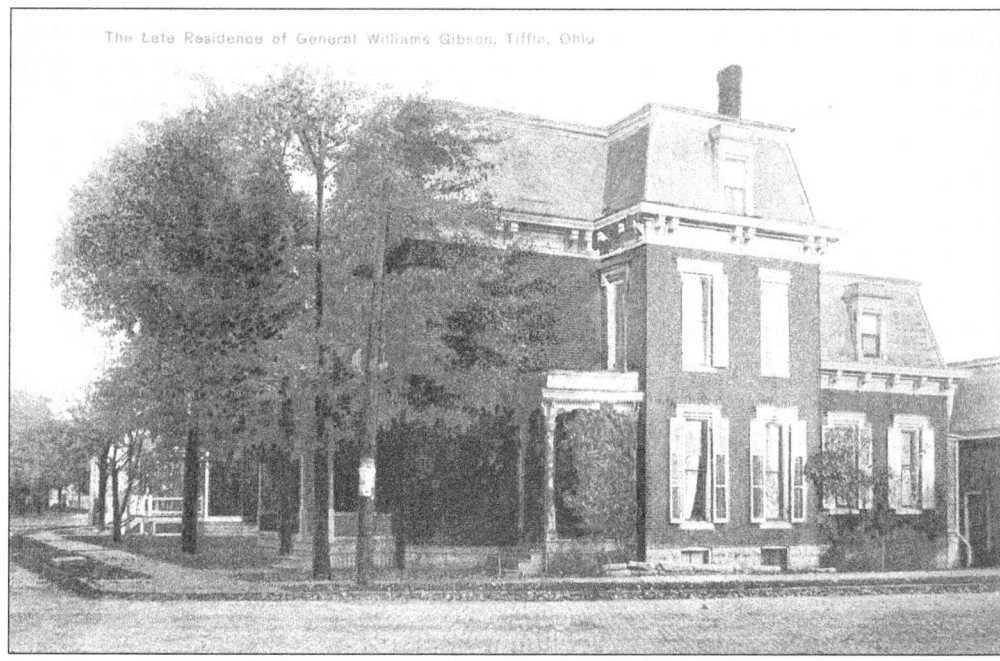

In his later years, Gen. William Harvey Gibson moved to this house near what would become the site of the Soldiers and Sailors Monument. When the famed, silver-tongued orator dedicated the memorial to his fellow Civil War veterans in 1885, he needed only to step outside his front door to make the speech. Following the Flood of 1913, this house was relocated onto Miami Street.

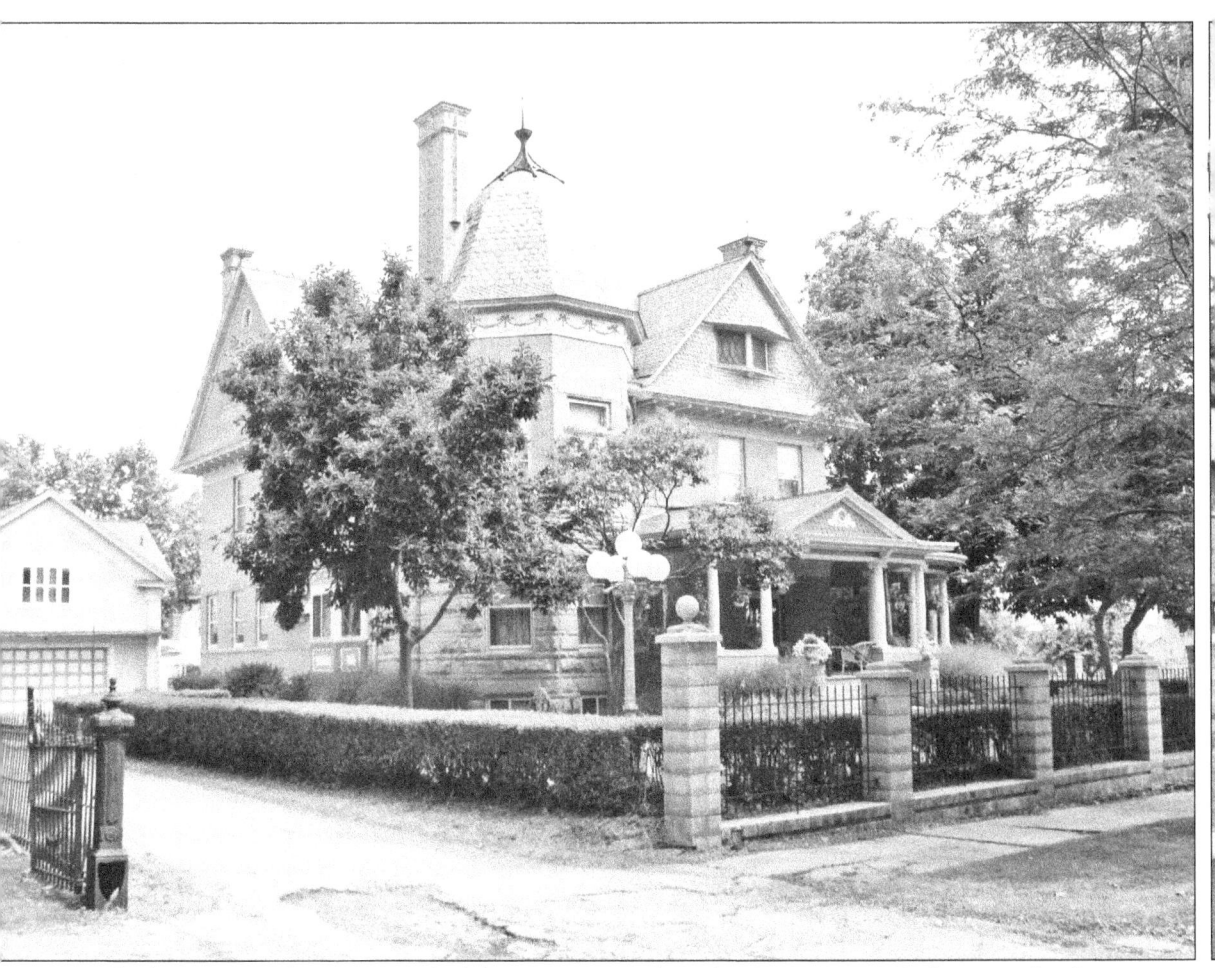

The house at 14 Clay Street was built by in 1896–1897 by Judge George Seney for his second wife, Anna, who had been shunned from Tiffin society as a result of the pair's scandalous extramarital affair. Seney, a civil law authority and four-term congressman, thought the Queen Anne mansion would endear the pair to Tiffin's social scene—it did not. (Authors' collection)

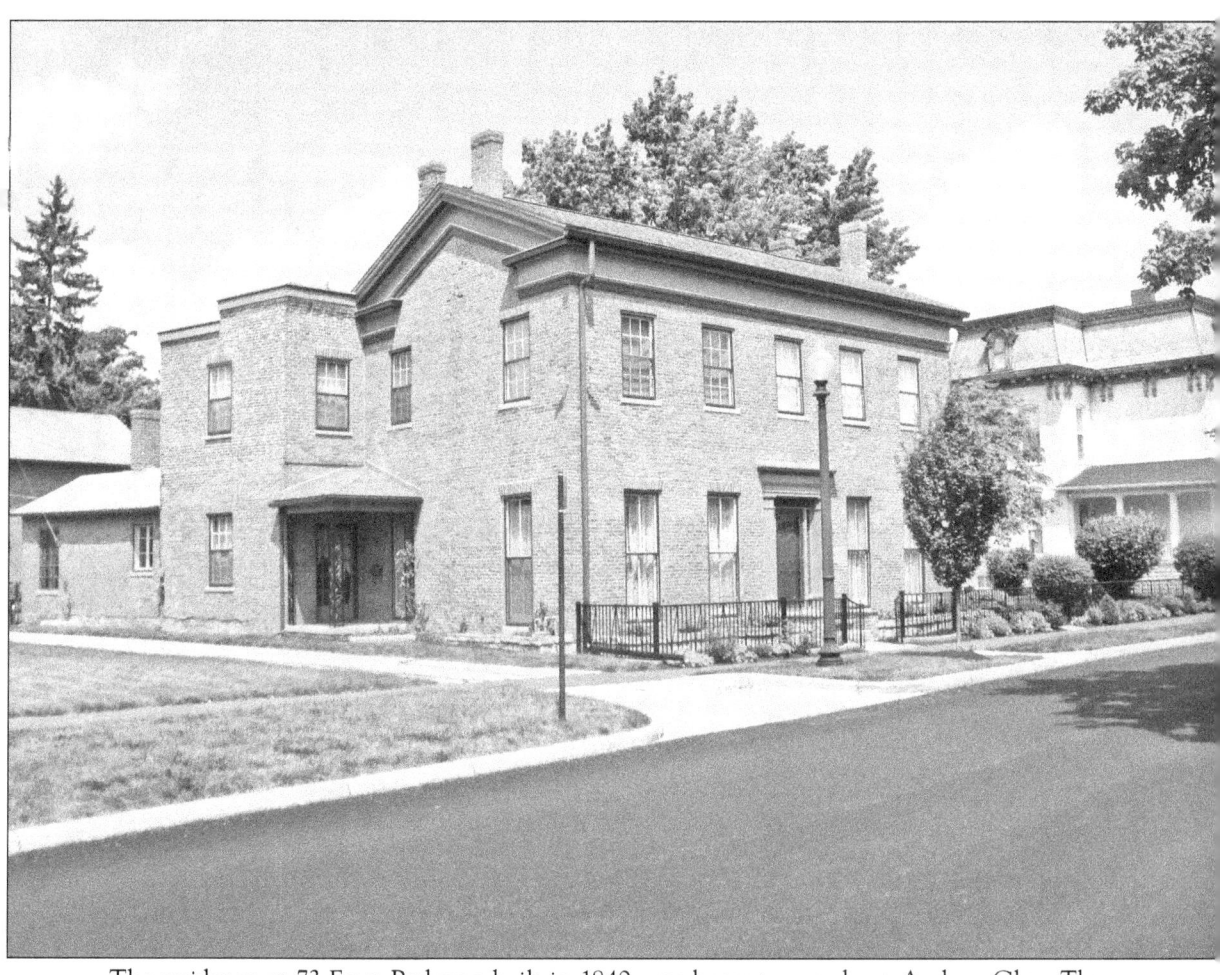

The residence at 73 Frost Parkway, built in 1840, was home to merchant Andrew Glen. The Federal-style home also features a two-story carriage house in the rear. The property later was owned by Tiffin historian and Seneca County Museum director Myron Barnes and his brother, Paul. (Authors' collection.)

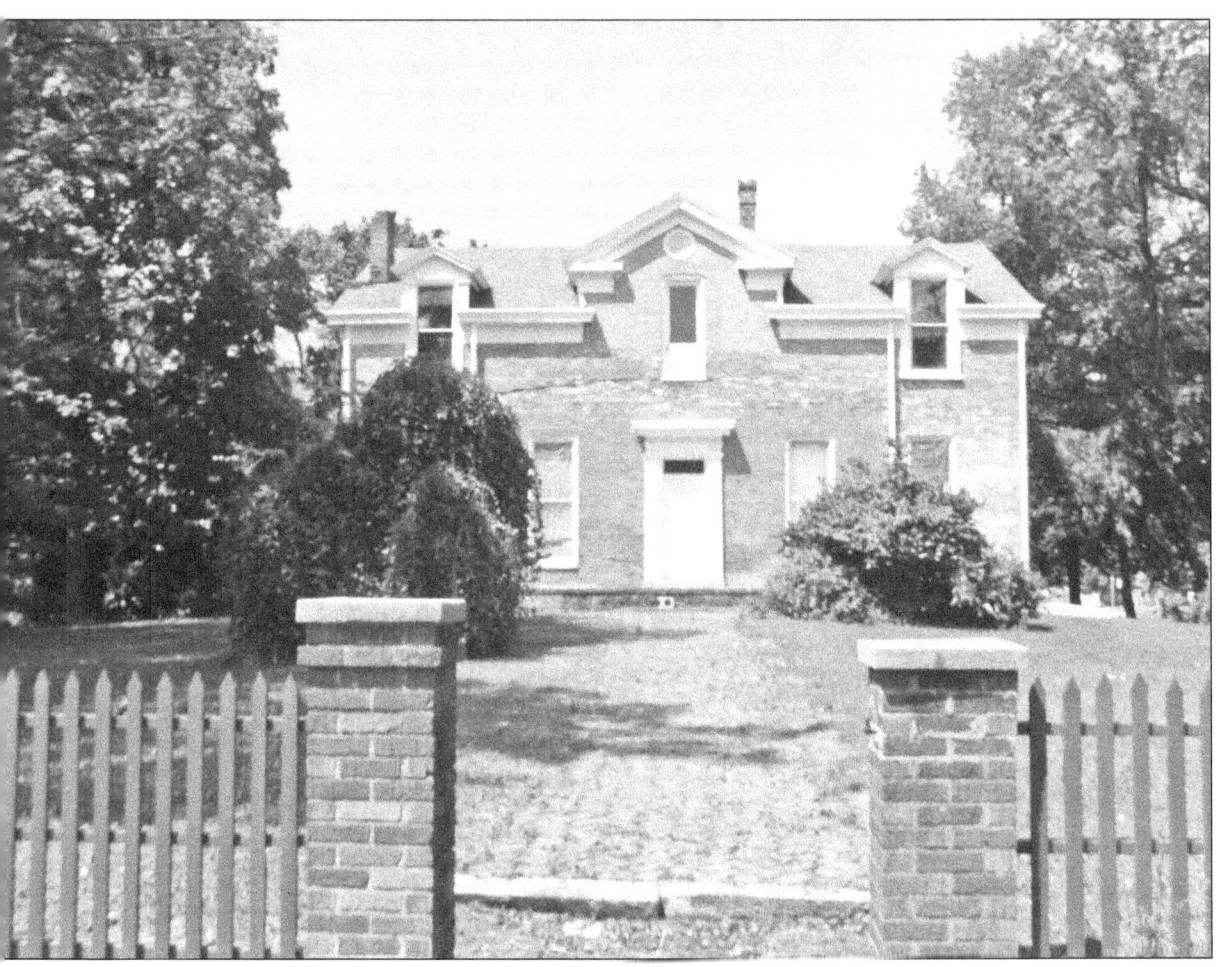

Louisa K. Fast (1878–1979) was known as Tiffin's first lady. The women's activist and world traveler maintained her base at 115 North Sandusky Street. Orphaned at an early age, Fast became a ward of family friend William McKinley, who was an occasional visitor to the Tiffin residence where Fast grew up. A longtime librarian as well as an advocate for education, Fast also organized the archives of the Seneca County Museum. (Authors' collection.)

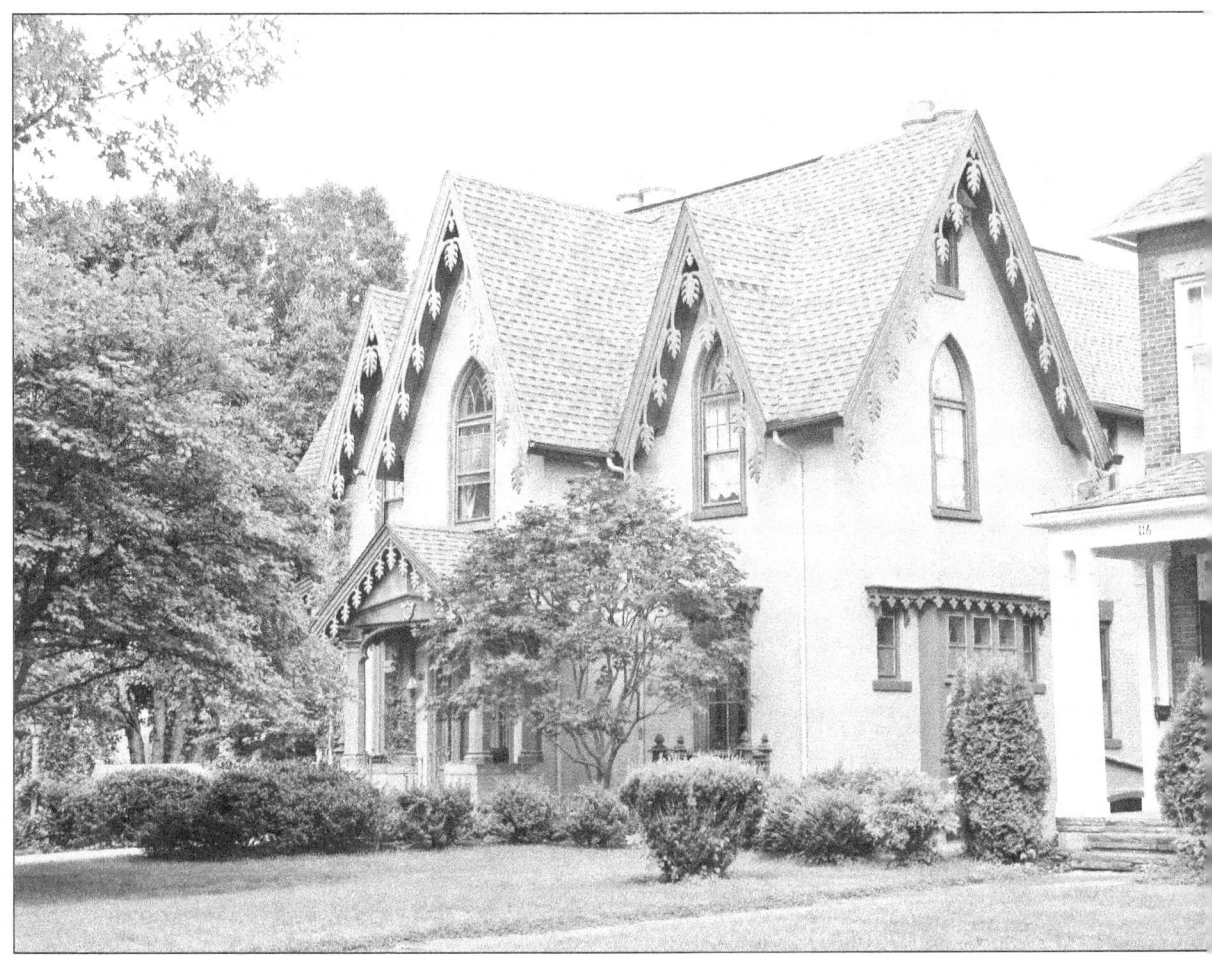

Tiffin's own House of the Seven Gables is at 120 North Sandusky Street. The Gothic Revival home was built in 1855 by Truman Bagby who was, among other pursuits, a staunch abolitionist. In more recent times, the building, with its distinctive grape cluster adornments, has served as home to the First Church of Christ, Scientist. (Authors' collection.)

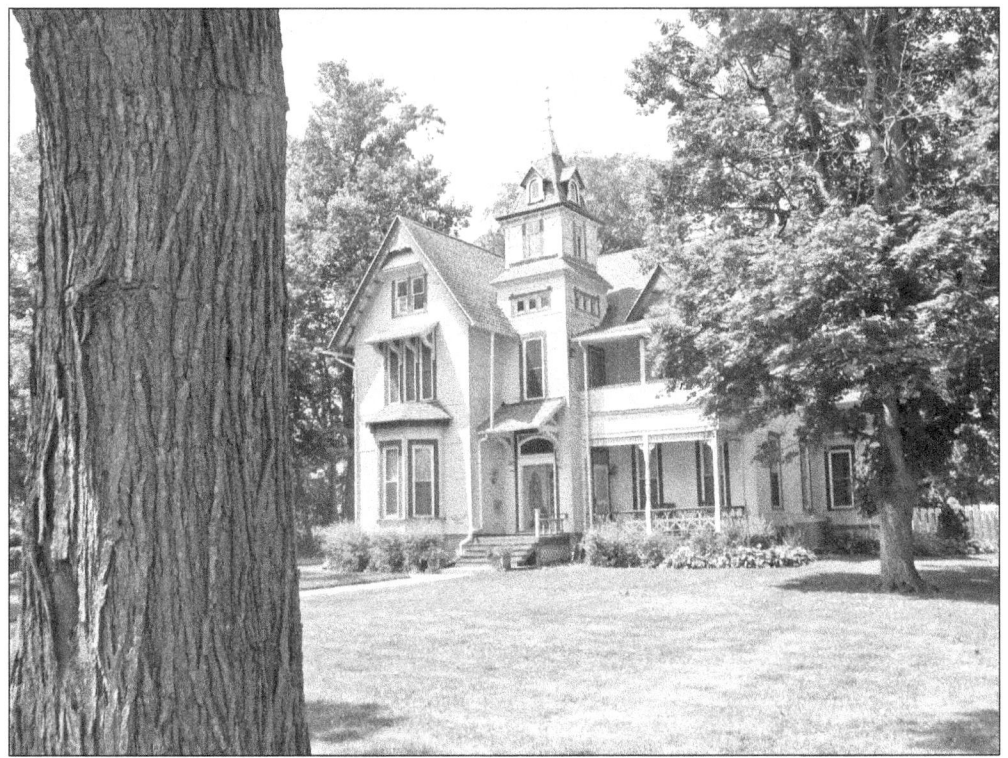

The elaborate Victorian home immediately north of the Fast House, at 139 North Sandusky Street, was built by Civil War veteran, doctor, lawyer, politician, and journalist James "Doc" Norton. In its day, it featured a fountain and an elaborate fence. In later years, it served as a Tiffin University dormitory. (Authors' collection.)

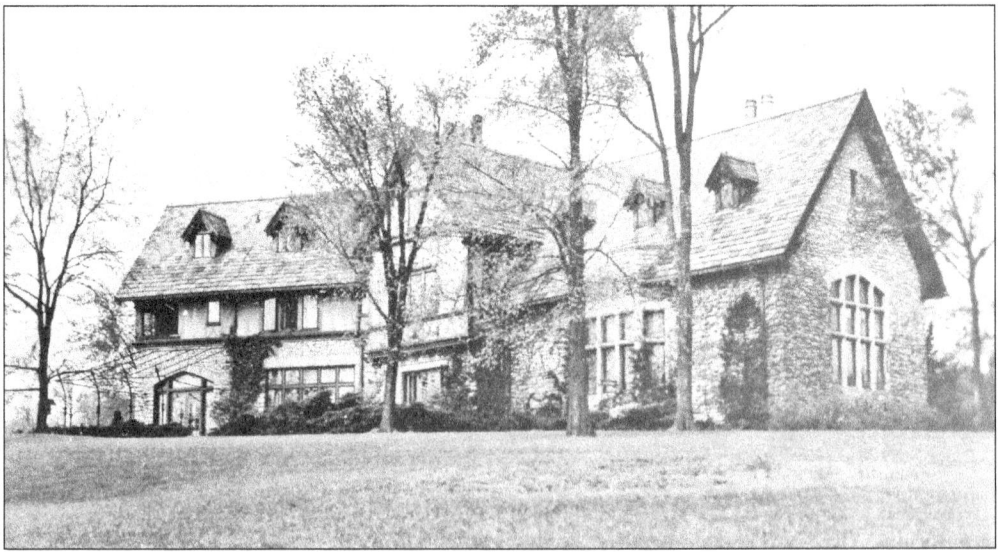

The Tudor-style home of George Kalbfleisch is a distinctive Tiffin landmark. After a tenure as secretary of Tiffin Art Metal, Kalbfleisch served as the longtime chief executive officer of the Great Western Pottery Company (a forerunner of Tiffin's American Standard plant). He also was president of the town's library board.

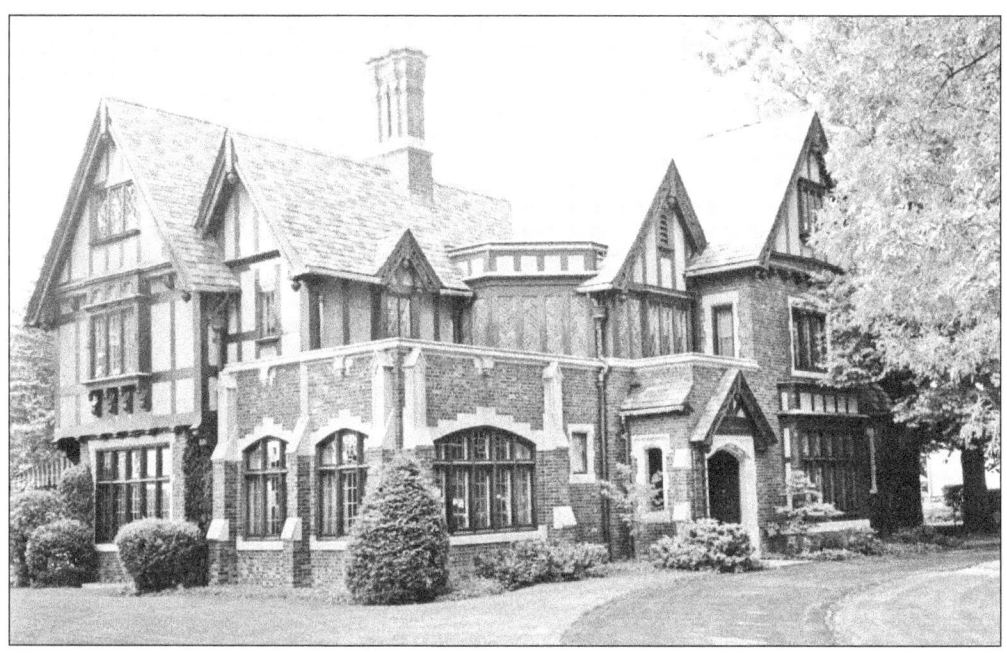

This Tudor Revival residence at 170 Sycamore Street was home to Carl Kalnow. Kalnow and his family members made their name by investing in Tiffin Enterprise. Enterprise Manufacturing started in 1876 as a woodworking/cabinetmaking factory. A century later, Tiffin Enterprise was supplying insulating material for the Alaskan oil pipeline as well as wood products.

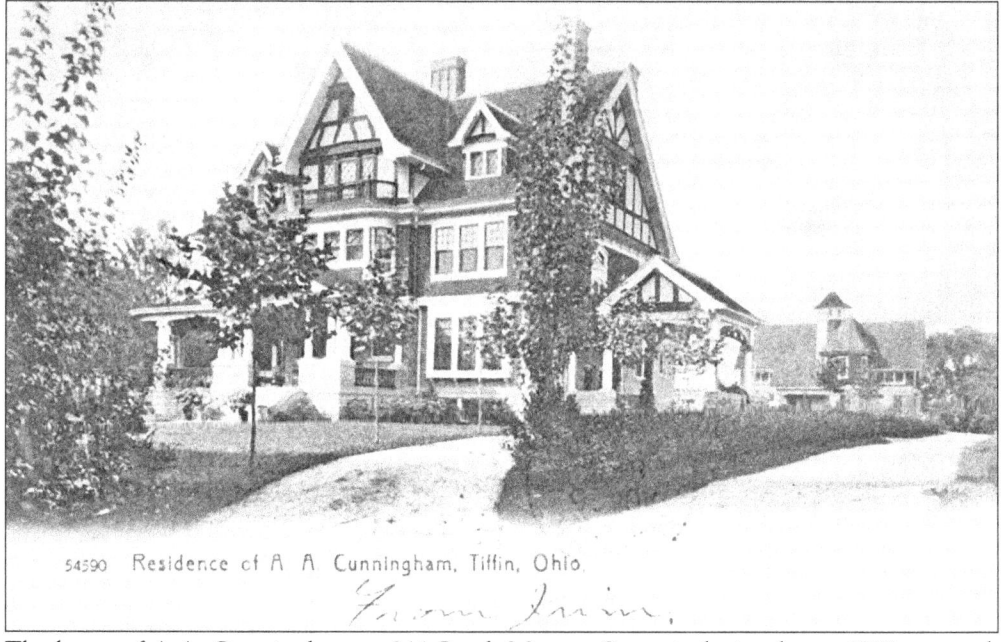

54590   Residence of A. A. Cunningham, Tiffin, Ohio.

The home of A.A. Cunningham at 244 South Monroe Street is depicted on a 1908 postcard. The money Cunningham earned from milling interests—grist, flour, and saw—begun by his father enabled him to construct his residence next door to Tiffin's Union School. Grain elevators also were part of Cunningham's holdings. His former home now houses the offices of Tiffin City Schools.

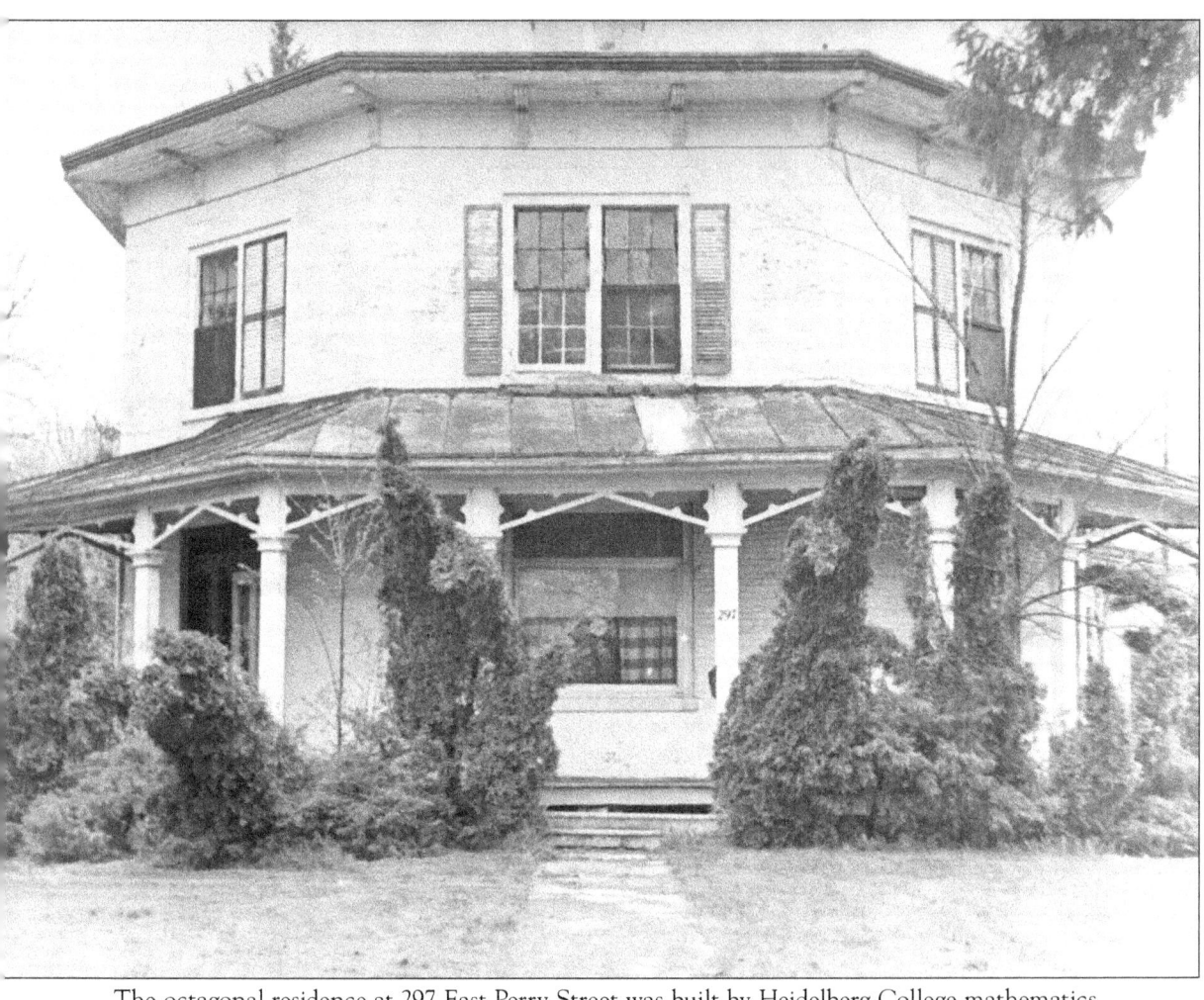

The octagonal residence at 297 East Perry Street was built by Heidelberg College mathematics professor Jeremiah Good as his home in 1852. Good also served as pastor of Tiffin's German Reformed Church for 15 years and was president of Heidelberg's Theological Seminary. After passing through a succession of owners, the octagon was divided into two apartments.

Ten

A CITY ENTERTAINED

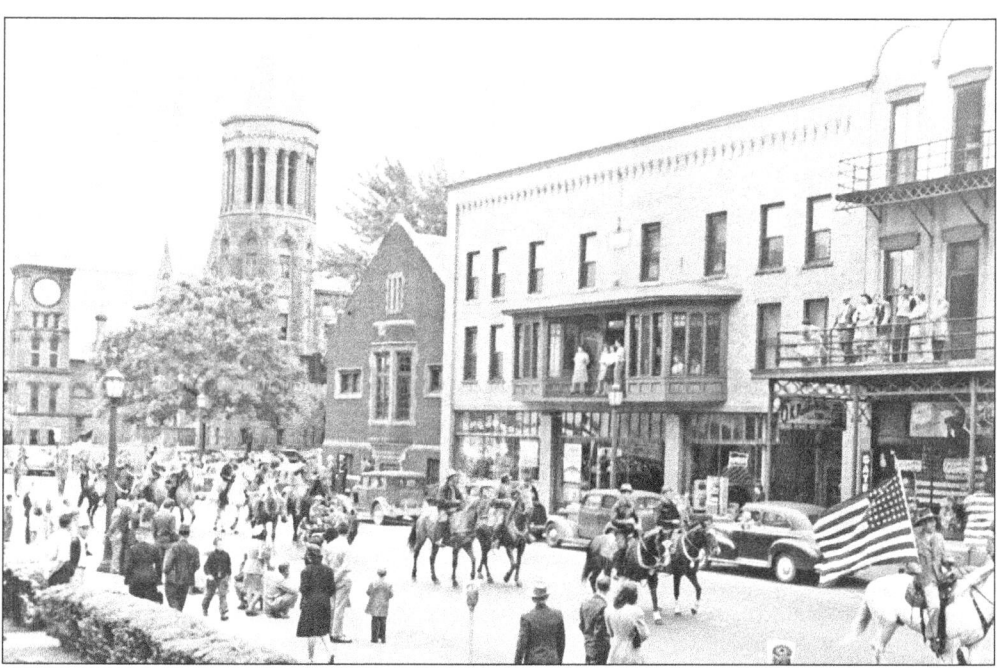

The June 15, 1947, Flag Day parade, long before the era of Tiffin's one-way streets, makes its way west down East Market Street. Among the landmarks in the background are the tower of Columbian High School and the public library building directly across Jefferson Street. Spectators watch the parade from street level or from apartment balconies, including one above a tire store at the far right.

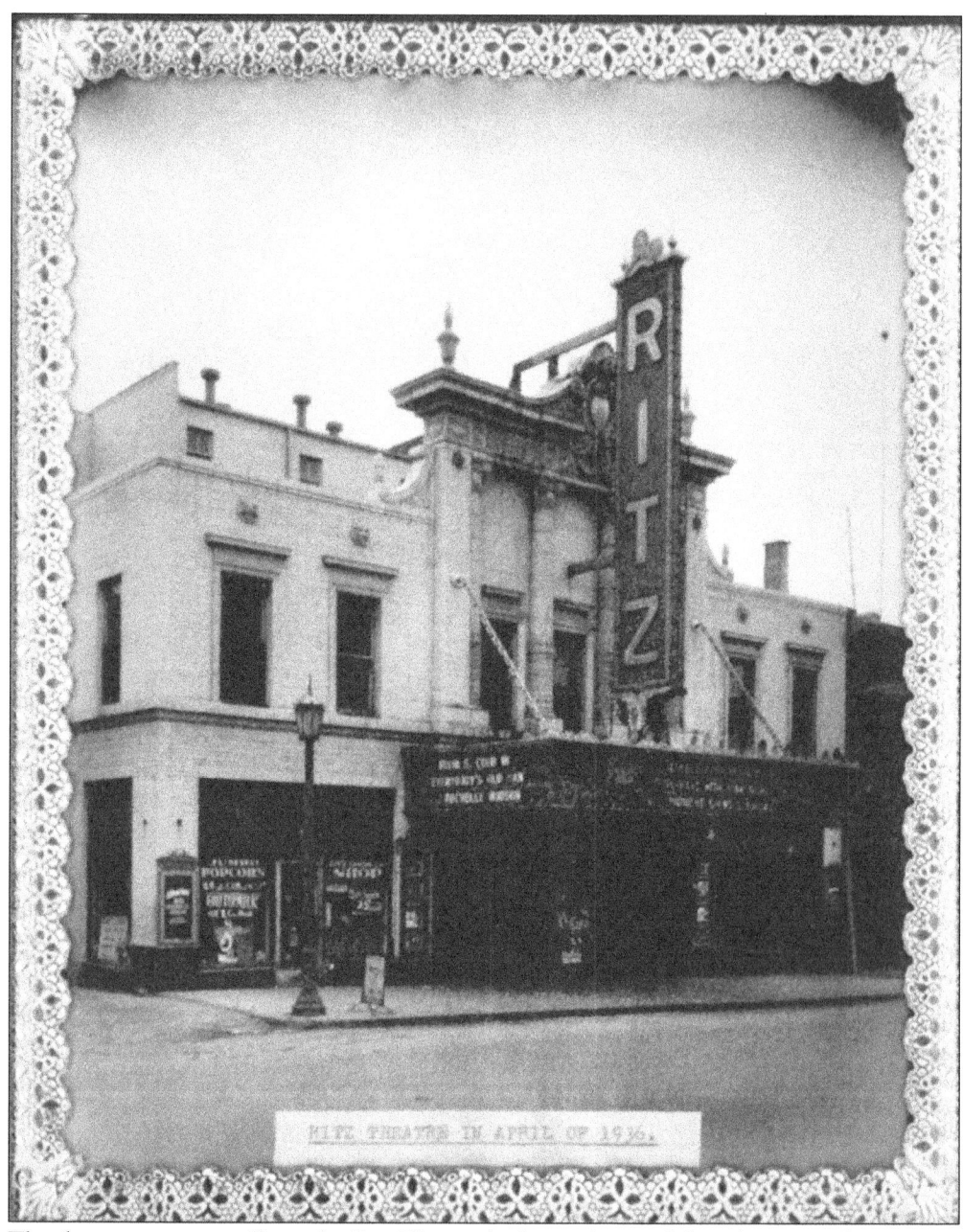

Thanks to restoration efforts, the Ritz Theatre looks much as it did in the years after its 1928 opening. Built in nine months at a cost of $250,000, the Italian Renaissance–themed Ritz features a 1,200-pound, 20,000-piece crystal chandelier suspended over the auditorium's 1,260 seats. Renovation of the auditorium was completed in 1998, and an annex was finished in 2002. (Courtesy of Ritz Theatre.)

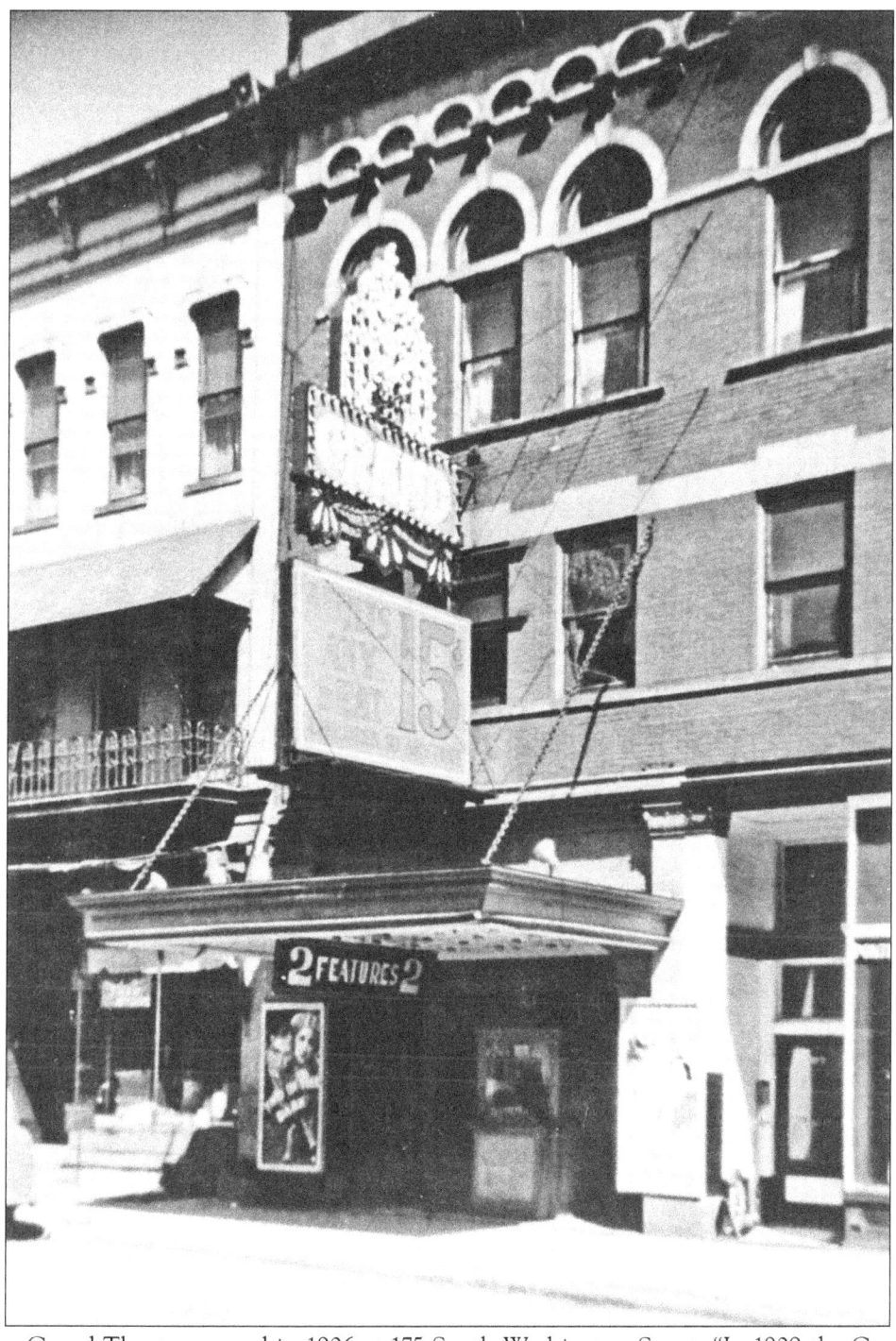

The Grand Theatre opened in 1906 at 175 South Washington Street. "In 1909 the Grand showed the first really long movie, *Les Misérables*, but patrons became too tired and walked out," reports an early Heritage Festival guide. The Grand debuted the first talking movie in Tiffin, and vaudeville shows were a popular weekend attraction. Between 1907 and 1923, the Grand also hosted Columbian High School's graduation.

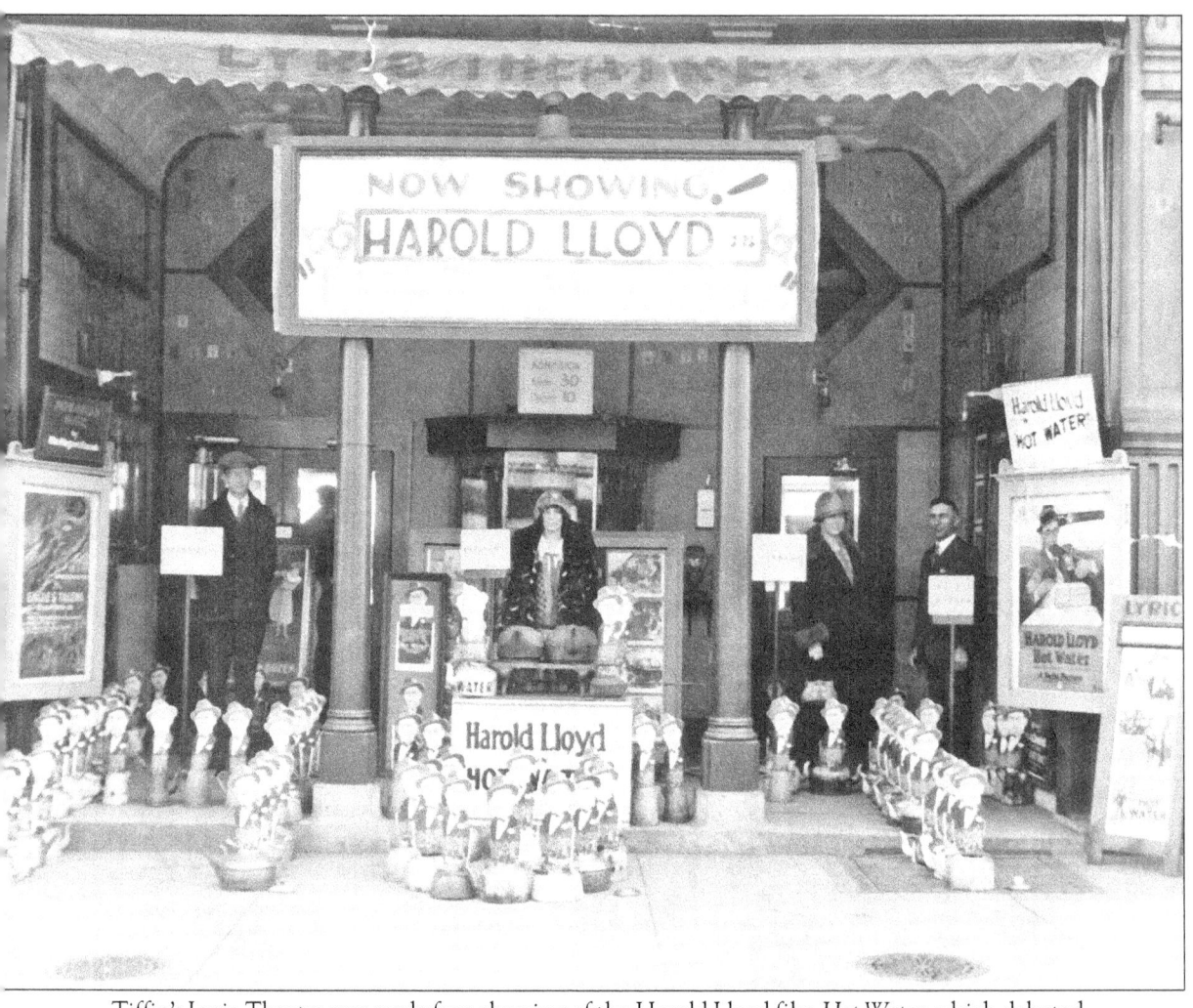

Tiffin's Lyric Theatre was ready for a showing of the Harold Lloyd film *Hot Water*, which debuted in October 1924. Cutouts of the comedian in various teakettles are on display as the Lyric staff poses in the background. From left to right, as identified by their signs, are the projectionist, organist, cashier, and "main gazook," possibly proprietor Otto J. Motry.

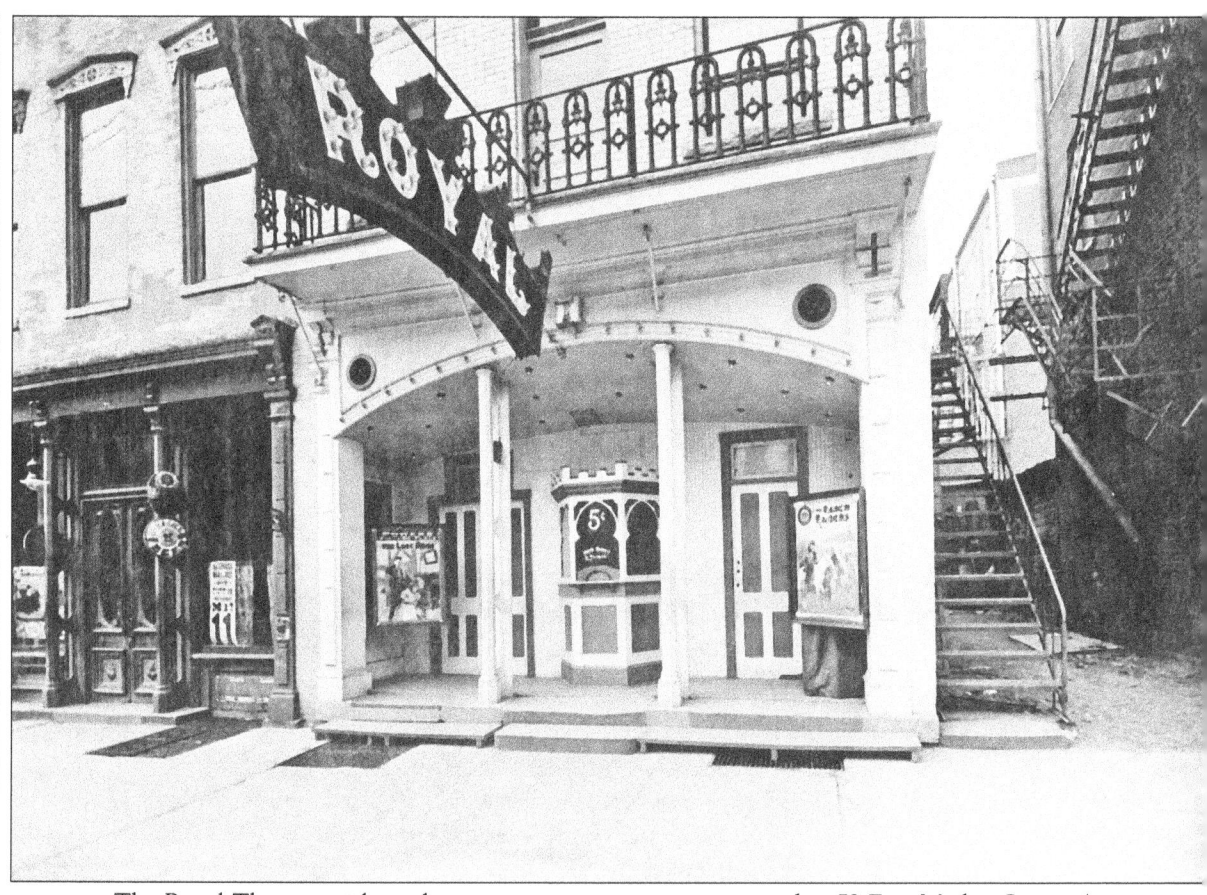

The Royal Theatre, with its distinctive crown marquee, operated at 73 East Market Street. At a nickel a ticket ("How many tickets" asks the words painted on the center ticket window), patrons could catch a double bill of *The Last Rose* and *The Ranch Raiders*, which likely dates the photograph to 1911. The bar next door has an advertisement for a different kind of entertainment, a frontier show.

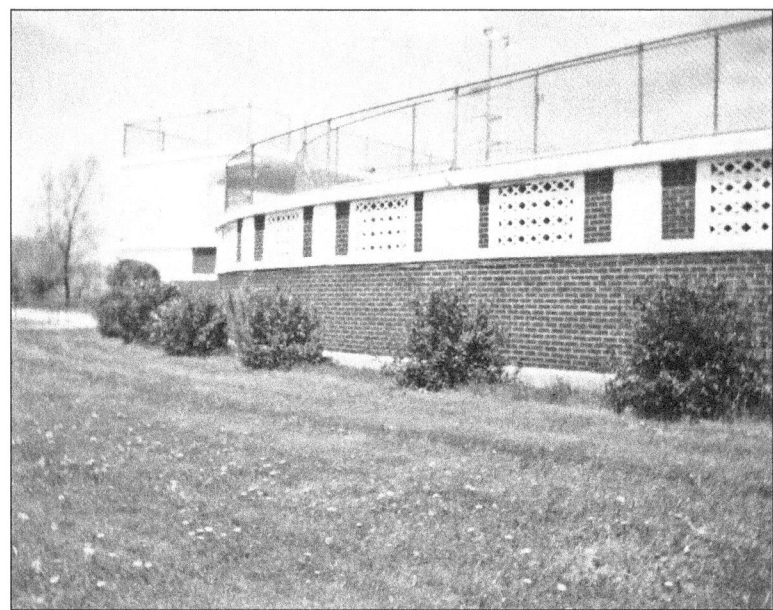

The sundeck is visible in this outside view of the former Hedges-Boyer Park swimming pool. Lockers and changing rooms were located on ground level, and the pool itself, with its pair of diving boards, was accessed through a staircase in the locker room. A wading pool for younger swimmers was also part of the complex.

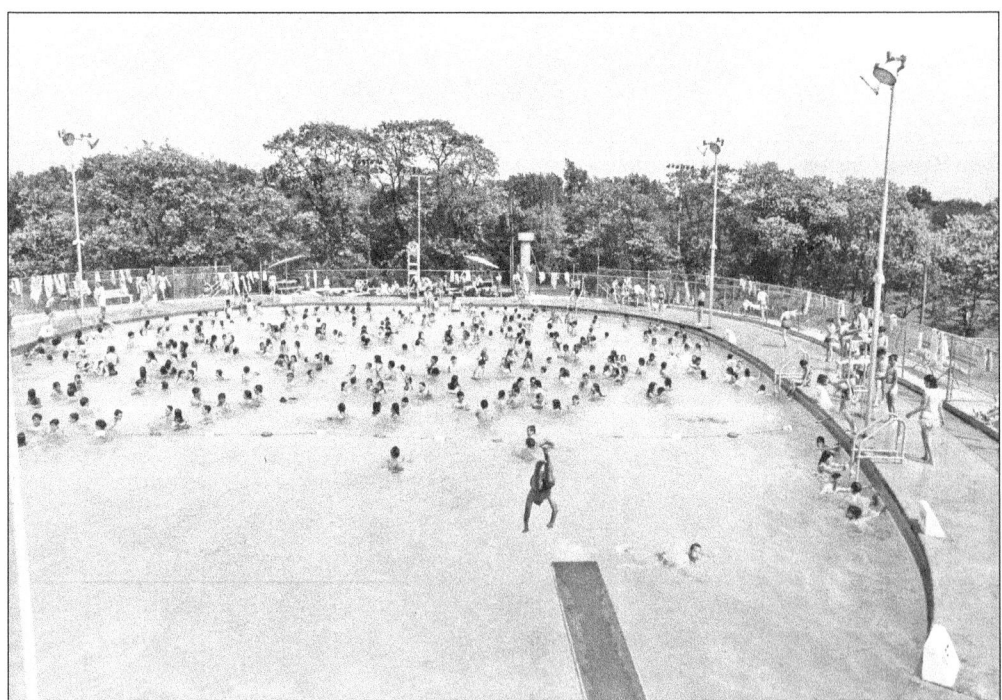

The shallow end of the 1970s municipal swimming pool at Hedges-Boyer Park is packed with swimmers on a warm summer day, while the deep end is much less populated in this view from the pool's sundeck. Also a cool treat for swimmers and other park patrons were the frozen Zero candy bars and other refreshments available at the concession stand next to the pool.

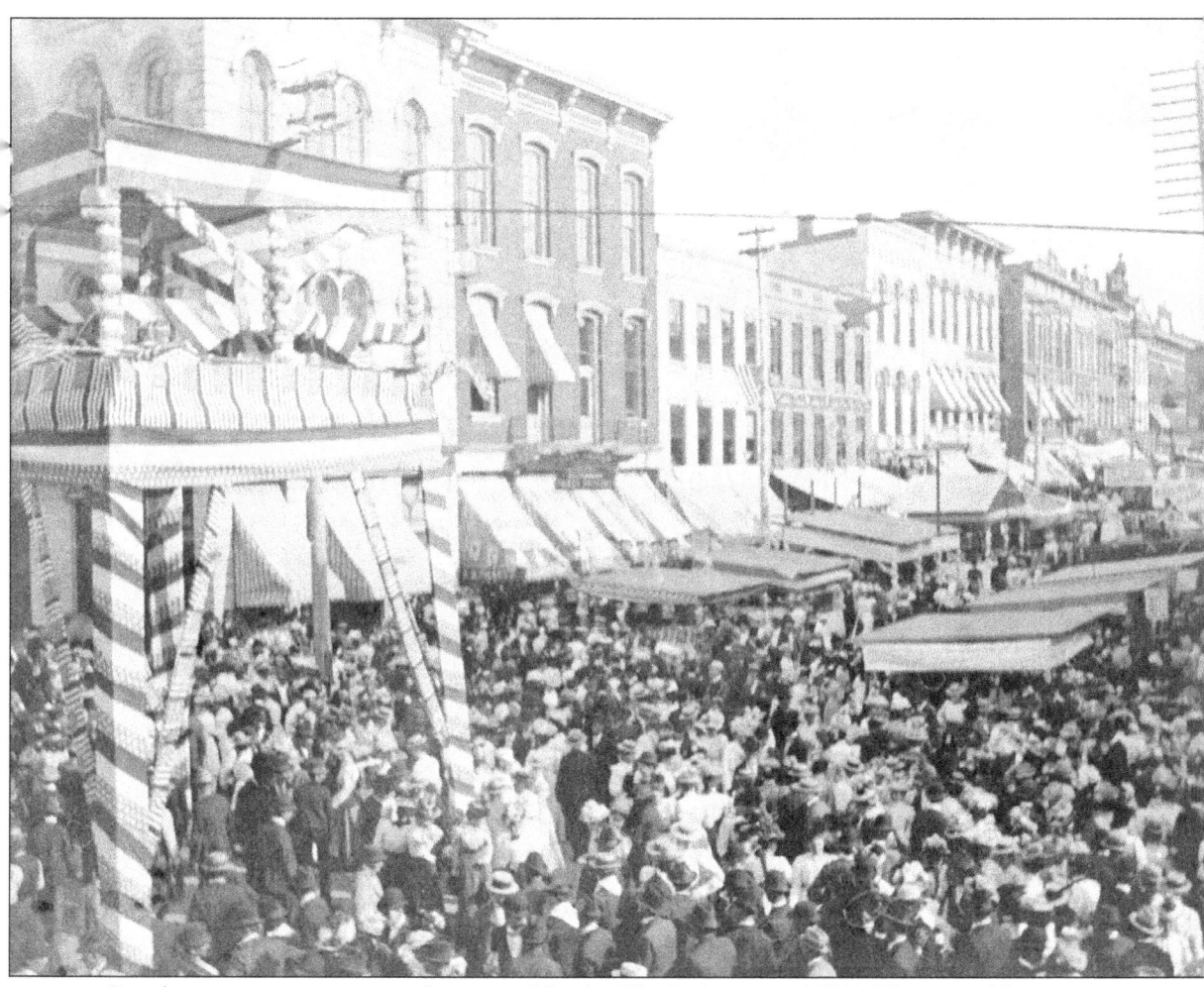

Revelers enjoy a street carnival sponsored by the Elks Lodge around 1910. The annual fair was a fundraiser for the construction of a new lodge. A Heritage Festival program from 1981 describes how "Washington St. was closed from Perry to Madison, and Market from Monroe to Washington. There were side shows, games of chance, a ferris wheel and a merry-go-round." Minstrel shows replaced the street fair from 1913 to 1923.

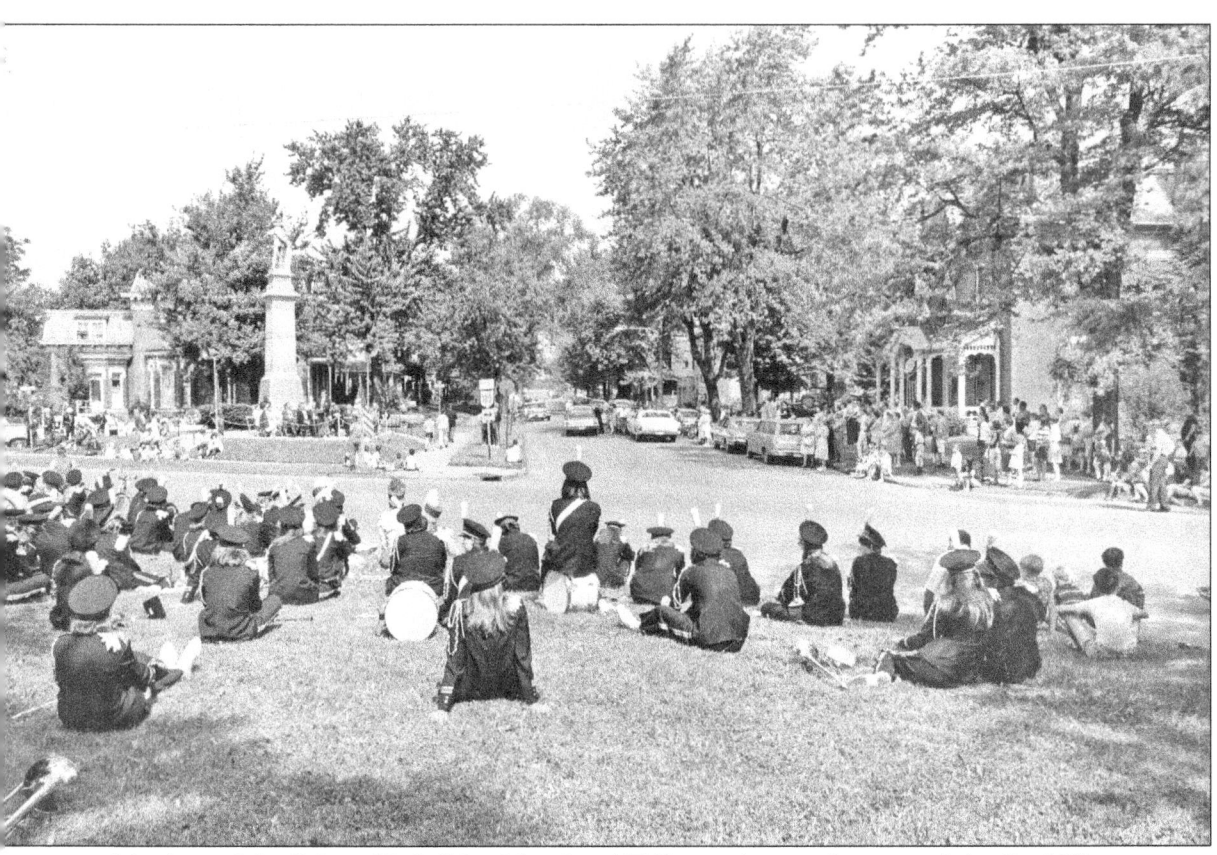

Members of the Calvert High School band and Tiffin residents gather around the Civil War Soldiers and Sailors Monument for a 1970s Memorial Day celebration. Over the years, the triangular-shaped parcel (bounded by Frost Parkway, Adams Street, and North Monroe Street) around the original monument has been upgraded to include commemorations to Tiffin's veterans of subsequent wars.

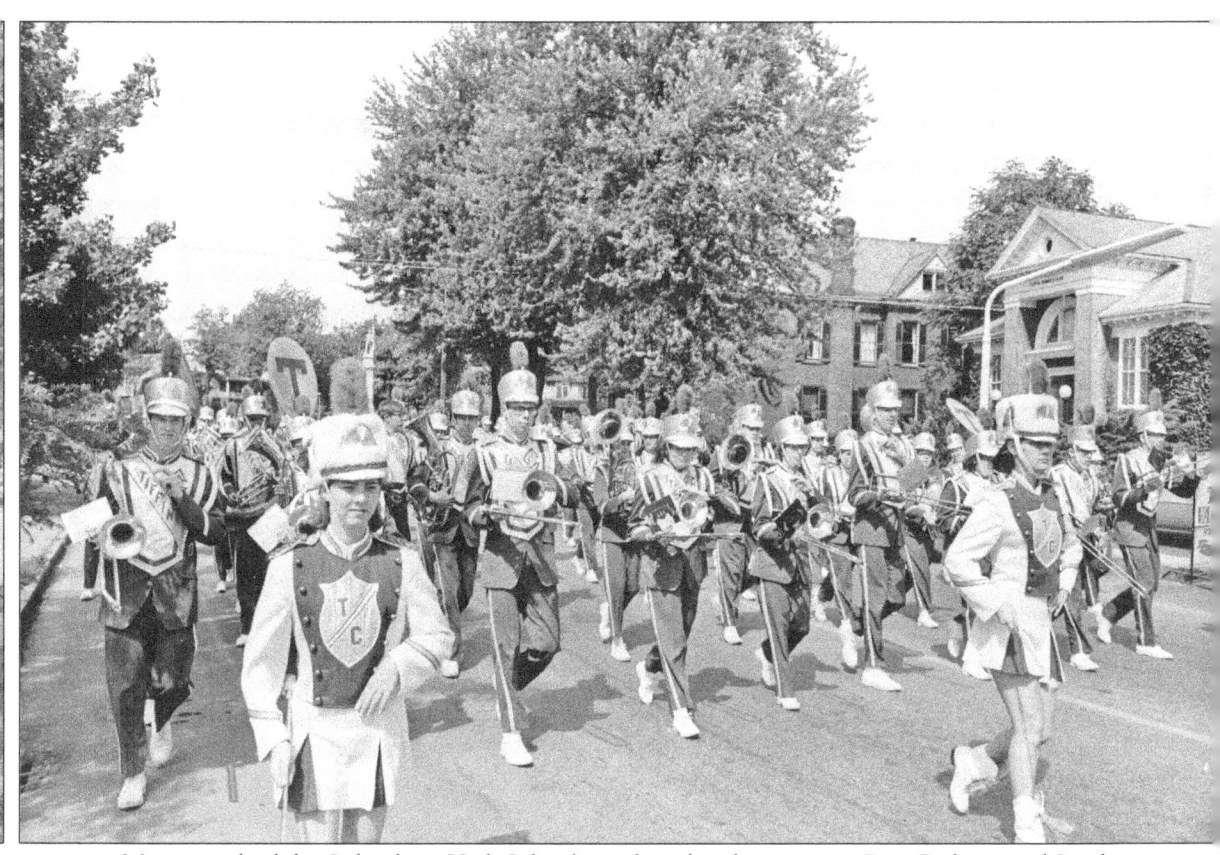

Majorettes lead the Columbian High School marching band to a turn at Frost Parkway and South Washington Street during a 1970s Memorial Day parade. Multilayer woolen uniforms and tall hats ensured that marchers would be as warm in May as during a Christmas parade in December.

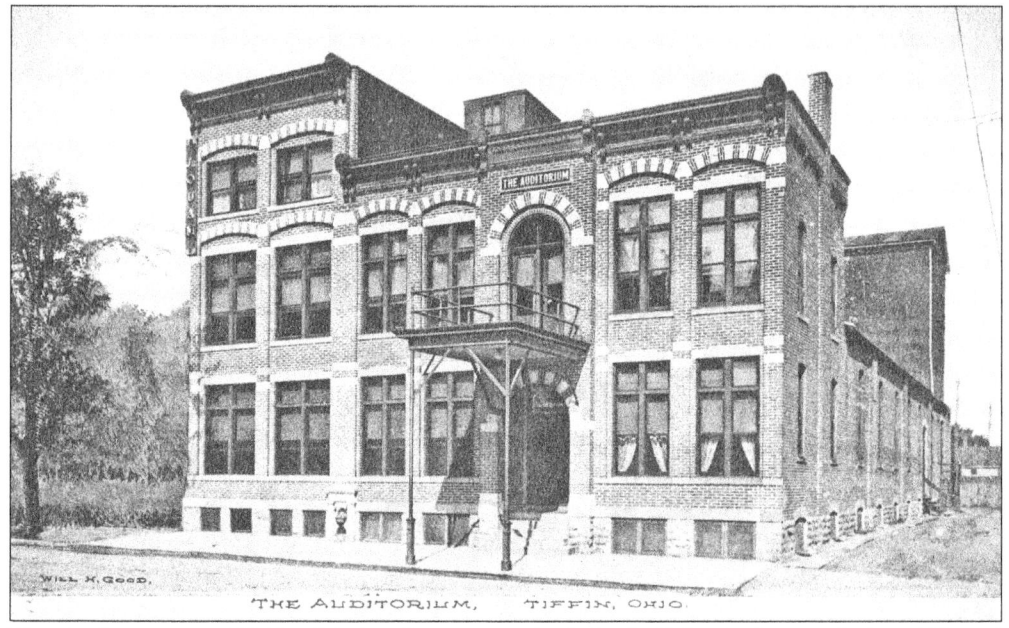

The Auditorium, at 155 East Market Street, was the lodge hall for the Junior Order of United American Machinists, but it became the center of relief efforts after Tiffin's Flood of 1913. Hot meals were available three times a day for victims in the days of the flood, fires, recovery, and reconstruction. The Auditorium was also host to an appreciation dinner for soldiers who had aided in flood efforts.

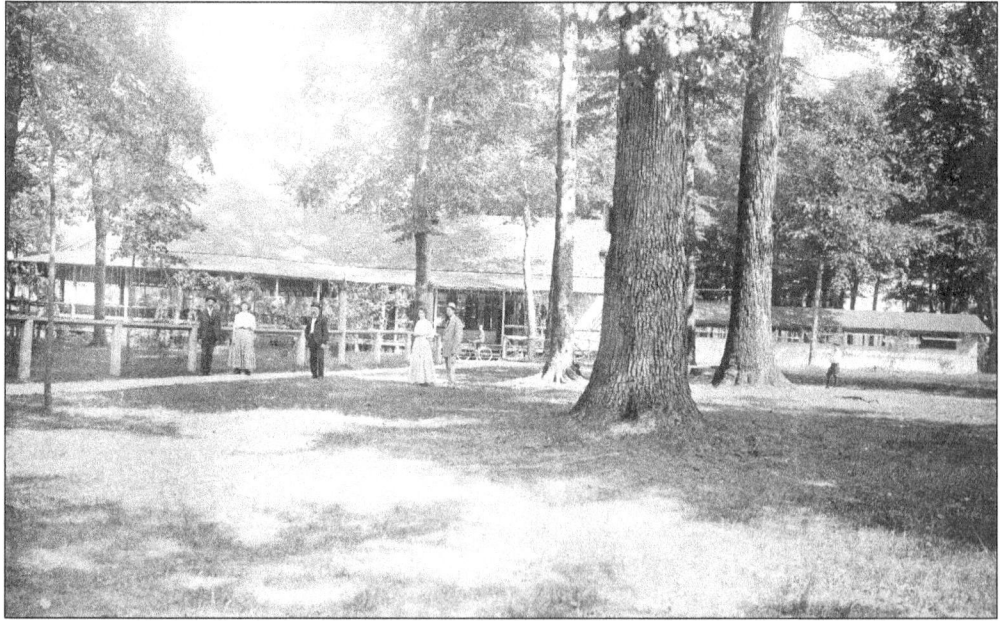

In this photograph from about 1905, Tiffinites stroll near the pavilion at Riverview Park. Patrons arrived at the 25-acre park on streetcars, and once there could partake in activities such as boating, swimming, bowling, tennis, baseball, and family picnics. A bandstand offered plentiful concert opportunities. The park fell out of favor in the post–World War I era, and the land was sold to the Junior Home.

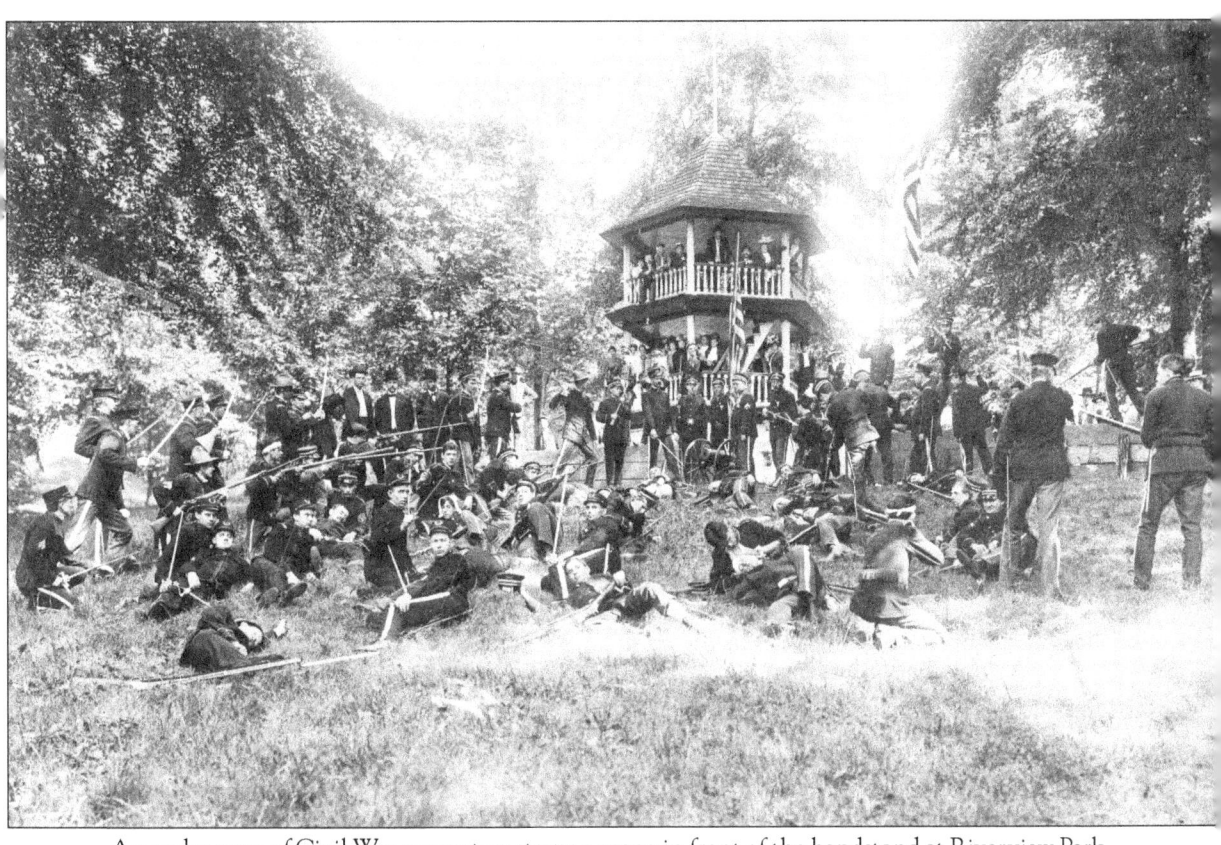

An early group of Civil War reenactors stages a scene in front of the bandstand at Riverview Park in 1896. Swords and bayonets are much in evidence as a pair of buglers sounds the call. A crowd watches the proceedings from the two levels of the bandstand as well as from behind the lines.

Bibliography

1856–1956 Centennial: Monroe Street School. Tiffin, OH: Sayger Printing and Publishing Company, 1956.

Art Work of Sandusky and Seneca Counties. Chicago: W.H. Parish Publishing Co., 1895.

Barnes, Myron. *Between the Eighties: Tiffin, Ohio 1880–1980.* Defiance, OH: The Hubbard Company, 1982.

Centennial Committee of Seneca County, Ohio. *Tiffin-Seneca Sesquicentennial: Pictorial Issue.* Tiffin, OH: Sayger Enterprises, 1967.

Daughters of the American Revolution, Dolly Todd Madison Chapter. *Ohio: Early State and Local History.* Tiffin, OH: 1915.

historynotebook.com

Lang, William. *History of Seneca County, From the Close of the Revolutionary War to July, 1880.* Springfield, OH: Transcript Printing, 1880.

Leeson, Michael A. *History of Seneca County, Ohio.* Chicago: Warner, Beers & Co., 1886.

Reid, Whitelaw. *Ohio in the War.* Cincinnati, OH: Moore, Wilstach & Baldwin, 1868.

Swickard, Lisa. *Calamity and Courage: Tiffin's Battle During Ohio's Deadly 1913 Flood.* Melmore, OH: Virgin Alley Press, 2010.

Tiffin High School Athletic Association. *Historical Sketches of the Churches and Schools of Tiffin, Ohio.* Tiffin, OH: W.H. Good, 1903.

Wilde, Davis S. *Seneca County, Ohio History & Families.* Nashville, TN: Turner Publishing Company, 1999.

Winter, Nevin O. *A History of Northwest Ohio: A Narrative Account of Its Historical Progress and Development from the First European Exploration of the Maumee and Sandusky Valleys and the Adjacent Shores of Lake Erie, down to the Present Time.* Chicago: Lewis Publishing, 1917.

INDEX

Visit us at
arcadiapublishing.com

· ·

www.ingramcontent.com/pod-product-compliance
Lightning Source LLC
Chambersburg PA
CBHW080421190526
45161CB00004B/250